**To Alice,
and
Lucy and Krikor before us**

contents

figures
and
illustrations

introduction

This volume presents the basic ideas and information needed by the elementary classroom teacher to understand, prepare, and put into practice a progressive and effective art curriculum. Our emphasis here will be on what children know about art as much as on what they make with art materials. This focus reflects a significant body of current thought as well as points to possible future developments. Like all else, art education, the study of the teaching of art, is changing its character; it is moving from an almost exclusive concern for creating art to a greater preoccupation with its appreciation.

There are three main principles upon which this book is based. The first is founded on the confidence that neither the prospective teacher untrained in art nor the child is totally ignorant of or inexperienced in aesthetic response to works of visual art, but that their experiences—broad and rich in our complex, highly visual culture—have been most often in other than fine arts contexts and, generally, have not been as technically informed as they should be or might be. For this reason the book has been organized so that the first five chapters are similar in form and content to my earlier volume designed to be used by secondary-level pupils and adults untrained in art (*The Arts We See: A Simplified Introduction to the Visual Arts*, Teachers College Press, 1982).

The second principle is that knowing about art is at least as important an elementary school concern as making art. It is not that there are no benefits provided to youngsters by the making of art. Rather, these developmental gains have, in the past, been exaggerated at the expense of "consumer" benefits, that is, benefits provided through viewing and appreciating the arts we see. Furthermore, most of us will never become proficient creators or performers of art or music or drama or dance, but all of us can and should become as learned and insightful about the arts as the schools can promote.

The third principle has been developed out of the history of art education itself. There is as much theory that is inadequately conceived and practice that is pointless and wasteful as there are theory and practice that should be endorsed and supported. For example, theoretical concepts such as general creativity, which has had an overbearing and, in many ways, an unfortunate influence on the teaching of art, are, when subjected to unbiased analysis, inappropriate to art education. Consequently, the rationale for teaching art that is presented in the sixth chapter (along with an exploration of these theoretical concepts) does not include such ideas. Instead the ideas about the teaching of art which structure that chapter and the entire volume are those which seem to hold up under careful scrutiny. Nevertheless any intellectual bias contains its own problems. The reader is urged to continue the study of art and art education in whatever ways are available and desirable. Fortunately, there seems to be no such condition as too much knowledge; this is no less true in art than it is in other areas of human concern.

There are three types of material common to most elementary art text books which do not appear in this one. These are: elaborate illustrated instructions on how to work with art materials; pages of pleasant but rarely significant transcriptions of conversation among children and between children and teachers; and often pedantic reports of specific empirical researches in art education or the behavioral sciences. However, when specific research reports do appear highly relevant, notes are provided so that the reader can refer to those sources in a library. Fortunately, these instances are infrequent.

Other materials, such as descriptions of projects involving "hands-on" productive activities, have been omitted because they will be more meaningful when provided by the instructor of the college elementary art education course in conjunction with a specific activity in that class. Nor does this work cover the history of the visual arts, even in outline form. Such material is much too vast in scope to be attended to properly in a small textbook. Moreover, there are some basic histories of art that provide this material adequately. This book deliberately has been kept brief and concise. It is not that art—or any human behavior for that matter—is a simple affair, but, rather, that brevity and precision are effective characteristics of instructional materials.

This volume is primarily designed for use in elementary art education classes which prepare teachers during their college experiences. However, teachers already practicing in the schools will also profit from the ideas and information it contains by finding ways to improve their art programs. At the same time, administrators, parents, and community leaders will find the material of some interest, particularly in light of the fact that it presents a different view from the customary one as to what the teaching of art should be in the elementary school. To the extent that the reader is willing to countenance new ideas, this book will be provocative and interesting. Those who do not like to have their sacred cows questioned should go no further than this page.

Part I ————————

THE VISUAL ARTS

Overview

Part I is about the visual arts, the arts we see. It does not deal with plays, opera, and dance even though we see those arts as well. We usually say that we "watch" those art forms because they change as we look at them. We do not say that we watch the visual arts since they do not change while we view them, except for special cases such as mobiles and kinetic (moving) sculptures. What they show us remains the same even if we look at them for hours. They do not have the character of images changing over time or "sequence." The arts we see are usually objects, not events.

Part I does examine motion pictures and television even though these media are not visual art forms. They change over time and should be explored and understood as art forms quite different from paintings, architecture, or billboards. They belong in a classification by themselves. On the other hand, both motion pictures and television have inherited some of their techniques from the visual arts and, thus, can and should be studied in the same book, as long as we do not confuse them with the arts we see.

The material in this section is mostly about the fine arts, those visual arts we see primarily in museums and galleries, even though more and more of the visual arts today are found in advertising, architecture, commercial and industrial design (packages, cars, chairs), and photography. It is assumed here that most of us, young and old, know a good deal about these popular arts and mass media, but very little about the fine arts, and that we might be able to use some help in learning how to look at what museums and galleries have to offer us. The more we know about any of the arts we see, the better able we will be to understand and enjoy all of the arts we see.

Although this volume uses many paintings, sculptures, buildings, and other art works as examples and illustrations of its content, it is important to remember that the reproductions in the book are very different from the original works. Most often the pictures in the book are much smaller than the art work itself, so that we are not seeing the work in true scale or size. Often the images in the book are in black and white, and we do not see their original colors. Some works of art, particularly architecture and sculpture, were designed to be seen in a particular setting, a place where they fit into their surroundings. You will not be able to see them in their settings in the book. Last of all, some of the art works we will talk about and illustrate are three dimensional, that is, in the round, and obviously, a flat picture cannot do them justice. These limitations exist because this is a book and cannot replace seeing the actual art work. It is important to remember these limitations as you read and look at what follows.

This section has been written for those whose background in art has been limited. The approach used here is based on the belief that the fine arts should not be a mysterious encounter for special people who know its secrets, but, rather, a part of life to be enjoyed by all of us. Remember, you do not have to "like" all that you see and read about here. All that you have to do is try to understand it—with some help from this volume. What you like or dislike is your own business, as long as you are not cheated from enjoying something simply because you do not understand it.

All the arts we see that were ever made belong to all of us. This section will help you take from that part of the world you see around you as much as you can of what is yours, to value and enjoy.

CHAPTER 1

the purposes
and
nature of art

In order to explore the basic content of the subject of art, we will start by examining some of the purposes for which works of art have been made. Next we will review some ideas about aesthetics, the study of the nature of art and how and why we respond to it. Although aesthetics has been one portion of the concerns of philosophical speculation, it is by no means unapproachable or incomprehensible. Stated in simple terms—as they will be here—the ideas of aesthetic theory can be understood even by children, who today can understand and correctly use a word as difficult as "astronaut" and a term as complex as "fair," meaning "just."

Further, the ideas about aesthetics which will be reviewed here purport to describe responses all of us seem to experience, even though we do not usually question the nature of these responses. Such insight as we can generate about this part of our lives might help us to expand the range of these experiences and, perhaps, to intensify their quality. This review of ideas about aesthetics will also introduce the reader to the foundations upon which conceptions of art teaching and curriculum will be developed in the second part of the book. Later in this chapter we will also look briefly at the contemporary world of the fine arts and at the artists who make them.

THE PURPOSES OF ART

Perhaps the least problematical statement one might make about the visual arts is that they seem to appear from earliest history and in every part of the world. In fact, a good portion of our knowledge of earlier societies derives wholly or in great measure from their artifacts. In the absence of written records or when these are meager, as in the case of ancient Egypt or Mesopotamia, much of what we know about how they lived and thought is based on their architecture, carvings, and household objects. Further, it might be observed that these objects represent a multitude of purposes from basic shelters and the embellishment of tools to expressions of important thoughts and feelings.

Archaeologists and art historians tell us that even primitive people of the Old Stone Age (20,000 to 15,000 B.C.) created art. Figure 1 shows us a bison or buffalo carved into and painted on the rock wall of a cave in Altamira, Spain, at a time when a good part of Europe was still covered by glaciers. We think that the caveman, for whom the bison was an important source of food, made paintings such as this one in the belief that, by some magic, painting the animal would help him in hunting it. Many years ago, the native American of our own continent carved and decorated his club, bow, or tomahawk in order to make it, magically, more powerful in war. Figure 2 shows an Apache medicine man's shirt worn by a scout to make him invisible to the enemy. The same shirt is still worn today, although its purpose is no longer considered to be magical. Like the Apache shirt, the World War II "Flying Tiger" aircraft of the U.S. Army Air Force, shown in Figure 3, was decorated to emphasize its purpose.

Often in the past, works of sculpture or architecture were created as an attempt to remember or recognize the greatness of someone who had died or to show the wealth and power of a political or military leader or a large and wealthy organization. The Taj Mahal (Figure 4), completed in the 1600s, is a monument to the wife of an Indian shah. Even today, memorials are built for famous people. Figure 5 is a memorial to pioneer settlers of the western United States. In much the same way, skyscraper offices of large corporations demonstrate the wealth and power of these business concerns. Figure 6 shows the New York offices of Lever Brothers, a firm which manufactures household products.

In addition to the purposes of magic, memorial, and prestige, art has also been created by making useful objects attractive. Almost all the implements we make and use are designed with this idea in mind. Dishes, pots, tableware,

(continued on page 8)

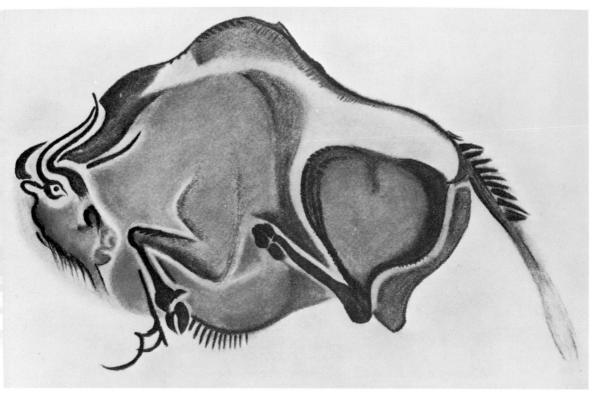

1. Crouching bison turning its head. The Cave of Altamira, Spain, by Abbe Brauil and Hugo Obermaier. Courtesy of The American Museum of Natural History

2. Apache medicine man's shirt, painted buckskin, c. 1860–1880. Courtesy of the Smithsonian Institution

3 (top left). "Flying Tiger" fighter aircraft. Courtesy of the Air Force Museum

4 (bottom left). The Taj Mahal, Agra, India, c. 1632–1653. Courtesy of The Information Service of India

5 (top right). The Gateway Arch, St. Louis, Missouri, 1965. Eero Saarinen and Associates, architects. Courtesy of The Chamber of Commerce of Metropolitan St. Louis

6 (bottom right). Lever House, New York City, 1952. Skidmore, Owings and Merrill, architects. Courtesy of Lever Brothers Company

furniture, and automobiles are designed and decorated with colors, textures, patterns of all kinds, and a variety of materials to make them attractive to look at. Young people sometimes decorate their surfboards and automobiles (Figure 7), adding their own personal embellishments to already designed and decorated, but mass-produced, objects. Sometimes decorations serve other purposes besides simply making the object more attractive. Figure 8 shows the medieval French cathedral of Notre Dame in Amiens, with its hundreds of skillfully carved figures. These sculptures provide religious inspiration and tell the story of Christianity. Thus, these decorations or embellishments have served a practical as well as aesthetic or artistic purpose, just as the building itself has been a useful object made attractive by the way in which it is arranged or designed.

Often in our industrial world, an object designed primarily to serve a useful purpose is impressive and handsome, even without decorations, and becomes for us what we can call an art object. Figures 9, 10, and 11 are examples of such machine forms. They have little in them or on them that is simply decorative. Instead, they depend for their attractiveness on the way they have been put together for their use. The idea that a useful object can be beautiful when it has little or nothing on it or in it except what is needed to make it work is sometimes called "form follows function."

7 (left). Painted automobile, c. 1978

8 (right). Cathedral of Notre Dame, west façade, Amiens, France, c. 1220. Courtesy of A. Dean McKenzie

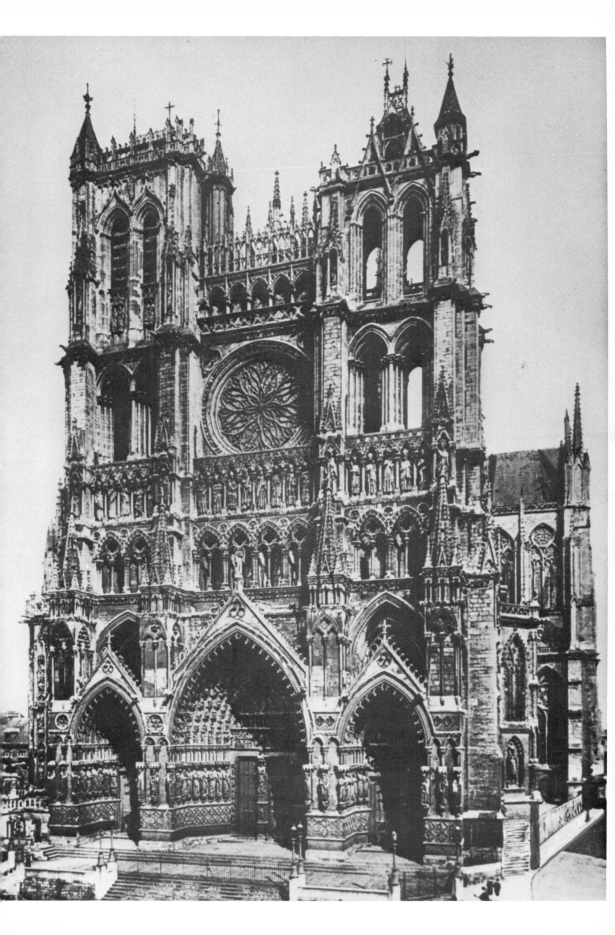

9. Museum desk clock, porta-
ble desk version. Courtesy of
Howard Miller Clock Co.,
Zeeland, Mich.

10. Harley-Davidson panhead,
1948. Courtesy of James
Lanier

The same effect can be seen in simple, handcrafted objects from earlier times or from less industrialized societies. Figure 12 is an example of an object designed for use that we might view in much the same way as paintings, buildings, or industrial forms. It also illustrates the idea of form following function. Objects much older than this chest used the same principle, although a hundred years ago the idea was not expressed that way.

What is thought to be beautiful or valuable in an object's design or decoration changes from era to era and sometimes from year to year. If we compare Figure 8 with Figure 6 we can see a considerable difference in viewpoint about building design between approximately 1200 and the 1950s. The surface of the Gothic cathedral is covered with intricately carved stone patterns and figures, while the contemporary office building depends on the relationships of its materials—glass, steel, and stone—for its handsome appearance. The same kind of difference over a period of time can be seen in a much smaller and more common object such as a chair in Figures 13 and 14.

Another reason people make works of art is to express important ideas and feelings or to show what they believe to be of value. Just as in music or poetry or dance, artists can be excited by something in themselves or in the world around them and express these feelings by painting or carving or drawing. A Japanese artist of the thirteenth century, a Frenchman drawing in the 1870s, and a Spaniard who died in 1974 were, all of them, disturbed by the horrors of war and expressed these feelings in works of art, as seen in Figures 15, 16, and 17.

(continued on page 17)

11. Boeing 747. Courtesy of Boeing Commercial Airplane Company

12 (top left). Oak buffet, American, c. 1920. Courtesy of James Lanier

13 (top center). Carved and gilded walnut armchair, French, eighteenth century. Courtesy of The Metropolitan Museum of Art, Gift of J. Pierpont Morgan, 1907

14. (top right). Modular seating unit. Photo Courtesy of Herman Miller, Inc.

15. (bottom). *The Burning of the Sanjō Palace* (detail), handscroll, 41.3 × 699.7 cm., Japan, Kamakura period, thirteenth century. Courtesy of the Museum of Fine Arts, Boston, Fenollosa-Weld Collection

16. Honoré Daumier, *Conseil de Guerre*, lithograph, 1870. Courtesy of The Metropolitan Museum of Art, Schiff Fund, 1922

17. Pablo Picasso, *Guernica*, oil on canvas, 1937. Prado, Madrid. Formerly on loan to The Museum of Modern Art, New York. © S.P.A.D.E.M., Paris/V.A.G.A., New York, 1982

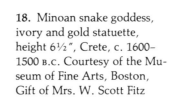

18. Minoan snake goddess, ivory and gold statuette, height 6½", Crete, c. 1600–1500 B.C. Courtesy of the Museum of Fine Arts, Boston, Gift of Mrs. W. Scott Fitz

19. Buddha (Dainichi Nyorai), crypotomeria wood, Japan, A.D. 947-957. Courtesy of the Museum of Art, Rhode Island School of Design, Providence, R.I.

Religion has inspired some of the world's art. Figures 18, 19, and 20 show us a figurine of a Minoan snake goddess from 1600 B.C., a tenth-century Japanese statue of Gautama Buddha, and an engraving by Albrecht Dürer (1471–1528), all of which seem to express religious ideas and feelings. The Cathedral of Notre Dame, Figure 8, and most other places of worship of the world's religions serve the same *expressive* purpose. As with all architecture, however, their primary purpose is to create enclosed spaces in which religious activities can take place. When they are arranged or decorated to express religious feelings—as they often are—they serve this second expressive purpose as well. Many other objects which we call works of art share this double purpose. For example, Figure 21 (page 19) is both window and artistic expression.

Sometimes artists are so deeply involved with political issues—such as war or social injustice—that their work can be called "propaganda" for a particular point of view, as in Figure 22. Some art critics feel that when a drawing, painting, or print is overly devoted to expressing a political point of view, it becomes mainly propaganda and might lose some of its value as a work of art. In the end, it is the viewer who will have to judge whether this is so in each individual case. For example, Figure 23 (page 20) is one of the many murals or wall paintings found in some of our cities today that seem to express, and can be understood to show, pride in the ethnic and cultural heritage of some Americans of minority groups. They are used, as this one can be used, to bring people of that heritage together; thus they serve a propaganda as well as an art purpose. Some of them are done by trained artists, often working in groups. Others are done by people without much schooling in art. They are, in any case, very much an instance of propaganda, a political message, in what is called "people's art." You, the reader, can decide for yourself to what extent this political purpose interferes with its qualities as art.

Oddly enough, while it is perfectly possible for a work of art to express viciousness or hatred, this is rare in the history of art. This is probably not because artists all are "good" people with healthy ideas. It may be because the experience of art usually has to do with beauty (however we explain that term), and it is not easy for anyone to think of beauty and hatred at the same time. Artists throughout history, as well as in our time, have created works of art which deal with cruelty, greed, intolerance, and ugliness in human experience (Figure 24). Yet our total response to this kind of work and the way in which we interpret the artist's attitude toward his subject usually reflect both human compassion and a sense of the beauty of our visual experience. In fact, it is probably the power of this visual response that makes the impact of the human situation presented more stirring and memorable. This is a difficult problem and one that needs a great deal of investigation.

Works of art are created to express thoughts and feelings about important issues other than war and religion that can affect all people, such as a concern for the welfare of one's fellow human beings, as in Figure 25, or the love of one's family. Part of what the artist wants us to recognize in Figure 25 is the terrible vulnerability of the mother. Often works of art express emotions or ideas far less intense than the horror of war, the glory of religion, or the brutality of injustice. The artist simply may wish to show joy in living, pleasure in the

(continued on page 25)

20. Albrecht Dürer, *Christus am Olberg*, iron engraving, 8 5/8×6″, 1515. Courtesy of The University of Arizona Museum of Art, Gift of C. Leonard Pfeiffer

21. "Entry Into Jerusalem," stained-glass window, Canterbury Cathedral, England, thirteenth century.
Courtesy of A. Dean McKenzie

23 (top). "Viva la Raza," mural, Los Angeles, c. 1973. Courtesy of Peter Schellin

33 (bottom). "El Castillo," Mayan pyramid, Chichén Itzá, Mexico, c. 900–1200

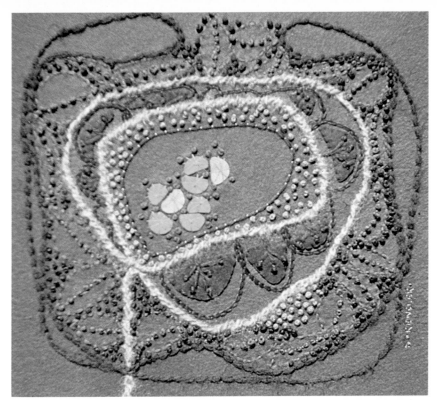

47 (top). Barbara Kensler, *Spring Rain,* yarn on felt, with appliqué, 1966. Courtesy of the artist

80 (bottom). Row houses, Eugene, Oregon, 1980. Courtesy of Unthank, Seder, and Poticha, Architects, P.C.

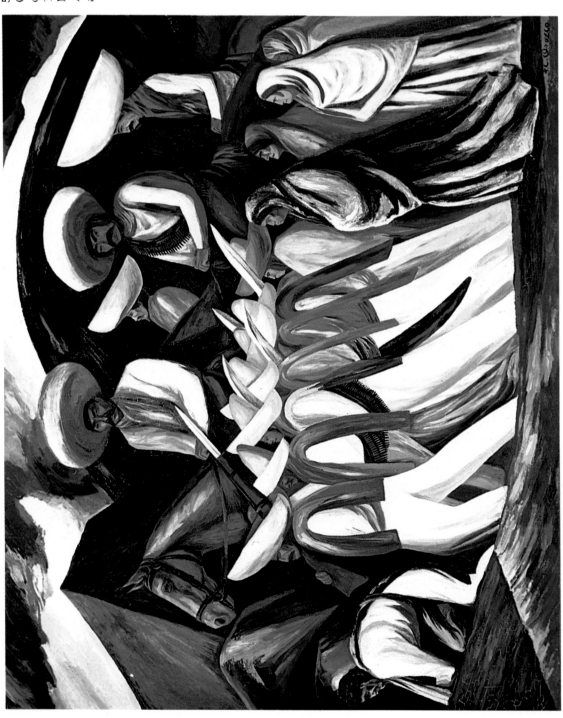

51. José Clemente Orozco, *Zapatistas*, oil on canvas, 45 x 55". 1931. Collection, The Museum of Modern Art, New York, given anonymously

22. Peter Blume, *The Eternal City*, oil on composition board, 34 × 47 7/8", 1934–37? (dated on painting 1937). Collection, The Museum of Modern Art, New York, Mrs. Simon Guggenheim Fund

24. Jack Levine, *Dramatis Personae*, oil, 11½×5½", c. 1942. Courtesy of The University of Arizona Museum of Art, Gift of C. Leonard Pfeiffer

25. Francisco Zuniga, *Mujer de Pie con Manos en la Cara*, bronze II/IV edition, 81 1/8× 21 5/8×17 7/8", 1976. Courtesy of The University of Arizona Museum of Art

beauty of nature or small children, or fondness for simple, everyday objects and activities. There are art works of bowls of fruit, of backyards, as in Figures 26 and 27, and of the cities in which many of us live (Figure 28). One group of American artists was called the "Ashcan School" and an English group the "Kitchen Sink" painters because they chose to paint the ordinary side of life. Nothing in human experience seems to be too large or too small but that the artist can use it to show the way he or she looks at what all of us see.

Sometimes, the purpose of visual art is to tell a story or provide information. Many signs, posters, book illustrations, magazine "picture stories," and some paintings have been made more to tell us about something than to make us feel strongly about something. The billboard is a good example. The purpose of this visual material is primarily to communicate information about some product or person. Although the information is usually provided in as attractive a fashion as possible and can be beautiful for its own sake, new breakfast cereals or nearby motels are hardly subjects about which most of us can have strong emotions and important ideas.

However, communicating information alone is not a very significant reason for the creation of art. Words are usually a more efficient way of communicating information. Those who study language believe that the alphabets of our languages started with picture symbols or what we call "pictographs" (Figure 29). Eventually these picture symbols evolved into symbols, signs, or "letters," as the chart indicates. Each letter alone stands for a sound and letters in groups make up words. It seems reasonable to assume that this development occurred because words were more effective in communicating complex thoughts and information than were pictures, if communication of ideas is the only purpose involved.

Many artists in the past hundred years have not tried to achieve any of the purposes we have talked about. Instead, they created works simply to please and excite you visually, without a particular subject or natural image. Picasso's *Guernica* (Figure 17) is about the subject of war and Cézanne's painting in Figure 26 is a still life. Both of these paintings have a subject and may be said to show us how the artist sees, thinks, and feels about it. Kandinsky's painting in Figure 30, on the other hand, is just lines, shapes, values, colors, and textures; it is "nonobjective." If we have strong feelings and many ideas when we look at this work of art, they are caused by these elements and their relationships, rather than by a subject. In any case, by the beginning of the twentieth century, artists had become interested in the possibilities of arranging the basic elements of what we see, such as shapes, colors, and textures, regardless of whether or not these elements, when arranged, made objects or told a story.

So much of recent painting, sculpture, and printmaking reflects this general approach that this arranging of visual elements might be called a purpose in itself. Most of the art that is familiar to us has combined one of the purposes described before with this last one: the careful arrangement of visual elements to attract the attention and arouse ideas and feelings in the viewer. Just as we design or decorate a building to make it more impressive, we design a poster or paint a picture not only to express how we feel about something but to make a

26 (top). Paul Cézanne, *Still Life with Apples*, oil on canvas, 27 × 36½", 1895–1898. Collection, The Museum of Modern Art, New York, Lillie P. Bliss Collection

27 (bottom). John Sloan, *Backyards, Greenwich Village*, oil on canvas, 26 × 32 inches, 1914. Collection of the Whitney Museum of American Art, New York

28. Edward Hopper, *The City*, oil on canvas, 1927. Courtesy of The University of Arizona Museum of Art, Gift of C. Leonard Pfeiffer

"beautiful" work, one that will suggest ideas and feelings about the way it is put together.

Finally, it would be fair to say that any object we see, whatever its original purpose, can be called art if we look at it that way. For example, Figure 31 shows a particular way of braiding hair that comes from Africa. While we do not usually think of a hair style as art, it is obvious that looking at it (even in a photograph in this book) makes us realize that it can be valuable or exciting or attractive to look at, to us or to someone else. It can give us, through our sense of sight, very much the same kinds of meanings—that is, thoughts and feelings—that we find in seeing a building or a painting. What is important to us is our experience of the object, not what the object might be called.

Some of the objects around us that give us that kind of experience are called fine arts; others are called popular arts and folk arts. Still others are not called art at all, since they are natural objects, not made by people. Thus we can see that the important question to answer about art is how we describe that experience we have of any object we see when we look at it as art.

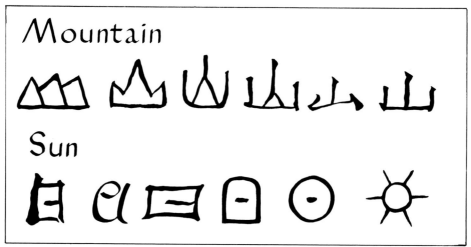

29. Two examples of the development of Chinese letter symbols from pictographs during a 3,000-year period. Prepared by Cheng An-Chih for *From Cave Paintings to Comic Strip* by Lancelot Hogben. Courtesy of Chanticleer Press

THE NATURE OF ART

The study of the nature of art or the study of "beauty," as it has been called in the past, has a long and complicated history. From the time of the Greek philosophers to the present, concerned thinkers have developed numbers of theories about the arts and how people respond to them. In fact, most major philosophers, who built systems of thought in answer to the primary questions of their field (the nature of reality, how we attain knowledge, what constitutes value—particularly moral value), have also confronted the issue of aesthetics. Although even a fragmentary review of these often elaborate aesthetic theories is not a necessary part of our content here, knowledge of some of the major positions on aesthetics can be of value. The teacher should keep in mind that none of these theories appears to be an adequate description, that is, one which can answer all the questions that might be asked. However, the theories that follow may be of worth if for no other reason than to assess the suggestions of this volume in the context of other options.

the aesthetic transaction

Some writers divide their questions about aesthetics into a number of particular points of focus. One recent volume arranges this inquiry into three components: the interest of the subject or perceiver (I), the object of interest (O), and the relationship between them (R).[1] Berleant describes the "aesthetic field" as composed of the artist, the performer, the work of art, and the perceiver.[2] Within the body of writings on the teaching of art proper, Efland suggests four elements which most theories of art recognize and discuss: (1) the work of art itself; (2) the artist as the work's creator; (3) the audience to whom the work is

30. Vasily Kandinsky, *Extended No. 333,* 1926. Collection of The Solomon R. Guggenheim Museum, New York, photograph by Robert E. Mates

31. African hair arrangement. Courtesy of the model Grace Hampton and the photographer Mark Bailey

addressed; and (4) the universe represented in the work, that is, what the work is about.[3] These patterns of components are quite similar, and each one has characteristics of merit. The first appears to be the clearest and most economical. The aesthetic field (to borrow Berleant's term) suggested here will be the *object,* the *history,* or the social environment in which both object and viewer have developed and presently operate, and the *viewer* or perceiver. The second element could more accurately be called "story," rather than history, since history is usually associated with the past and no such limitation is implied here. However, story has the connotation of subject matter or of fiction and is less appropriate as an identifying term.

The relationships among object, history, and viewer can be divided into a sequence of functions: apprehending or seeing (or hearing), appreciating, and understanding.[4] These steps can be used in the classroom to explain how the aesthetic field operates. However, it should be clear that these functions need not proceed chronologically in the sequence in which they are listed, although the process might occur in that fashion. Further, identification of these functions is not meant to suggest that the viewer can isolate each function in his or her own mind easily during the process of viewing and responding.

Also, use of this sequence does not imply here (as Berleant does) that apprehension is "precognitive."[5] The act of apprehending involves more than the reception of sensations. Apprehending is applying meaning to sensation, and this process is very much a function of cognition. To develop a construct such as an intuitive or precognitive phase in our responses to stimuli is to drive too massive a wedge between thought and other response behaviors. It is to treat cognition as if it were the icing on a cake. Human sensations are processed cognitively, not as an amoeba or a camera might process them, automatically and mechanically.

The Object. The object is the most obvious consideration within the aesthetic transaction, but it is also the source of much confusion. Aesthetic experience is often called "art experience," the object in the aesthetic relationship being identified solely as the work of art. The use of a term like art experience can be misleading in that it supports a severe discontinuity between aesthetic responses to a work of art and what appear to be at least similar responses to other objects not likely to be called art works, such as natural forms, popular and folk arts, and industrial arts. It might also be misunderstood to imply a sharp separation of aesthetic experience from other experiences (e.g., practical, moral) on which consciousness is dependent. This is a division which would seem far too drastic to be accurate.

While there is theoretical precedent for these disjunctions (as, for example, in the works of Clive Bell and Roger Fry), there is also clearly adequate support that argues for continuity. Significant endorsement can be found in the writings of Dewey, while Berleant asserts:

> These ideas all try to render aesthetic experience distinct from the involvement in a matrix of transitory means and ends by which one is bound up in practical experience, distracted from the qualitative nature of the world around us. Yet in

attempting to keep the experience of art separate from the pulls and pushes of practical activity, these proposals, as we have seen, tend to place the experiencer in a distant seat where he becomes more than disinterested; he is left remote, detached, and uninvolved. The immediacy of our response is discouraged and may vanish altogether.[6]

Further, the widening of scope of potential aesthetic stimuli from art objects alone to any object assures that responses to the fine arts will not be viewed mistakenly as some special esoteric exercise desirable or available only to middle-class, or educated, or especially sensitive individuals. Aesthetic attention can then be seen as it should be seen, as a part of everyday experience accessible to everyone, given the knowledge appropriate to the particular context.

A second consideration in dealing with the object in the aesthetic relationship is to decide upon some system of classification for the wide range of such materials. For the most part, such formulae are arbitrary although some attention to empirical observation is useful. For example, one valid classificatory distinction can be made between natural and humanmade objects, another between popular art works and fine or museum art works. In both instances, gray areas blurring the division are prevalent but not frequent enough to overwhelm the distinction. The distinctions remain tenable in a gross sense. Chapter 2, which describes the techniques and materials of art, will provide particulars on classification. Suffice it to say here that the prevailing principle to be emphasized is that all of the objects in our spatial world are capable of evoking aesthetic response. Classification is simply a way to arrange these multitudes of objects into some primitive sort of geography for further study.

A third issue concerning the object which ought to be studied is that it usually has immediate sensory qualities organized in a formal structure. In some recent work such as conceptual art, our experience appears to be as much or more a question of intellectual reaction as it is a product of visual stimulus; in Figure 32, for example, the idea or concept presented is more important than the visual elements of the art work. Nevertheless, in most aesthetic response the formal structure of the object is a critical (though not the sole) focus of attention, in contrast to the ways in which we usually attend to objects in nonaesthetic experience. One can ignore the visual structure of a machine like a power saw when concentrating on its practical function, unless one has an interest in its specific technology. However, attention to visual structure in the same object cannot be avoided when it is viewed from an aesthetic posture. In fact, when we shift our attention from the practical uses of a mechanism to its formal character (with comments such as, "That's a beautiful machine"), we seem to be moving toward what can be called "aesthetic contemplation."

In most of the visual arts, these sensory qualities and the ways in which they are structured impose a particular character to our experience of them which is significantly different from our experience of other art forms such as music, dance, drama, or literature. One important difference, which should be carefully explored in any learning situation, is the spatial/temporal distinction, which is that all but the visual arts are sequentially presented, changing internally over time. One can "watch" a play or ballet or film, but not a paint-

32. Wayne Enstice, *Stick Gum Up Sweet V,* improvisatory floor work in medium of match-books and reconstituted rag paper, 7½ × 56″, 1982. Collection of Wayne Enstice, courtesy of the artist

ing. The mobile (see Figure 39) and some other contemporary art forms, as well as some of the paintings of the Futurists, illustrate attempts to circumvent the purely spatial character of the visual arts.

A fourth consideration in discussing the object is that all made objects have grown out of a context, a particular place and time and, in the case of many objects (especially art objects), the life and work of a particular person. Indeed, it might be said that it is often the context which identifies the object and how it might be or should be viewed. This idea is illustrated by Dewey's instance of the handsomely shaped rock in the art museum which was attributed to an anonymous artist until it was discovered that the rock was, in fact, formed by the movement of the ocean. At that point, it was removed from the art museum and placed in a museum of natural history.

The History. History as an element in our inquiry refers to the circumstances or context of the aesthetic experience as well as to the background of the object itself. These should include the setting in which the object is seen (a view from a window, a television screen, or a gallery room), the time and place in which and purpose for which the object was made, the life of the person who made it, and the background of other objects similar to the one in question. The assumption on which this element of the aesthetic field is based is that nothing is seen in isolation from the rest of our experience; our viewing is continuous with all that is happening to us. Nor is anything seen to which we do not bring some previous knowledge or experience. Cognitive psychologists often take what might be called the extreme of this position, that we see only what we know how to look for.

Some conceptions of aesthetic functioning and art criticism suggest that these "historical" circumstances of context and background interfere with our negotiation of the object or art work. We are not seeing the object as it is when we see it through a filter of so-called extra-aesthetic considerations. One must, according to these *formalist* conceptions, suspend or put aside irrelevancies and attend to the properly aesthetic factors of the object, such as its organizations, its shape, or its colors.

It is assumed here that the history of an object in many of its ramifications contributes to the meanings, and thus to the potential for response, that object has for the viewer. Stolnitz puts it this way:

> In the aesthetic experience, any and every sort of awareness—sensory, perceptual, intellectual, imaginative, emotional—may occur. The definition of "aesthetic attitude" presented in this chapter does not exclude any of these *a priori*. It tries to do justice to the facts that men find aesthetic enjoyment in the smell of freshly cut hay, in novels and plays, in the mathematical-logical properties of "perfect" circles and trans-finite numbers. Thus we attempt to be faithful to the evidence and also avoid narrowing our investigation of aesthetic experience at the outset.[7]

As part of the history of the aesthetic situation, the setting or context in which the object is seen has several components. One of these is the physical setting itself. Some objects which evoke aesthetic response are seen as one portion of a wider view. For example, a striking rock formation may be part of a desert vista, or a handsome building may occupy the background of a film scene. In other instances such objects are viewed through or in a frame: an automobile window, the screen of a television set, the mat and edging of a framed print, the irregular framing of a hand on which a piece of jewelry is seen. In still other instances, the site may enhance aesthetic impact. The hilltop castle of Peñafiel in central Spain would probably not be quite as impressive on a flat plain. The room in the Prado in which Goya's *The Third of May* is shown is barely large enough for one to stand back and absorb this huge painting. The same work placed in a larger room might be even more impressive. Sometimes the setting even defines the object. Some of the 1960s sculptures of Robert Morris and David Smith would appear to be piles of construction material on a building site. In a gallery or museum they are seen as works of art.

Another aspect of the setting may be the climate. Or, the setting might include the physical or psychological conditions of viewing, such as the amount of lighting in a gallery, or the foot fatigue of a museum visitor, or the reluctant viewing of one who has been forced by social pressure to go to a gallery. In every case, some aspect of the setting might influence the nature of the viewer's response and, therefore, should be borne in mind, when deemed appropriate, particularly when one's response appears to be controversial or problematical.

There are the wider scale predispositions one brings to viewing, such as the attitude that gallery art is only for educated people, or that South Sea Islanders' art is "primitive" and thus unworthy of serious attention, or that all the art of the USSR is propaganda and, consequently, inherently inferior to so-called apolitical art. An attitude opposite to these, that all art is worthy of attention, might also operate as a factor in viewing. Whether we wish them to do so or not, each of these attitudes might contribute to the way in which the object is seen and, also, to our judgment of it. In a very real sense they are parts of the history of the object or, more specifically, the history of the circumstances in which the object is or has been negotiated by the viewer.

The social background of the object itself, as far as that is known, is still another element in its history and another way in which meanings can be generated from viewing an object. To know, for example, that Henry Moore's drawings depicting rows of reclining figures were done as representations of Londoners sheltered in underground stations during the German air raids of World War II is to add a level of meaning which is unavailable without that information. To know further that Henry Moore is a sculptor is to understand the vigorously three-dimensional quality of the drawings and to see them as what they might well have been, sketches for the powerful sculptural forms which Moore spent a lifetime creating.

Some levels of meaning one might obtain from an object—its symbolism, ramifications of its subject matter, the role played by the object in its society and the development of its medium—are to varying degrees available to us only through knowledge of its history. Without this kind of information the viewer is limited to negotiation of formal qualities and obvious content. For example, José Clemente Orozco's painting *Zapatistas* (Figure 51, page 22) provides even the uninformed with a powerful diagonal composition, rich colors, a dramatic pattern of dark and light, and the pictorial content of a mass of what appear to be civilians marching and riding off to battle. For those who do not know the history of the painting, however, there is no way of recognizing a further level of meaning in this work, which is its revolutionary message of peasant against landowner. Nor, by the same token, can one read it as a symbol of and outcry against oppression. The function of the work as part of the tradition of social realist art is lost to us without knowledge of its history.

One might argue, of course, that none of the Orozco painting's extraformal elements, such as the history of its subject, are properly aesthetic factors but are, instead, literary elements. Nonetheless, these literary considerations themselves appear to evoke aesthetic reaction; we can respond to them as "poignant" or "thrilling" or even "beautiful." In another sense they justify and extend the function of the formal elements; the diagonality and the dark and light intensify our reception of the subject and the symbolism of the painting. These formal elements are, as Ben Shahn put it, the shape of its content. A pattern of verticals and horizontals and gentle gradations of dark and light would hardly have presented the subject as appropriately. One can appreciate how effectively Orozco used the formal grammar at his disposal to present his content, and that appreciation becomes an additional increment of value to be gained from the work.

It is important to note that these informational materials accrue in large measure by means of words; the visual data in works of art (in all objects, for that matter) are meager without the background of all the verbal preparation which we accumulate unknowingly. Much of what we absorb from what we see is dependent upon what we have brought to the visual experience and much of that is essentially built upon a foundation of words. The sombreros of the peasants in the Orozco painting would give us no clues to one aspect of its subject if we did not previously know that these were the traditional headgear of the Mexican farmer. Thus it is easy and not uncommon to exaggerate the efficacy of the communicative powers of visual images, without realizing the function of verbal background in the process.

Reservations about the communicative efficiency of visual images do not necessarily imply that no information is contained in them, nor that the artists —in the case of an art work—do not insert or invest both cognitive and emotive content in what they create. It is quite obvious that pictorial material contains specific data; a photograph, drawing, or diagram of a horse does offer particulars about one representative of that species. This is, in fact, one of the problems of the visual image, that it can only present a particular horse and not the general idea of horse. The horse in a picture must be a mare or stallion, a bay or black, an Arabian or Percheron; it cannot be the abstract idea. Arnheim explains this point: "The visual world presents itself as a continuum . . . it is . . . a world of individuality. It shows the particular specimen or instance in the uniqueness of its details—its difference from other things of its kind."[8] In other words, images are restricted by their nature to concrete, single examples, literally illustrations, and cannot present abstractions. The latter activity is the function of verbal language.

This restrictiveness does not apply to images used as symbols. For example, the dove holding an olive branch can signify the concept of peace and the bull in *Guernica* is a symbol of Spain, precisely because the images are recognized in those instances in the same way as verbal symbols. But one cannot comprehend their meaning unless one knows enough of the context of the image to apply the correct interpretation.

With language, general knowledge of word meanings will usually enable one to interpret meanings correctly in any verbal situation. Even here one can be confused or misled by uncommon or poetic usage and defeated completely by a foreign language. Written language did, in fact, start out with pictorial forms, or "pictographs," which, apparently, were too cumbersome or ineffectual (see Figure 29). We occasionally return to them in special cases of contemporary use such as international road signs.

The frequent use of the word "communication" in writings about art and art education has led to the assumption that the visual image, like verbal language, actually transmits information, that is, that there is a substantial correspondence between what the maker of the object (the artist) inserts and what the viewer on the other end of the transaction withdraws. What has been overlooked—in addition to the inherent inability of images to negotiate abstract ideas—is that much, if not most, of the information we obtain from visual images is carried through or brought to us by ancillary verbal language. We read or hear about the art work, then attach those meanings to the image, believing, mistakenly, that they are encased for our removal in that image.[9] This ineffectuality of visual cognitive communication is greatly increased in the case of emotive communication. Obviously works of art evoke feelings, but how can we know that those feelings correspond significantly to what the artist placed in the work? Perhaps it is this potential for ambiguity which is the visual arts' most valuable contribution to aesthetic experience. The viewer can use the work of art as a basis for imaginative thinking and can enjoy the emotional and intellectual rewards such "flights of fancy" might provide.

Finally, the most relevant material in a review of history is that information which describes the society and the times in which the object was fashioned and its role in the development of those styles in which similar objects were made. Ludwig Mies Van Der Rohe's Barcelona chair and a Chippendale chair each represent a social context and an era and, also, a stage in the progression of single seating units. Fortunately for this aspect of history, there is, in the case of many art works, a considerable amount of information about these issues. The problem would seem to be to decide which data are the most significant for particular groups of students. It is difficult to conceive of a general rule on this question; the answer is more likely to be found in the specifics of each work. However, some history in the sense of geography, chronology, politics, economics, culture and artistic style, is often relevant. Chapter 3, dealing with the perception of art from a slightly different perspective, will review and enlarge these points.

The Viewer.   The third factor in the aesthetic transaction is the viewer. Since the viewer is also the subject of the instructional situation, that is, the pupil in the school, it would be appropriate to inquire at first into the nature of the experiences the pupils themselves presently designate as aesthetic. Growing out of such dialogue could be the necessity to examine on what basis one might characterize a response to an object or event as aesthetic. The history of aesthetic theory provides us with a number of alternative answers.

Theories about the nature of art or of aesthetic experience are grouped in a variety of categories in writings which deal with the subject. Berleant categorizes aesthetic theories as: imitation, emotionalism, expression, communication, formalism.[10] Stolnitz offers divisions such as: the "imitation" theories, formalism, emotionalist theory, and the theory of aesthetic "fineness."[11] Rader with Jessup suggests: art as imitation of nature, art as the expression of values, the theory of fusion, and the theory of formal resemblance.[12] Weitz lists such headings as: formalism, voluntarism, emotionalism, intellectualism, intuitionism, and organicism.[13] Efland, writing in an art education context, groups the major ideas as: mimetic, pragmatic, expressive, and objectivist.[14]

The categories of aesthetic theory offered here have been designed to simplify these materials without undue disservice to the breadth of content. These will be entitled: imitation, emotionalism, formalism, intuition, and valuation. Although preference for one of these positions as the most practicable in the teaching situation will be indicated here, it is wisest to approach these ideas in the spirit suggested by Weitz: "It behooves us to deal generously with the traditional theories of art; because incorporated in every one of them is a debate over and argument for emphasizing or centering upon some particular feature of art which has been neglected or perverted . . . it [aesthetic theory] teaches us what to look for and how to look at it in art."[15]

1.   Historically and logically, the first group of ideas is made up of those which suggest that *imitation* is the essential characteristic of art. Thus, we know we are dealing with a work of art when it is a faithful reflection of life. Historians of aesthetics tell us that imitation theories can be located in the writings of Plato, Aristotle, Samuel Johnson, and Sir Joshua Reynolds. Some imitation theory emphasizes *simple imitation,* in which art mirrors life as realistically as possible. The *imitation of essences,* on the other hand, asserts that art should portray or reveal those universal qualities of an object or event, the main characteristics which define what an object or an event really is. Thus a church should have an uplifting or spiritual quality and should not look like a fast-food shop. Still other types of this group stress the *imitation of the ideal,* just as Nefertiti and Cheryl Tiegs have been pictured as ideal images of what handsome people should look like. Whatever its particular emphasis, each of the imitation theories is primarily concerned with the content of the work of art, the area in which verisimilitude or the accurate representation of life can best be portrayed.

Imitation theories are deceptively simple. On the one hand, it is difficult to deny that, in one sense, all art or all the arts do in fact "picture" some aspect of life, for without this correspondence they would have little meaning or value for us. On the other hand, it is also easy to see that this explanation does little to clarify why we react strongly to a work of art or to any stimulus which provokes an aesthetic response, often more strongly than we might to the actual experience of which the work is an authentic or an essential or an ideal reflection. Also, this theory does not account for natural objects, which are not works of art, nor for the formal qualities of art works, the ways in which they are arranged. While it may explain some of how and why we react aesthetically, it fails to cover the entire range of our responses.

2.   The second cluster of ideas gives us more information about this question. *Emotionalist* theories suggest that it is the feelings aroused or communicated by the work of art that constitute its uniquely aesthetic character. Writers such as Leo Tolstoy and I. A. Richards assert that art is the expression of an artist's feelings and that we respond to these feelings or, in fact, share them through the art work. In psychoanalytic terms, these emotions are or may be subconscious expressions of the artist's feelings that are, in turn, subconsciously recognized by the viewer.

Emotionalist ideas about aesthetic experience seem to be, at first, more satisfactory than imitation theory, for indeed art does deal with feelings. We do, after all, "feel" the beauty or importance of a work of art. However, these theories do not tell us nearly as much as we need to know about the subject. People have emotions outside of aesthetic experience. Is the emotion aroused or communicated by a work of art some special kind of feeling and, if so, what is its peculiar nature? Further, it is clear that some significant portion of our response to art is not emotional at all; rather it is cognitive or rational or intellectual. This inadequacy, in addition to those problems relating to the issue of communication discussed earlier in this chapter, hampers the explanatory power of an otherwise attractive conception of aesthetic response.

3. *Formalist* theories attempt to fill this void. British aestheticians such as Clive Bell and Roger Fry, writing at the turn of the century, explain the impact of art by suggesting that its experience is unique and separate from any other human experience and that its uniqueness is to be found in its "significant form," those formal qualities of visual relationships that structure works of art. The distinctive and definitive feature of a work of art is its composition or "design." All those other considerations involved in dealing with art are non-aesthetic, in particular the "representational" element.

But to know that aesthetic response is provoked by significant form does not help to explain the nature of aesthetic response itself. Nor does it account for other factors involved in dealing with art (such as content), which appear to influence our responses. Further, the isolation of aesthetic emotion from other behavioral elements is far too severe to be authentic; it seems unlikely that humans are quite that segmented in their activities. Nonetheless, this is an appealing aesthetic theory that seems to have more than a little currency in art teaching since it supports our traditional preoccupation with learning about visual relationships.

4. Another group of ideas about aesthetic experience can be called *intuition* theory and is represented in the works of writers such as Benedetto Croce, Henri Bergson, and Sir Herbert Read. This theory assumes some manner of transcendental or spiritual reality, a realm of being in which reside universal harmonies (and, sometimes, moral laws) of which the material world is a reflection or expression. Art, then, is the direct, intuitive confrontation of this reality. For those who take this position, art is a suprarational recognition of truth, and its revealing of this ultimate reality accounts for the power of its impact, its aesthetic quality.

Intuition theory is, perhaps, less fruitful in revealing insight about aesthetic activity than are the other categories of ideas, for while intuition theory avoids some of the limitations of the other ideas discussed here (it does not reduce aesthetic functioning to a single factor nor does it promote discontinuity within human response) it depends for explanation on a controversial assumption, the existence of a more than physical reality. This is by no means a necessary assumption about the world, nor does it follow, having made the assumption, that we must see art as the mechanism for breaking through to that metaphysical realm. Like the significant form of the formalists, this confrontation of transcendental truth is not helpful to our task, since both substitute an unexplained or unexplainable concept in place of aesthetic experience.

5. A final group of ideas and the one favored here for school use can be called *valuation* theory. To writers such as D. W. Gotshalk, Alfred N. Whitehead, John Dewey, and some Marxist aestheticians, aesthetic response is the placement of intrinsic value on an object or event. We recognize our experience as aesthetic when it is unconcerned with its consequences; the experience

assumes value to us for its own sake. Thus a vintage automobile can be viewed as aesthetically valuable even though it cannot be driven or ridden, even though it has no utilitarian or moral value as a consequence; it has a value or virtue in itself. Dewey calls this characteristic "self-consummatory" and broadens the domain of the aesthetic beyond art to any experience having this quality. Thus, the aesthetic experience is resolved and complete within itself. He writes, "Art is a quality that permeates an experience . . . in it [aesthetic experience] a body of matters and meanings not in themselves esthetic, *become* esthetic as they enter into an ordered rhythmic movement towards consummation."[16]

However, we sometimes call a tool or machine "beautiful" simply because it performs its practical function so effectively. This would seem to be a conferring of aesthetic status on the basis of consequences. Nor can value theories of aesthetics easily explain how one such experience is recognized as more powerful than another, except by asserting that the internal resolution of one experience is more complete than that of another, which is not as helpful to us as it needs to be.

Despite these problems, however, value theories at least avoid the main pitfalls of the others. They do not reduce all the experience of art to one of its characteristics. Also, they provide a reasonable continuity between the experience of art and other human experiences. Finally, they account fairly well for the tremendous diversity of stimuli designated as art or as beautiful by human beings throughout history—objects and events as varied as the sight of a bomb burst (by Vittorio Mussolini during the Ethiopian War) to twenty miles of white nylon fence across Marin County by the American artist Christo. Just as science can be said to be made up of propositions of fact about the world which can be verified with varying degrees of certitude, art can be said to be made up of those materials which represent the views or visions of others as to what is of intrinsic value. Thus, while a sunset is aesthetically valuable because it strikes us as important enough to be attended to for its own sake, the monoliths of Stonehenge are valuable, in part, because they were deemed to be of value by their creators. Even if we do not know all the reasons for their valuation (as we do not with any certainty in the case of Stonehenge), we recognize that the effort involved in its construction signifies prior valuation. When we do know the reasons, when we have adequate information on the history of the object, we have access to still other motivations to prize that object. If we were to discover, for example, that the structure is a testament in stone to the sun (in a religious sense), we might respond to that expression of value of the creators by a further increment of valuation of our own. It may be that each portion of significant information about an object—knowledge of the Latin name of a shrub, or the life style of the sculptor—promotes additional layers of viewer valuation in the process of aesthetic contemplation.

It is important to note that this placement of value is not an exclusively intellectual, nor yet a wholly emotional process. We can say with equal conviction and justification, I think this is valuable or I feel this is valuable, the former statement suggesting that one can provide reasons to support the observation. Nevertheless, the concept of valuation itself suggests desirability, which carries the obvious connotation of some degree of emotive investment. Perhaps, as with individual differences among people, too much has been made of this distinction in writing about art. Fortunately, in the context of valuation theory, aesthetic experience is seen as both cognitive and emotive, both objective and subjective, both formal and representational, depending for its parameters on the specifics of the particular situation. It embraces all of the variety of possibilities available in what is reported as characterizing aesthetic response. It is able to explain how evil and horror can evoke what seems to be aesthetic response and how what appear to be purely cognitive transactions with literal meanings in a work of art elicit the same reaction (though it would probably be more accurate to suggest that there are no purely cognitive functions, as all cognition can be said to have affective or emotive reverberations, while all feelings have cognitive cues). It is not dependent on the creator of the object, the artist (or the performer, if it is that type of work), nor upon social recognition such as acceptance into the world of museum or gallery art. That which can be said to evoke aesthetic response is that object or event which one determines to be of importance, hence of value, for its own sake.

Best of all, for the purposes of schooling, this idea responds to all sorts of stimuli, from natural events to Old Masters, from the mass media to antique artifacts, from the most abstract instances of conceptual art to the paintings of the nineteenth-century French Realists. It most adequately satisfies the requirement which Arnstine, writing about aesthetic education, describes:

> Aesthetic quality, then, may characterize virtually any sort of experience at all and is in no reasonable sense limited to confrontations with what are traditionally called works of art. The special significance that works of art do have lies in their capacity to emphasize and heighten the qualities of experience that we meet only accidentally when confronting other things and events in the world. Aesthetic education which ignored works of art would thus lose a valuable resource. But aesthetic education which ignored examining the rest of the world in its artistic dimensions could only result in a sharp distortion of both art and the world.[17]

It is a theory genuinely egalitarian and universal and, thus, can be used in an educational context to structure understanding of viewer behavior.

Much like the other ideas presented here, valuation theory has its limitations. Perhaps chief among these is that the concept of aesthetic functioning as the placement of intrinsic value does not explain all that we need to know about the process. In contrast to some of the other theories, it is too broad in its view rather than too narrow. As presented here, it fails to describe the specific mechanics of this value investment, or what part is played by our intellectual response and what part by our feelings, or what aspects of the object promote these conditions. Perhaps, as Weitz asserts, aesthetic theory conceived as definition is "logically doomed to failure."[18]

Other factors in viewer activity which influence aesthetic response and which merit classroom discussion include the attitudes toward aesthetic experience and art of one's family, friends, and subcultural group, the relationships of the object or art work to nonaesthetic (i.e., practical, moral) considerations, and personal associations elicited by the object. For example, cues in the Orozco painting such as the sombreros might bring to mind another fictional or real-life event within the experience of the viewer and occasion further aesthetic (or, for that matter, nonaesthetic) response. These memories are necessarily unique to that viewer and the nature of such response is clearly subjective. The sombrero is an objective datum, but its interpretation is dependent on individual biography. In chapter 3 these factors are further discussed.

One final aspect of viewer behavior which needs to be mentioned is judgment. When this act might occur within the continuum of seeing-appreciating-understanding is far from obvious. It is most likely that judgment takes place at different times during the aesthetic encounter, depending on the specifics of each aesthetic situation. Nevertheless, we can say, as will be suggested later, that while we might and should suspend judgment, we cannot avoid it. The human organism seems to be, by virtue of its biological history, a judgmental mechanism, ever alert to both threatening and gratifying factors around it. What we can do in the aesthetic transaction is to try to hold each controversial judgment in abeyance until we have certified it with a rationale. As Ecker once put it, to say that one likes an object (such as a work of art) is simply to provide a psychological report, a bulletin proclaiming one's state of mind. On the other hand, to say that the object is a good example of its class for the following reasons is to make a substantive and educationally useful comment about it. It is what Ecker called a critical or value judgment.[19] Education should strive to habituate the latter type of statement in order to generate student dialogue.

Insisting on critical judgments in place of, or in addition to, psychological reports within a school context can serve to monitor talk about art and other related visual experience, so that it might enhance the precision of understanding in aesthetic response. This precision might, in turn, promote more adequate comprehension and appreciation in future aesthetic encounters. Whether, in fact, the enlargement of understanding influences or even conditions the viewer's taste or enjoyment, is difficult to judge. It is probable that we tend to enjoy what we know about. Nevertheless, it is quite possible to appreciate, in the sense of recognizing value (what Berleant in the volume previously cited calls "appraising" rather than "prizing") without deriving likeable sensations. The journey from knowledge back to Ecker's "psychological report" is an open question. Perhaps this is just as well, since to influence pupils' likes and dislikes might be seen by some as beyond the prerogative of education. Our moral traditions suggest that there should be some differences between education and indoctrination and, as the Latin proverb has it, in matters of taste the individual is (and should be) the final arbiter.

Further, having to make critical judgments will allow us to suspend our evaluation of the object in view until we have had a chance to interact with the object, its context, and its background. We should try to "give it a fair shake" before we form a judgment. Also, postponement of evaluation can help us to determine which historical considerations are appropriate to our negotiation of the object. While there are no general criteria for determining the relevancy of these considerations, time for careful assessment might permit us, at least, to become aware of what they are.

Elements of viewer activity might collectively constitute the most stimulating material available to the art teacher in that they are personal and self-exploratory to the pupils. Nevertheless, traditional writings on art and art education often avoid such material, in part because they direct attention away from the work of art and the artist, those areas of concern most highly prized by scholars. There is, of course, a vast body of aesthetic speculation and debate which has been omitted here on the basis that such information is valuable but not critical to the initial classroom task of understanding aesthetic behavior. This chapter presents the basic ideas in this context.

This review of aesthetic theories, brief and incomplete as it is, provides us with some information on the basis of which we can answer the kinds of questions pupils in school are likely to ask. In fact, if the children do not ask significant questions about the nature of art, the teacher should pose these questions and answer them. The most obvious of these queries, whether it is raised overtly or by implication, is: What is art?

defining a work of art

As we said in an earlier part of this chapter, art is "humanmade." We also noted in the discussion of the purposes of art that what people make to be seen—at least when it is called art—must have importance or value to us; it must stand out in some way from our experience of other objects around it. It must have meanings; it must cause us to have thoughts and feelings, which make it stand out. It might also be said that this importance or value must be of a special kind: the object must be of value for its own sake—not valuable only because it is of use to us. Thus, for someone who finds old automobiles exciting and beautiful, a 1937 Buick which no longer runs is important and valuable to look at even though the car cannot be driven. It is a work of art. On the other hand, when we are concentrating on what an object can do for us, like the efficiency with which a power saw cuts wood, we are less concerned with how it is put together and how it looks. It is important to us for another reason than its artistic or "aesthetic" qualities.

If we put all these ideas together, we might say that *a work of visual art is a made object we see that we value for its own sake.* Although this statement is far from a sound or even a complete definition of art, since there are questions about art it cannot answer, it may help us to understand the nature of art.

One problem with this explanation of art, which one might notice right away, is that it does not make clear whether the meanings we value and are talking about are in the work of art or are put there by the viewer. Our best judgment is that both ideas are true, that the meanings of a work of art are an exchange between the viewer and the work. For example, it is clear from this explanation that a work of art is usually an object whose maker, at least, thinks it to be of value for its own sake. When a cabinetmaker builds a fine chest of drawers (Figure 12), he makes it not only to hold clothing and other items, but to look good or important as well. Even if we know little else about an object from long ago (such as Figure 33, page 20), we can often tell, from its size or where it is placed or how it is made, that someone thought of it as valuable in this way. Thus, we, too, can give it the same kind of attention: we can look at it as a work of art. If later we learn more of the meanings—the thoughts and feelings the people had who made it and looked at it when it was made— we might see those meanings ourselves. This is one reason why it is of help to us to know something about art works. It makes sense to take this view, just as it makes sense to know the rules of basketball, so you can really "see" what is going on in the game.

It is probable that we sometimes find meanings in an art work or think it is important for reasons very different from those of the maker of the work or those of people who lived at the same time as the artist. This is particularly true of older art works, but could be just as true about objects created today. Art works have meanings in their own times and places. Or it may be that the work will remind you as an individual of something in your own life which no one else can share. There is no good reason why we cannot do this; art is not a rigid message system with right and wrong answers. But it does make sense to try to find out what an art work might have meant in its own time and place and see if we can find the same meaning or importance in it. After that we can be free to see what we wish in it or to like or dislike it.

Now that we have looked at some of the ideas people have had about the nature of art, we can examine what *meanings* works of art might have for us and how they are placed in a work by the artist or by the society in which the artist lived or by us as we look at the work. The reasons for making art are varied and, consequently, the meanings in works of art are varied as well. If we use Pablo Picasso's *Guernica* (Figure 17) as an example, at least four different kinds of meanings can be described.

First of all, it is obvious that the object is a work of art since it is in a museum (the Prado in Madrid, Spain) and, therefore, is thought to be important for its own sake. Secondly, the subject of the painting—the twisted, distorted figures with expressions of pain and horror—seems to express the artist's shock at something in the world around him. Actually, we know that Picasso, who was a Spaniard, was horrified at the bombing of civilians in the small town of Guernica during the civil war in Spain in the mid–1930s. Third, the painting also has symbolic meanings, in that particular signs or images stand for specific ideas. Some believe, for example, that the bull in the upper left-hand portion of the painting represents the pride and courage of Spain. For those who recognize the symbol, this meaning, too, is clear. Not so obvious, however, is another kind of meaning found in the same work, which is made up of emotional response to the diagonal slashes of line, the jaggedness of the forms, the sharp contrasts of dark and light—the arranging of the visual elements by the artist. These arrangements heighten the impact of the second meaning, for would *Guernica* be as forceful with quiet, horizontal and vertical lines, and gently curved forms? Even if the painting were not about war and the figures were not recognizable forms, the visual arrangement alone can provoke strong emotional response. Two examples are Figures 34 and 30. In the first, the human

form is barely recognizable, while in the second the shapes are primarily geometric rather than representational.

Almost all art that we know of contains this fourth type of meaning, stimulating our response by its visual arrangement or the way in which the parts
have been put together, or what we call its "formal qualities." In fact, a description of what art is, up to quite recently, would have had to include formal
qualities as an essential characteristic. However, recent art frequently con-
fronts us with images or information which seem deliberately to avoid a concern for qualities, but depend, instead, on other meanings. So strong
was this a characteristic of Pop art (Figure 35), for example, that some writers
spoke of it as "anti-art" while others considered it the liberation of art from its
limiting traditions. Indeed, some artists avoided making any image at all. Instead they presented the thoughts with which they had been concerned, often
in the form of a written statement. This style or idea became known as "conceptual art."

If these are some of the ways in which meanings occur in art, how strong
do our responses have to be before we can characterize an object as an art
work? It is tempting for the writer on art to say the stronger the better, or the
stronger the emotion aroused, and the more important the ideas, the greater
the work of art. Yet, art, like living itself, is not always a matter of intense feelings or great ideas. The grace of an elegantly curved staircase or the charm of a
bright yellow flower photographed against a soft blue sky can cause delight,
which is certainly a substantial emotion, though not a powerful one. The feelings we have about, and the ideas we get from, a work of art must, at least, be
more than ordinary; they must be strong enough to set the work of art apart
from all the other things we see.

What are these meanings that exist for their own sake? Aside from the example of the 1937 Buick, a useful illustration is that of money. Certainly a dollar bill is a humanmade object which we see and which can have meanings.
Yet, for most of us the feelings and ideas inspired have to do with what can be
purchased with the money rather than with the bill itself. For some very few
misers, the money itself and for its own sake arouses emotions. At this point,
the dollar has become, for them, almost a work of art or at least an object that
causes an aesthetic experience. Another more familiar instance can be found in
watching a football game, when, for example, someone comments that the last
play involved a "beautiful pass." The fact that the pass was also incomplete, or
not caught, is not always important. Sometimes an athletic action can be
thought of as beautiful for its own sake, for the way it was performed, regardless of its consequences.

This description of the nature of art gives us a useful concept with which
to answer questions such as: "When is a dish or a chair a work of art?" or "What
makes a building Architecture with a capital A?" or "Why is a painting of a
Campbell soup can (Figure 35) called a work of art?" At least part of the answer
in each case would be that these humanmade objects are works of art because
meanings and value are placed in them by those who make them, by the society in which they function, and by those who look at them in later years.

The author clearly recalls an incident, which took place during the 1965

art education conference at Pennsylvania State University, that relates to this question. In the midst of the vigorous dialogue professional meetings sometimes provide, one of the participants asked, "Yes, but what is art?" From the back of the auditorium came the booming voice of Harold Rosenberg, then art critic of the *New Yorker* magazine. He said he knew what art was, it was what was on exhibit in New York, London, and Paris (it is hoped that the author's memory is accurate and that this paraphrase does justice to Rosenberg's remark). As facetious as the comment may sound, it is, in fact, a sturdy rule of thumb in determining what objects are art—in the sense of fine art. We know an object is art when museums, galleries, art critics, and artists tell us it is art.

One question which our description of the nature of art does not answer is whether the meanings drawn from the work of art by an observer must be the same as those placed in it by the artist. This is why we have not emphasized the idea of art as clear-cut communication. In some cases, art does communi-

34 (left). Stanley William Hayter, *Tarantelle,* engraving and soft ground etching on copper, 21 11/16×13", 1943. Collection, The Museum of Modern Art, New York. Edward M. M. Warburg Fund

35 (right). Andy Warhol, *Campbell's Soup Can,* silkscreen on canvas, 1964. Photo Courtesy of the Leo Castelli Gallery, New York

cate effectively. The feelings of the observer are likely to be close to those intended or felt by the artist, or by the society in which the artist lived, as in Figure 20, for example. In other instances, such as Figure 30, it is unlikely—or at
least very difficult to determine—that much of the intent of the artist is clearly
communicated to the observer. The only reasonable position is that meanings
are placed in and taken from works of art, and that the correspondence or the
degree of similarity between the two sets of meanings depends upon the particular circumstances, such as the style of the artist and the amount of knowledge
of the observer. Certainly artists—in the overwhelming majority of instances
we know about—do wish to communicate their feelings. But this probably
does not happen very often. What the artist does is to stimulate our thinking
and feeling about what has been created, even if our responses do not correspond to the artist's intentions.

Another question this description does not answer is who or how many
people must find meanings in an object before it can be called a work of art? Is
one person's judgment enough or must there be several or many? Must the
judgment be made by the artist, or by other artists, or an art critic or museum
director, or can each one of us make these decisions? The only answer that
makes sense is that what is called art is decided by different groups of people at
different times. In the Middle Ages, tradition, in the form of craft guilds and
monasteries, kept a fairly steady point of view of what meanings made an object a work of art. In our own day, at least in the United States and Western
Europe, a small group of artists, art critics, and museum and gallery directors
most often decide what shall be called art, just as disc jockeys, singers, and
band leaders together often decide which popular tunes shall be "hits," or, as
we have described it here, have highly significant meanings.

In the end you and I must decide what is art for ourselves. You must decide what you enjoy or what you think is of value. If what you decide is different
from the judgments of those in the art world, you will have no way to change
their ideas—unless, of course, you become an artist or art critic. Some of us enjoy being independent in this way, others do not. Whatever our preferences,
we should at least understand how these judgments are made.

RECENT CHANGES IN WHAT IS CALLED ART

The continual and often striking changes in styles of art during this century
provide useful evidence of the wide variety of types that have been accepted
as art by those who make up the art world. We have had art that dealt with
social problems, sometimes called "Social Realism," as in Figure 24. Another
style has been called "Surrealism," using symbols that are supposed to come
from our dreams and from the subconscious mind (Figure 36). In this painting
the deep shadows, the irregular perspective of the boxlike shape and the building, and the banners blowing in the strong wind might remind us of dreams—
vivid, yet not always realistic. Other artists created "Op" (optical) art works
such as Figure 37, designed—in a sense—to play tricks with your eyes. Still

36. Giorgio de Chirico, *The Nostalgia of the Infinite,* oil on canvas, 53¼ × 25½″ 1913–14? (dated on painting 1911). Collection, The Museum of Modern Art, New York

37. Bridget Riley, *Hesitate,* acrylic on board, 1964. Courtesy of Sotheby Parke Bernet © 1980

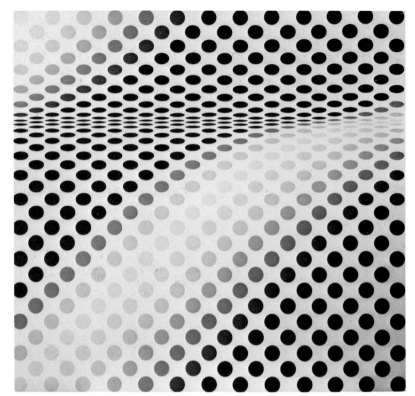

38. George Segal, *The Dinner Table,* 1962. Courtesy of Seymour Schweber, Schweber Electronics

others developed "Pop" art, such as Figure 35, in which visual symbols of our popular culture, like comic strips or consumer objects, were represented and, in one sense, questioned.

Art critics and art historians find many reasons for this wide range in styles: the expanded questioning of all traditional values and patterns in the twentieth century; the impact of two devastating world wars; and the awakening resentment and revolt against social injustice. It is probable that all these reasons together are correct rather than just one or two of them. These and other pressures make today's world tense, uncertain, and restless. The artist, like all of us, lives in this world, is uncertain and restless, endlessly searching for new ways to look at what is around us.

The decades of the 1950s and 1960s (at least in America) seem to have been a period during which art styles and techniques were increasingly experimental, often developing new devices for creating visual images. Some of these devices were special ways of painting; others went beyond painting or traditional sculptural techniques altogether. Some had particular names, others did not. "Frottage" in painting, for example, involved pressing an oil-painted canvas against an irregular surface and scraping away the paint where the canvas touched the high spots of that surface. Another device used twigs, leaves, machine parts, or any "found" object, dipped in paint and pressed on canvas. Still another attached these objects on the painted canvas and left them there as part of the image. Another process called "decalcomania" squeezed wet masses of paint between two canvases much like folded-paper ink blots. One step further carried us to dropping paint or turpentine or dripping it from a stick onto the canvas on the floor. An even greater degree of accidental effect was created when a French painter fired a rifle at bags of paint hung on a wall or when firecrackers were set off in bags of paint on a surface. One unusual technique was to drive an automobile back and forth over a painted canvas. All these forms have been called art and have been placed in museums and galleries.

Sculptors also attempted new processes of image making. From old automobiles squeezed by a huge press into cubes of tightly packed, twisted metal to "Environments" in which life-size plaster figures are set into real interiors (see Figure 38), the sculptor moved further away from the traditions of the artistic past. Artists have wrapped large buildings in huge sheets of polyethylene plastic; built a block of packages of $1.00 bills (totaling, in one case, $250,000) and exhibited it as sculpture; dug mile-long furrows and mounds of earth in the desert; collected one day's paper litter from a floor of the New York Stock Exchange and exhibited it on the roof of a midtown building; and assembled contributions from thirty artists for a show of "Your Worst Work." These new forms, shocking at first in their novelty, became tame and "old-hat" as even more unusual forms were developed. These ever-quickening changes appear to create pressures for even newer styles.

One of the most unusual developments in the visual arts of the 1950s was the "Happening." Although it grew from the experiments of artists and was very much something that was seen, the impact of the Happening depended as much on what was heard and the drama-like quality of its process. As nearly as it can be described, a Happening was a series of actual events "acted" by real people in a carefully organized environment. Dressed in deliberately bizarre costumes, the participants (sometimes including the audience) performed un-related and absurd actions—such as destroying furniture, covering one another with trash, riding a motorcycle in circles—to the accompaniment of outlandish sounds. Some Happenings were completely spontaneous, others had carefully planned scripts. However it was engineered, the Happening seemed to be as far away from the traditional visual arts as one can get. From the point of view of this book, the Happening, and what have recently been called "Performance Pieces," move away from being visual art works entirely. They become, instead, a drama, an event, like television, motion pictures, or a play. We watch them; our attention and the meanings we get from them are a matter of changing images or sights over a period of time, unlike the tradition-al art work which does not change as we look at it. In this sense, these works are something like moving sculptures (Figure 39).

Of course, no harm is done if we call these events art or even fine art—as, in fact, they are usually identified—as long as their very different nature does not confuse us. The distinction made here between objects of art and events is simply for the purpose of understanding, as clearly as possible, what art is. It does seem as if the artist today, at least in some art forms, is more interested in the novelty and originality of what is created than in what is expressed. In a sense, the art is in the unexpected way in which it is made rather than in what is made. The process of making works of art rather than the products themselves is often seen as art. To some contemporary artists, what is left when they finish working is unimportant. In conceptual art, for example, a written or diagramed description of a planned or finished art work is sometimes placed on the gallery wall. This style is different enough from what we call traditional art to be puzzling and, sometimes, unattractive.

In addition to the restless changing of the artist's modes of expression, several important social and technological changes that influence the world of art have occurred during this century. One of these changes is the great in-crease in the number of "things" those of us who live in the affluent nations possess. Many of us have enough money to own automobiles, television sets, radios, refrigerators, washing machines, as well as furniture, clothes, and household objects. Not only are some of these manufactured items built to wear out quickly, but the styles of all of them change, usually every year. Thus, we own even more "things" during a lifetime, since they are replaced so often. Each object must be designed and, in many cases, its appearance radi-cally altered every few years in order to promote sales. This is why industrial design is such a large part of the visual arts of today.

Together with the growth of industrial design in the manufacture of mass-produced goods there have been tremendous changes in the quality and forms of advertising. With several firms making the same product and competing to sell it, advertising in magazines and newspapers, on billboards, posters, radio, and television, is seen as a necessity for influencing our purchasing choices, and advertising art is a significant part of the visual arts of today.

A third change, and one which is technological, is the development of photography and, through still photography, motion pictures and television.

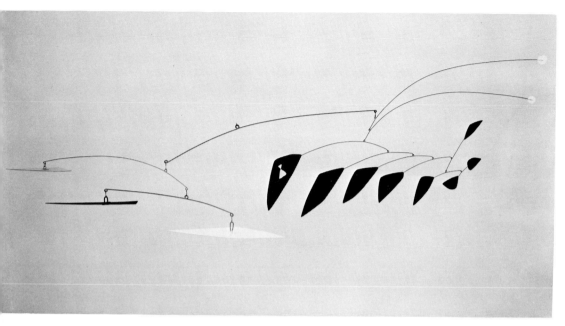

39. Alexander Calder, *Two White Dots in the Air*, metal, 1958. Photograph Courtesy of the Perls Galleries, New York

The last two combine all the major arts—bringing together visual arts, music, and literature in the form of drama and the older theater arts of stage and costume design, pantomime, dance, and acting. Still photography and television are likewise vital forms of, or parts of, advertising.

A fourth and striking change is the overwhelming spread of the popular arts. Even fifty years ago, although there were both folk arts such as painted decorations on furniture and popular arts such as newspaper drawings and cartoons, these were small in number and limited in type. Today, the scope in types of popular arts, their incredibly vast quantity, and their frequently excellent quality (from a technical point of view if no other) have created a situation in which no one in the United States, no matter how isolated, can escape exposure to some form of popular art. Music, of course, is the clearest example of how the popular arts saturate our surroundings. Transistor radios, television sets, jukeboxes blare out popular tunes wherever we go. But the visual popular arts are just as widespread, though, perhaps, not as obvious. Magazines, clothes, personality and psychedelic posters, and billboards beam millions of visual images toward us; and their number and vigor seem to grow each year.

The appearance of these new art forms—such as advertising and photographic media, the expansion of industrial design, and the popular arts—has not only widened the range of objects we make and look at as art, but has also raised questions about what we believe art to be. There are those, for example, who would deny that the popular arts have or can have any of the stature of the fine arts; that there is, in fact, a hard and indelible line of distinction between the two, and that the former is inherently inferior. Others, such as symphony orchestra conductor and composer, Leonard Bernstein (who narrated an hour-long TV program called "The Pop Revolution"), defend popular music as capable of having significant art qualities—that is, in terms of our description of what art is, containing significant meanings. Another instance was the case of the Beatles films, *Help, A Hard Day's Night,* and *Yellow Submarine* which were frequently cited by serious movie critics as excellent examples of cinema art.

Whatever problems our century may have raised in the arts, there is no question that it has also brought, through advancing technology, a staggering wealth of visual images to all. Even fifty years ago, most Americans depended upon a few newspapers, infrequent book illustrations, and expensive reproductions of paintings and slides, since original works of art were not near enough to visit. Now with television, movies, picture magazines, paperback books, and reproductions, all of us can easily look at the contents of the world's greatest museums, and at architectural masterpieces from far away and long ago, even if we can never go to see the originals. This is perhaps the greatest contribution of technology and social change to the arts we see.

The careful reader will have noted that paintings dominate the visuals used as illustrations in this book. This is not because painting is thought of as a more important art form than any of the others described in chapter 2. It is simply because many of the questions raised and answered about the arts we see can be most easily illustrated in drawings, paintings, and prints. To many, the most significant visual art forms of the present day are those which represent the popular arts, particularly still photography, product design, and advertising.

It might also be noticed that most of the illustrations used in this book represent American and Western European art works, old and new. This is certainly not meant to suggest that we have any monopoly on past or present works of fine or folk art. In Asia, Africa, the Middle East and Latin America, these art forms have a long and proud tradition and are practiced today with skill and significance. On the other hand, it is difficult enough to understand thoroughly the arts of our own culture, much less those from other cultures and, thus, we have concentrated here on our own. It should be clear that the arts we see are everywhere and that all of them are worth looking at and learning about.

Finally, it should be noted that the illustrations in this volume are but a very, very few of the literally thousands of objects of art of all kinds—from buildings to record-album covers—which people have created and are still creating. As much as one might wish to collect and present all of these, or even many of these to the reader, it is, of course, quite impossible. One can only hope that the reader, armed with the knowledge provided in this book—as incomplete as it is—will seek to find as many of these objects as a lifetime will permit. They are enjoyable enough to be worth looking for.

THE ARTIST

Some people still think of the artist as a weird, unconventional character who cuts off his ear to offer as a gift (Vincent van Gogh), or abandons his family in order to paint in the South Seas (Paul Gauguin), or lives a generally disreputable life. To be sure, there were and are artists who behave in similar fashion. However, most artists live just as you and I do. The difference between artists and other people is that they see portions of the world around them or their own ideas and feelings in patterns or relationships of shapes, colors, and textures and have the ability to arrange these meanings—feelings, ideas, patterns—into combinations of physical materials which we call paintings, photographs, and other visual art forms.

Most artists go through a very thorough and specific training, learning the skills of the art form they plan to work with, often in an art school or a college. Fine photographs are not usually made simply by pointing a camera at a fascinating scene, nor are fine paintings made by casual slashes or dribbles of paint on canvas—even though the works may give the appearance of being done this way. All artists think mostly in terms of visual qualities, and must not only put a great deal of thought into their work but also obtain knowledge and skills to produce these qualities.

The ways in which artists approach and solve visual problems are much the same in all the arts we see. Yet there are striking differences. These are principally the particular qualities of the materials they work with, such as paint or stone or colored light; the functions or uses of what they create, such as houses, costumes, or dishes; how the art object is to be seen, as from a distance, or on the page of a book. These differences make it unusual, for instance, for the painter to be an expert architect without special study, although some of the training both artists receive is the same. Perhaps this is something similar to the abilities involved in playing musical instruments. The expert pianist does not necessarily play the guitar well, but does, however, understand how musical sounds are made on the guitar and can probably learn to play it well much more quickly than one who does not play the piano at all.

In some societies and in some periods of time in the history of Western culture, the artist was almost an anonymous figure, a highly skilled worker rather than a unique personality. For example, six or seven hundred years ago, medieval artists carved stone sculptures all over the cathedrals of Europe. But they did not sign their works, and we know very few of their names. In the same way, the wood carver of Samoa today may be just an inhabitant of the village who makes art, but again does not place his or her name on what is created. In contrast, many artists sign each major work of art to identify it as their own, and sometimes museums and collectors will buy a painting or sculpture because of the reputation of the artist rather than for the work of art itself.

Many who write on art and artists make the mistake of romanticizing the abilities of the artist. They credit the artist with some sort of supernatural wisdom and insight although history suggests that these attributes are more characteristic of individuals than of classes of people, such as artists or politicians or scientists. There are those who claim, for example, that artists—painters in particular—predicted nuclear fission. Others believe that artists, as a class of people, have some mysterious pipeline to universal laws of good and evil. Still others maintain that the artist possesses a shortcut to fundamental truths about the universe.

All these ideas may be interesting to wonder about, but they do not stand up under any kind of critical examination. Nor do they recognize the artist's unique talent, namely, to call to our attention that which is important and beautiful to see. The artist is not primarily interested in what is in the world, at least not in the same way as the scientist—although some artists have studied the world scientifically, as Leonardo da Vinci did in his drawings of the structure of human anatomy. Nor is the artist centrally concerned with moral problems—though some artists make moral statements in their art, such as Daumier in Figure 16. The artist's chief involvement is with what is visually significant; and when this concern is dealt with brilliantly, the artist can give us visual experiences that are important and exciting. In short, the artist is neither a superperson, nor a peculiar individual. The artist is probably a gifted person and usually trained to see and create what is especially worth looking at.

Although it is difficult to construct strict categories that make it possible for us to value one artist over another or one work of art over another, there are unquestionably some artists, in each of the arts we see, whose works have so greatly influenced other artists as well as generations of viewers that they merit the term "great." Painters such as Rembrandt, whose high rank in the minds of the viewing public makes him outstanding among artists, and Cézanne, whose innovations in the creation of an orderly space with paint on canvas changed the development of painting, would seem to be examples of candidates for greatness. Yet most people in the arts are less concerned with ranking artists than they are with making sure that what every artist has to offer is thoroughly understood and, if possible, enjoyed.

In this book the words "artist" and "designer" are used interchangeably, even though there is at least one striking difference between the two activities. A designer arranges the form of an object which performs some practical function in addition to having expressive qualities. Thus, the architect and the landscape architect are called designers. The term "artist" is used for people who deal primarily or exclusively with expressive qualities in art forms, such as the painter or the sculptor. Still, since the basic attitudes and ways of thinking are the same, it is more important to emphasize these similarities by using the terms interchangeably than to stress the differences. If, by doing so, we think of all the arts we see as equally capable of giving us important or exciting meanings—at least in their potential—we can expand our range of visual enjoyment.

CHAPTER 2

the techniques
and
materials of art

When we use a word like "consumer," we think immediately of something we buy and use up. There is, however, another equally legitimate sense of the term. Every one of us consumes works of art in one form or another, just as we consume food and air. In some cases we use the art primarily, or only, for the enjoyment or sense of value it provides; in other instances we "use" it in some very practical way as well as enjoy it, for example, when we sit on a chair or wear a piece of clothing.

We can divide all the objects we see around us that we value for their own sakes into five categories: natural objects; folk arts; popular arts; practical arts; and fine, or expressive, arts. These are not, of course, hard and fast divisions. One object might easily serve two of these categories at the same time or at different times. A piece of driftwood picked up on the beach—a natural object—might be an expressive object when it is placed on a table in our home. Or, a painting of a landscape—an expressive object—might give us information about the place it pictures, serving in that case also as a practical object. Whatever the original use or purpose an object might have had, our use of art is mostly a matter of how we look at it. Nevertheless, in a broad sense, this rough classification helps us to organize what we know or can learn about the arts we see.

An important idea which should be remembered in reading this chapter is that the divisions made here (natural/folk/popular/practical/expressive) do not suggest that one of these kinds of objects is any more worthwhile than another simply because of its classification. We might value any one thing (for its own sake) more than another, whatever its origin. All visual materials are capable of providing aesthetic value, regardless of source or purpose.

In this chapter, we will concentrate on two of these categories: *practical arts* and *expressive arts*, although natural objects, folk arts, and popular arts will be looked at briefly. The reasons for this concentration are several. First, most of us—probably all of us—are familiar with natural objects, folk arts, and popular arts as sources of value and enjoyment. Second, most of the folk arts and popular arts are essentially practical (that is, they serve a useful purpose) or, in some cases, expressive in their technical nature and purpose. Third, the number of these objects, particularly popular arts, that exist around us is staggering. We could never hope to attend to them adequately. As long as the reader will realize that all these objects are of potential aesthetic value, the omission of natural objects, folk arts, and popular arts in our review of where we find the arts we see and how they are made should not be confusing.

Aside from natural objects, the arts we see exist in many forms, from very small pieces of jewelry to huge planned areas of cities, from ancient stone carvings to recent record-album covers. Some of them have histories almost as old as humanity; others have just been created. The arts we see are very easy to find if we know how to look for them. All of us live in buildings, sit on chairs, dress in clothes, read magazines, and use dishes and silverware. Some of us go to museums where there are works of art made in the past as well as today.

Each of us has preferences in our daily lives: some of us like dogs, others like cats; some enjoy apple pie, others, blueberry pie. No one can tell us what to like, but others can tell us what there is about something that we might like. Usually, when we want to find out whether or not we are going to like something, we try it; we taste the particular food, try on the coat, or sit on the chair. It does not make much sense to say that we do not like pecan pie unless we have tasted it. In much the same way, if we want to know what kinds of art we are going to like, we have to try them by looking at them and by learning something about them. This chapter will present basic information about some of the art forms we see, so that we can understand how they are made and how they are used. With this information, we can look more intelligently at the arts we see around us. We will follow our system of classification: natural/folk/popular/practical/expressive.

NATURAL OBJECTS, FOLK ARTS, AND POPULAR ARTS

Some of us live near the ocean, others on the plains of the Midwest, and others near the mountains. All these places can be enjoyed, valued for their own sakes. All of us share the sky, sunshine and darkness, clouds and rain. Even those of us who live in cities can find trees, grass, rocks, and flowers to enjoy. Most of us value or enjoy natural objects such as these without having to learn anything about them. Just as the objects are natural, so, it would seem, is our appreciation of them.

Perhaps if we knew something about the histories of natural objects, they might possess even more meaning for us. If we learn, for example, how to distinguish one type of tree from another—pines from firs, elms from maples— we might enjoy trees even more than we now do. Or if we are looking at the Pacific Ocean, we may be aware that its waters wash the shores of Japan, Australia, New Zealand, Hawaii, and Canada, as well as the continental United States, and that knowledge may make our view of the ocean more exciting.

The *folk arts* refer to objects made by people usually untrained in art, most often for a practical purpose and for the most part in the same ways in which others before them made the same kinds of objects. For example, when people sew quilts just the way their mothers and grandmothers did, they are carrying on a folk art tradition, one which is slowly making its way into museums and becoming a "fine art." When people who are interested in CB radios prepare and exchange CB cards (some of which have drawings and other "artistic" material on them), they are creating a folk art form which in a small way could become a tradition itself. The recent growth of interest in "collectibles," objects which exist in some quantity but are all different from one another, is an illustration of the enjoyment and valuing of folk art. Just as some people collect stamps, others collect varieties of beer-bottle caps, old toys, quilts, dolls, baseball cards, old picture postcards, rocking chairs, old shoes—in fact, almost anything one might name. When the collected objects are reasonably new and manufactured in large quantities, folk art is close to popular art; but there is no hard and fast line between these divisions.

The original concept of folk art, that the object was handcrafted in a traditional way, is slowly disappearing. In its place are some of the forms mentioned above and the crafts objects sold in fairs, bazaars, and shops. Also replacing the more traditional folk arts are objects such as wall paintings, spray-painted graffiti and political prints and posters created by those who are enthusiastic but untrained in art. These are often called "people's art," in the sense that they represent genuine and powerful concerns of large groups of citizens, who want very much to express their ideas and feelings in some visual art form, even though they do not have a technical background in that form. These works often have a political message and are essentially expressive arts just as much as those art forms we will examine under that heading later in the chapter.

Like the folk arts, the *popular arts* are mostly practical in purpose. The

40. McDonald's

most common of them are television, motion pictures, magazines, billboards, and posters. In this book, the first two forms are not treated as visual arts because of their character of changing over time as we watch them. The others are clearly popular visual arts, from record-album covers to personality posters, and include such familiar objects we all see, as in Figure 40. Sometimes they are expressive objects, just as much as paintings and sculpture; the personality poster is an obvious example. But more often they are practical arts, like designer jeans or brightly colored plastic-covered notebooks carried by pupils in school. Sometimes a particular art form—usually mass produced—becomes popular, but is so unimpressive when we look at it carefully or critically, that we might call it "kitsch," meaning an object that is so badly done that it has a peculiar kind of value or virtue of its own. All of us enjoy some objects of this kind, but not all of us think of them as art. Nevertheless, the kinds of meanings we get from them are very similar to what we can get from the expressive and the practical arts.

The popular arts, at least the way they have been defined here, have some particular qualities which should be noted. Some of them, which bring words and images to large groups of people, serve the purpose of advertising or "selling" products or ideas. Others, like posters and magazines, provide information and are called "mass media." In both cases they use the power of words and pictures to convince the public of the importance and desirability of their messages. This function is perhaps most obvious to us in the television commercial. It is important to realize that the art qualities of these objects have nothing to do with the accuracy or value of their messages. The most handsome and exciting magazine advertisement may try to sell a useless or worthless product.

A second particular quality of the popular arts as mass media is that technology has advanced some of them into new art forms that bring together the traditional art forms of literature, drama, dance (body movement), and music. Motion pictures and television are examined in a separate chapter because they are not visual arts in the ways that these forms have been described in this book. Nevertheless, it is important to understand that films and television use some of the skills, techniques, and ideas of the visual artist and designer. The frames of both media are often just as carefully arranged or composed to provide the desired effect on the viewer. Dramatic darks and lights and attractive combinations of color in a television commercial are rarely accidents of filming. They are carefully contrived, in much the same way that paintings in a museum or famous buildings are contrived to provide visual excitement and satisfaction, even though their social uses are different.

It is unlikely that the mass media we are talking about here will ever replace the visual arts, the arts we see. What they have done is greatly to expand the opportunities we have for some of the same sorts of experiences, in combination with other art forms. Learning more about the visual arts may help us to understand and appreciate motion pictures and television in new ways.

THE PRACTICAL ARTS

The practical arts include architecture, landscape design, interior design, urban planning, industrial and product design, and advertising design. As with all other art forms, the arts in this category all can be expressive in nature. However, these art forms are grouped together because they can also fulfill functions in the physical world in which we live; they are our homes, parks, school buildings, and cities, and most of the objects or products we use. Since the arts in this category are functional as well as expressive, they must do the job for which they are designed. A park that does not have adequate paths for people to walk on is not very good landscape design, no matter how handsome or expressive its arrangement or its flowers, shrubs, and trees.

architecture

One form of art which is all around us and which we have been accustomed to since early childhood, though many of us rarely look at it as art, is architecture. It is also an art form developed early in human history, as soon as people came out of the cave or natural shelter and began to build shelters. Then are not all buildings architecture and, by definition, works of art?

Although it is difficult to make this kind of distinction in general, it is safe to say that in particular cases we can look at the structure itself and try to determine the care with which the builder or designer of the structure has put together its various parts. When we see that the architect has carefully and sensitively proportioned the sizes and shapes of the walls, related these to the size and shape of the roof, and attempted to make the colors and textures attractive to the eye, we can regard the building or shelter as architectural art. However, architecture, as a practical or functional art form, has some special conditions to meet. No matter how beautiful its appearance, the structure must properly serve the purpose for which it was designed. Otherwise it is usually not considered good architecture and, probably, not good art. For example, the architect who designs a school must make sure that the building leaves enough open area for play on its site (the land on which it is built); that the structure has enough rooms with adequate space for classes; that the halls are wide enough for pupil traffic; that the exits are well placed so that the building can be emptied in case of fire or other danger; that the windows let in enough daylight; that some rooms can be darkened easily for showing films or slides; and that all the other functional requirements of a school building are fulfilled. Only if these needs are at least adequately met can we start to look at the attractiveness of the building to judge its claim as a work of art.

Architecture is the largest of the arts we see except for one we will describe later, urban planning. A building or shelter must be at least a little larger than the size of a man, like a sentry box, and can be as vast as the World Trade Center buildings in New York City. For this reason, along with urban planning, architecture is usually the most costly of the arts in its construction, except perhaps for some special cases of jewelry where rare and precious stones are used. Therefore, though architects often have considerable freedom to shape their structures, they are responsible for spending other people's money and must design efficient buildings. In this sense, the architect works within strict limitations—as well as being limited by climate, terrain (features of the ground), available money and, often, the desires of the client.

Architects can take either one of two basic approaches to the problem of constructing the walls or "skin" of the space to be enclosed. They can build walls that will carry their own weight and the weight of a roof if there is one. The Eskimo's igloo (a domed structure) and many brick- and stone-walled buildings without a framework or skeleton have this kind of structure. A second alternative is to use a framework or skeleton and to hang or attach the walls and roof to the frame.

In creating large enclosed spaces, the architect has three basic methods available. As far as we know, the first of these to be used was the post and lintel. Vertical posts are anchored in the ground and beams (lintels) are placed across the tops of the posts, in the way children build with blocks. Most of our private homes today are built in this way. Once the posts and lintels are in place, it is easy enough to attach a wall of boards, brick, stone, or even glass to the framework.

Because stone is too heavy to lay across posts, if the distance between them is too great, the arch system was developed. This technique consists of placing wedge-shaped blocks of stone in the form of an arch over the space between the two posts. Just as jamming a triangular piece of wood under a door as a doorstop holds the door open more firmly the farther in the wedge is pushed, so the greater the weight pushing down upon the wedged stones of the arch, the stronger the arch becomes. This method of building made it possible for architects and builders to construct much larger spaces inside stone structures than they could with the post and lintel system.

A third technique used by the architect grew out of the development of steel. Joining a number of steel beams together, usually with rivets, the architect can create a cage of steel framework and fill in the sides, bottom, and top of the cage with any material and in any fashion desired. This system is essentially the way in which all our very tall buildings, our skyscrapers, are framed. Since both steel and ferroconcrete (cement poured with steel supporting rods inside it) are very strong, a roof or other horizontal member such as a balcony can reach far out from the building without any supports directly underneath it in what is called a "cantilever." Curved structural parts of any shape can also be constructed of ferroconcrete. With the development of these materials, the architect has been freed to model the shapes of the enclosed space almost in the manner of a sculptor. This structural freedom accounts for some of the irregularly shaped buildings we see around us today. They may appear bizarre or weird at first, but they represent a step forward in the history of building. Imagine how peculiar the Lever House building in New York City (Figure 6) would look to people who had seen only Gothic structures like the Cathedral of Notre Dame (Figure 8).

landscape design

Just as the architect plans the enclosure or shell inside which people live or work, the landscape designer or landscape architect plans the environment in which the building is set. Using trees, shrubs, plants, flowers, grass or other ground cover, concrete, stone, or wood as materials, the landscape designer creates areas around the structure that are attractive and usable for outdoor activities such as parking, clothes-drying, garbage storage and collection, the delivery of goods, outdoor cooking and eating, or the outdoor assembly of large numbers of people, as in a park or playground.

As with every other practical art form, the art of landscape design is to make open spaces as efficient and yet as good-looking as possible (Figure 41). When landscape is tied to a building, as it most often is, the designer either must work closely with the architect or, if the structure is already built, must take into consideration the shapes and uses of the building. Even more than the architect, the landscape designer is limited by or bound to the climate and the terrain. Obviously, landscape treatment in the hot, dry, flat, barren desert areas of Arizona must be very different from that in the forested, rain- and snow-catching mountains of Kentucky. Whether the designer is working around a department store, a factory, a school, a cathedral, or a private home, all the factors involved in the problem at hand must be carefully considered to create the particular art.

interior design

Just as the landscape designer arranges the spaces around a building, the interior designer arranges the spaces inside the structure. Again, the designer must work along with the architect or, if the building is finished, with what the architect has done. The interior designer is responsible for selecting and sometimes even designing the furniture, lighting, floor coverings, draperies, and wall coverings, and selects the colors, textures, and shapes to make the inside of a building attractive and appropriate to its use. The interior of a library is usually not gaudy, dramatic, colorful, or exciting to look at, but would be better designed as quiet and restful. Theaters, large stores, or exposition halls usually can be gayer and more dramatically colored and lighted.

Although some architects do their own landscape and interior designing, these are usually separate functions and separate art forms. Since most of us cannot afford the services of an architect, landscape designer, or interior designer, we do most of these tasks ourselves. If we look at some of the many possibilities open to us in these areas in museums, books, magazines, and films, we can, at least, make more effective judgments.

urban planning

Urban planning deals with the arrangements of cities and towns. The word "urban" refers to city-type areas in contrast to suburban, and rural, open-country areas. By the middle of this century more Americans lived in cities and towns than in the country. Since almost all our urban areas grew to their present size without any consistent planning, all of them are extremely congested with pedestrian and vehicular traffic, and the air breathed by the inhabitants is polluted. The urban or city planner can design a new community or redesign an existing urban area to avoid these hazards and to provide a better functioning and more attractive city environment.

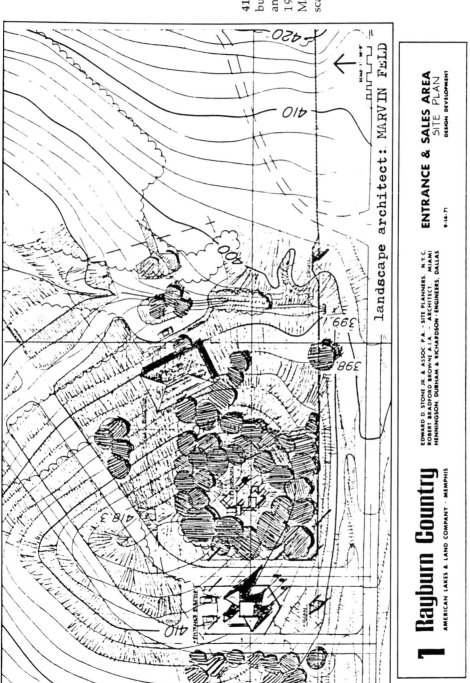

41. Site plan for Rayburn Country entrance and sales area, Memphis, 1971. Courtesy of Marvin S. Feld, Landscape Architect

landscape architect: MARVIN FELD

1 Rayburn Country
AMERICAN LAKES & LAND COMPANY · MEMPHIS

EDWARD D. STONE JR. & ASSOC P.A. - SITE PLANNERS, N.Y.C.
ROBERT BRADFORD BROWNE A.I.A. - ARCHITECT, MIAMI
HENNINGSON, DURHAM & RICHARDSON - ENGINEERS, DALLAS

ENTRANCE & SALES AREA
SITE PLAN
DESIGN DEVELOPMENT

9-14-71

The urban planner works on the largest scale of any artist and is probably responsible for the greatest expenditures of money. The problems are so vastly complex or intricate that it is impossible to work alone like the potter or painter or even in some cases the architect. The planner must work closely with community groups, government officials, businessmen, engineers, and educators, as well as with architects and landscape designers who plan individual structures and their grounds. Thus, it is easy to see that the urban planner must be a very different sort of person than the jeweler or printmaker, with substantially different training and even, perhaps, a very dissimilar personality. Fundamentally, however, the planner deals with line, shape, value, color, and texture, the elements common to all artists, though the "canvas" covers many square miles and the factors that must be attended to seem numberless. It might even be fair to say that for the planner the practical factors of the design problem often outweigh the aesthetic considerations.

industrial and advertising design

The growth of manufacturing and advertising in our modern world has given rise to a particular type of artist who specializes in designing industrial products or the advertising for these and other items. Some designers work in both of these areas, though most concentrate on one of them. Because of the vast number of manufactured goods and ads, the work of these artists is around us everywhere; and, just as with all other art forms, these works are capable of providing meanings for their own sake. They can be attractive, impressive, or exciting objects to look at, regardless of their purpose.

One frequent drawback to this category of art forms is that meanings other than those associated with the formal qualities (shape, color, and texture) are rarely of great importance. A transistor radio or a ski jacket, or a magazine ad for a cereal do not offer significant feelings and ideas about the world, although we can and do respond to the effectiveness with which the object or ad does its job. Most of all, we can enjoy the formal qualities of these objects, since, ordinary as many of them are, they make up so much of the visual environment of our daily lives.

Industrial and Product Design.   This category deals with the arrangement of the final form of a manufactured item. Often the object is deliberately designed so that it will be attractive as well as efficient. This usually is the case with consumer goods (items that satisfy people's needs) and occurs far less often or not at all with other industrial items such as carpenter's tools, printing presses, or railroad freight cars. Nevertheless, many industrial objects, designed solely to operate efficiently, have taken on a "beauty" of their own and are looked upon as objects of art. A classic example is the jeep, the original design of which evolved during World War II and reflects purely utilitarian considerations. Yet books on art have used it as an illustration of how the form of an industrial object can have its own beauty when reduced to those parts which make it function properly.

In the years before mass production, most common tools and household objects (except in the homes of the wealthy) were not considered important enough or were too costly to decorate, since decoration had to be done by hand by individual craftsmen. Consequently, most common objects such as hammers, ploughs, pots, skillets, and scales were made as economically as possible. The implement had nothing on it but what was essential to the performance of its function. As industry began to mass produce these utensils in the nineteenth century, the idea of what makes an expensive handcrafted object attractive was applied to the design of factory products. This attitude explains the design of objects such as that in Figure 42, which is a mass-produced machine dressed up in the decorations precious to previous generations. By the early twentieth century, this approach began to give way in favor of a return to simpler forms. Industrial objects and buildings were reduced to their functioning parts and still considered beautiful. This principle still governs some of our productions in these areas.

Although industrial designers create the form of almost every manufactured product—at least of those most of us use—only some of their creations are obvious or noticeable. Led on by advertising, we wait expectantly each year for the new-model cars to appear and are delighted or disgusted (according to our tastes) by their new grillwork, differently shaped contours, and bright colors. But homier, less imposing objects are also the designer's work. Refrigerators, radios, air conditioners, stoves, television sets, pots and pans, sewing machines, plumbing fixtures, sporting goods, silverware, tools, clothing, luggage, and even eggbeaters not only are designed but can be handsome and easy-to-use objects.

In the case of larger or more complex industrial objects, engineers and technicians work with the designer or may even decide much of the form of the item before the designer begins his work. An automobile, for example, must have a form that will operate efficiently and can be mass produced inexpensively. The designer has more freedom with some objects than with others. Telephones, lamps, and transistor radios, for example, can be and are designed in many different forms, all of which operate efficiently.

Clothing design, which is part of industrial design, has begun to assume some special importance as an art form in recent years. Even thirty years ago, most garments were drab and colorless compared with the bright, varied clothing being designed and worn today.

The clothing designer should not be confused with the fashion illustrator. The job of rendering the illustrations of fashion styles in newspapers, magazines, and brochures is the specialty of another art-trained person in the advertising field. As in the other design areas, the clothing designer has to consider much more than the beauty of the garment. Clothes—like cars, chairs, and eggbeaters—must do a particular job, so that the function of the garment is a serious consideration. A low-backed ski jacket or cardboard shoes might be designed to be very good looking but would be of little use in keeping out the cold and the wet. Most garments are mass produced; and, except for very expensive gowns and furs, the designs must be economical to manufacture. Per-

42. "The Turtleback," sewing machine, 1856. Courtesy of The Singer Company

43. "Fireball Y-8," package design by Hy Farber, 1970. Courtesy of the designer

haps most important of all, clothes must reflect particular "styles," which are usually created or promoted by clothing designers.

Advertising Design. This category is often called "graphic design" and as an art form it usually involves the creation of visual images intended to influence people to buy a product or service or to participate in some activity. The ways in which these messages reach us are called advertising media; they include television, newspapers and magazines, billboards, posters, handbills (the brochures, booklets, foldouts, and single sheets we receive in the mail, pick up on store counters, and find wrapped in packages), and, finally, the package itself. The cardboard cereal box, the shampoo bottle, and the record album, all serve not only to cover and protect the contents, but also to direct attention to them and make them desirable objects (Figure 43).

One characteristic of much advertising design today is its greatly increased dependency on the visual image. Figures 44 and 45 show two newspaper advertisements by the same company with an over forty-year difference in date between them. Whereas the early ad describes the virtues of the product with a long series of words, the more recent ad focuses on the photograph for its impact. The early ad is a page of type, dignified but put together without much consideration for its design qualities. The later ad, on the other hand, shows concern with relationships of line, shape, and value, and reflects also the considerable advantage of today's widespread and often technically excellent advertising photography. Sometimes, the advertising design even uses the image as a symbol with no other identification of the product being sold.

Advertising or graphic designers plan and in most cases provide the drawing or painting, the lettering or selection of type for the original billboard, magazine ad, or package. Like industrial designers and architects, they are very much a part of the practical, commercial world, and their work is everywhere around us. Yet, like all the other forms of visual art, the advertising design can provide some of the meanings of art; it can be enjoyed as part of the richness of what we see.

THE EXPRESSIVE ARTS

The arts described in this category include drawing, painting, printmaking, photography (Figure 46), sculpture, and ceramics. Though every art form noted in this chapter can serve the purpose of expression, the art forms in this category are grouped together because they usually have no other purpose than expression. Murals and sculpture do sometimes decorate a building, for example, and prints can illustrate a book or a magazine story, but these are for the most part exceptions.

drawing

Drawing is the process of making images on a surface, usually by means of a hard, dry implement or tool as opposed to a soft, wet one. For example, we

(continued on page 72)

44. "Down from Canada," newspaper advertisement, 1923. Courtesy of Canada Dry Corporation

45. "The Only Soft Drink That Doesn't Treat You Like a Kid," magazine advertisement, 1966. Courtesy of Canada Dry Corporation

46. James Lanier, untitled photograph, 1981

draw with pencil, pen, charcoal, or crayon, while we "paint" with a brush, which is soft by comparison and almost always wet. Drawing is usually thought of as producing lines, or shapes created by lines, though we might draw with the side of a crayon and produce a solid shape rather than a line. Drawing has been thought of, historically, as producing a likeness of something, although, as many artists of today have shown, it does not need to be representational.

There are many tools with which the artist can make a drawing. The most familiar one is the lead pencil or, more properly, the graphite pencil, which, when rubbed against a sheet of paper, leaves particles of graphite pressed into the surface. The amount of pressure determines the darkness of the lines. A common instrument of the same kind is the pen, which leaves a deposit of liquid ink in one or another color. Drawings can also be made with crayons, charcoal sticks, colored chalks (pastels), and felt-tip pens. The last is a wet rather than a dry drawing medium, but it can be classified as a drawing tool since it produces lines and dries very quickly. Various types and qualities of crayons and chalks are used in drawing, ranging from the wax crayons used by children to the fine-grained conté crayon used by the professional artist. Much of the quality of a drawing—its subtlety and variety of tones—depends upon the character of the tool used. Additional drawing techniques include scratch drawings, in which the figures or forms created by lines are scratched out of a crayon-coated paper or out of a board covered with dark tempera paint. This last medium is often called "scratchboard." One can also draw with colored or black inks and a pen, or a brush from which most of the ink is removed before each line is made; this technique is called "drybrush."

Any object which leaves a mark on a surface can be a drawing tool. Twigs, nails, cardboard edges, cloth, string can all be used as drawing tools. Artists prefer to use tools and materials that will allow them to work freely, yet provide richness of texture and a good range of shades and color (if color is desired). This is why charcoal is so widely used in art classes as a drawing tool. Although it lacks color, it gives sharp or soft lines, varied textures, and extremes of dark and light with the least amount of physical effort.

In the past, drawings were looked upon, for the most part, as preparations for some more important work of art. Artists made drawings to perfect the over-all arrangement of each of the parts of a painting or building. A preparatory drawing of this type is called a "study" or a "sketch." In recent times, drawings have become much more widely accepted as major works of art in themselves, having qualities of freshness or experimentation different from, but no less worthy than, the qualities of a finished painting or building. This is why exhibits and books of drawings are more popular today than they have been in the past, and why the drawings of some artists are bought by museums for large sums of money.

painting

Painting is the process of making images on a surface, usually by means of a soft, wet implement. The most frequently used painting tool is a brush. Painting is also commonly associated with color; thus, "to paint" the walls of a room means to cover them with color. Paintings are the first works most people think of among the arts we see, although there are a great many others. When someone says that he or she is an artist, we often assume—at least at first—a painter, although the person could be a sculptor, potter, designer, or jewelry maker. This is probably because we are most familiar, through books, motion pictures, and television, with the artist who paints.

Many thousands of years ago people painted on the walls of caves (see Figure 1), and paintings are still made on the inner and outer walls of buildings (though, because of the cost involved, these are usually public buildings). In fact, we have a particular name for paintings done on walls. They are called "murals" from *mur*, the French word for wall. The alternative to wall painting is called "easel" painting, because the canvas (or other material) is small enough to be placed on an easel to be worked on, or, if very large, is not part of a wall or meant to be fixed to a wall.

Not only are there many surfaces on which paintings are done: plaster, canvas, wood; but the materials used to paint with, namely, the brushes and paints, are varied. As a result, the specific effects that are possible and the general appearance of paintings vary considerably as well. The most common kinds of paints are watercolors, tempera or poster paints, oil paints, plastic paints, and encaustic paints. Perhaps the best way to describe these materials is by the effects they achieve.

Watercolors, as the name suggests, are water-base paints usually in cake or tube, and their principal quality is that they are transparent—that is, the color is thin enough so that the paper on which it is placed shows through. Since the medium is very thin and wet, watercolor painting requires fine-haired, soft brushes, such as those made of sable, and a heavy, porous paper which will absorb the water easily. These requirements are not strict rules, of course. Artists often look at their materials in an imaginative fashion, achieving effects that are exciting and pleasing to look at.

Since watercolors are transparent, they cannot be painted over the way other paints can. When a stroke is made with the brush, the artist is pretty well committed to that line and cannot change it, unless it is done quickly. A line may be "washed" out with a brush loaded with clean water. But this process can give the painting a worked-over appearance, which is just the opposite of the watercolor's distinctive fresh appearance.

Tempera or poster paints are opaque and thicker than watercolors. Since each paint medium is made up of the pigment (the chemical agent providing the coloring) and the binder (the material holding the pigment together), we can make a distinction between traditional tempera, which was made with egg, and modern commercial tempera. The animal oils of the whole egg were used with pigments to make an extremely durable, fairly thick paint. Most modern tempera has other chemicals that make paint of much the same quality but of less durability. Tempera is still used by some artists and, much more frequently, by advertising artists—hence the name poster paints. Most of the powder and liquid paints used in elementary and secondary school art classes are some form of tempera.

Another medium is oil paint, which is usually made with linseed oil as a binder and a chemical to give it its creamy texture. Oils are the most popular paints used by artists. They dry slowly but can be worked over again and again. They can be perfectly opaque—so that one cannot see through them—or they can be thinned down and used as translucent paint, so that some of the paint color or canvas underneath will show through. Some artists have capitalized on this; Rembrandt, for example, used bright yellow for under-painting, covering it with a thinned second layer of paint to produce colors with a glowing quality. Unlike watercolor and tempera, which can be used on paper, oils require a canvas surface or a roughened wood surface. The brushes used must be stiffer than those used for watercolors and tempera and are often made of pig's bristle.

Several other special kinds of paints are used for particular effects or specific situations. Casein paints, made with a milk curd and fat binder, hold firmly to most surfaces and can resemble watercolor, tempera, or oil. Encaustic is made with wax and turpentine or oils and must be fused with a hot iron after application to be permanent. So durable is this medium that Greek and Egyptian paintings done with it two thousand years ago are still found in good condition. Fresco painting, used in the making of murals, is done by grinding the pigments in lime water and then applying them directly to the still moist plaster.

The newest paint medium to be developed is polymer plastic paint, known also as synthetic or acrylic paint. The base of this material is water with fine particles of a colorless synthetic resin. When the water evaporates, the plastic forms a crystal-clear, elastic, tough, water- and oil-proof film which is highly durable. Plastic paints dry quickly, can be applied to almost any nonoily surface, and can be used with a variety of special ingredients to function and look like any of the media described above. Plastic paints are becoming more and more popular with artists and students alike and are the closest to an all-purpose paint yet found.

Another technique which is closely associated with painting is known as "collage," a name derived from the French word which means to glue or paste. A collage is an arrangement of objects or materials on a flat surface. The technique was developed by Pablo Picasso and Georges Braque in the early years of this century in France. At first it included newspaper, other paper, and fabrics in combination with paint to provide a greater range of texture and surface treatment. Now collage (Figure 90, page 119) includes almost any material which can be attached to a surface and often no paint at all is used.

printmaking

Printmaking, sometimes called graphics, is the process of producing an image by pressing paper or cloth against a surface which is unevenly covered with printing ink or other material, and transferring the ink from the surface to the paper. The process is similar to the printing of newspapers and other media which use words instead of pictures and is usually thought of as one which reproduces the same image many times. However, a technique such as the "mono-print," which permits only one impression from an inked surface, is considered printmaking as well.

The easiest way to understand the basic principle of printmaking is to take a coin, press it against a stamp pad to ink it, then press it against a sheet of paper. The result is a print. It is clear that the raised surfaces of the coin picked up ink from the pad, then transferred that ink to the paper, while the grooved surfaces did not pick up the ink and do not show on the paper. Much the same thing occurs when one takes a piece of linoleum or wood, cuts some of the surface away and then rolls printing ink over the whole surface. The portions of the surface that were not cut away, get ink on them. When the inked block is pressed to a piece of paper, these portions leave ink on the paper to make the image or picture. This procedure is called the "relief" process of printmaking and is one of the four basic ways in which this art form is produced.

Almost any method that creates an uneven surface for inking can be used for relief printmaking, though the traditional material used by the artist has been the wood block. There are, however, many different materials one might use. Objects such as bottle tops, sponges, sandpaper, string, pieces of wood, and cardboard can be inked and pressed directly on the paper leaving the mark of their shapes. Or these same objects can be glued down, ink rolled over them, and paper pressed to that surface. Each material has its own surface quality, giving the artist a vast range of textures with which to work.

The "intaglio" process of printmaking, used in engraving and etching, is just the opposite of relief printing. Lines are cut or incised into a sheet of metal with a sharp tool called a "burin." A "brayer," or roller, is then used for inking the lines, and the metal plate is pressed against paper in a printing press. The inked lines appear on the paper. Much greater pressure is needed here than in relief printing, since the inked lines are finer, and a printing press must be used. In an etching, lines are scratched through an acid-resistant coating which covers a flat piece of metal. When the plate is placed into an acid bath, the acid eats only into the scratched lines in the metal. The surface is then cleaned, and the plate inked and printed. Etchings and engravings have clear, sharp lines, very different in quality from other printmaking techniques (Figure 20).

The third major technique of printmaking is called "planography." Plane means flat, and planography is the process of printing from a flat, smooth surface, in contrast to the uneven surfaces used in relief and intaglio printing. The most common material used for the flat surface is stone, and the resulting print is called a "lithograph" (from *lithos*, the Greek word for stone). The artist draws with a grease crayon on the smooth, flat surface of the stone. The stone is then washed, dampened, and inked. Since the grease of the crayon resists water, the crayoned drawing remains on the surface and the oil-base ink sticks to the crayoned areas but not to the wet, clean surface of the stone. When the stone is pressed to the paper in a printing press, the resulting print reproduces every minute detail of tone and texture. Figure 16 is an example of a lithograph. This form of printmaking is in many ways the simplest and most direct, and it gives the artist much the same kind of freedom as in making a drawing.

Many prints can be pulled, or taken, from the same stone, giving exact copies of the original drawing.

Stencil printing involves inking or painting through holes or openings in some flat surface. The plastic or cardboard sheets with cut-out letters that students sometimes use are stencils. The most common form of this process as used by the artist is called serigraphy or silk-screen printing, and differs from the other printing techniques discussed here. Fine silk is stretched tight over a wooden frame to make the screen. Areas on the silk which are to be printed are left uncovered, while the areas that should not be inked or painted are blocked out with paper, a commercial film, a coat of glue, or some other substance that will resist the printing medium. Then a piece of paper is placed under the screen, and the ink or paint is drawn or pushed across the screen with a squeegee or rubber-tipped block of wood. Thus, the paint is forced through the screen only where openings have been left for it, and the image is printed (Figure 35). Whereas relief, intaglio, and planographic printmaking is usually thought of as a process using black, white, and grays, silkscreen printing is generally associated with color.

Photolithography is a recent development which combines photography and printmaking. One technique in the process involves making a collage or paste-up of photos, type, diagrams, drawings, or any other visual material, photographing the paste-up and transferring that photo to an aluminum plate. This plate can then be printed in a manner similar to commercial printing or on a lithograph press. The advantages of this process are that any visual material can be used, including other art works, and that it is not necessary to "draw" the subjects one wishes to use in the print.

sculpture

Works of art that are carved or cut away, built up, or put together so that they have roundness are called sculpture. Usually, sculpture is seen from all sides and, therefore, can be called sculpture in the round. Some sculpture is only partly round and is part of, or juts out from, a flat surface. This is called "relief sculpture." A common example is the face, figure, and words on a coin, which are "low relief," because they project out only to a small extent from the surface.

The earliest materials used to create sculpture were clay, stone, and wood —materials which our natural environment provides with abundance. Once people developed a command over the working of metals, these excellent and durable materials were added to the media used by the sculptor. Bronze, an alloy of copper and tin, was especially favored (Figure 25). Today, the number of materials used by sculptors is extraordinary, including almost every material one can name—steel, aluminum, plastic, synthetic stone, cement mixtures, wire, paper, cardboard, plaster, and glass as well as the original clay, stone, and wood. Some of the newer materials have made it possible for the sculptor to add color, movement, and even sound to the art created.

The three basic working techniques of the sculptor are modeling, carving, and construction. The most popular and pliable modeling material is clay, though many others are used. The most commonly used tools are the hands themselves; any cutting or shaping tool can be used in addition. With most of the pliable modeling materials, the artist can add on more and more material to build up the desired form and can also take away as much or as little of the material as desired. Thus, modeling is an "additive" and "subtractive" process.

Modeling can be done by shaping the form directly from a mass of material such as clay. Here the artist can easily and freely change the form while working, using hands or tools. However, the mass of clay or whatever material used is often solid or bulky and is too heavy to support itself. Modeling the figure of a person in clay, with arm stretched straight out, for example, is virtually impossible with direct modeling, since without support the arm will fall off. The device used to solve this problem is called an armature—a wire or pipe frame or skeleton of the desired shape over which the modeling material is placed. A much greater variety of shapes can be created over an armature than without it.

After the original sculpture has been modeled, a duplicate of it is frequently made, often of a different material. This is done by a process called casting. A mold, or negative cast, is made by pressing plaster, wax, or soft metal against the outer surface of the sculpture to take its impression, in much the same way as a dentist takes an impression of a tooth. Once the mold hardens (if the material needs to harden), plaster, clay, or molten metal is poured or packed into it. When the inside material hardens, the mold is removed, producing a reproduction. If the casting process was carefully done, it will be an exact duplicate of what was first modeled.

Carving is the process of cutting or scraping or taking away parts of a hard, solid mass to express the desired form. It is a subtractive process: once a piece of the material has been taken away, it cannot be replaced as in modeling, since the material is hard. Carving, therefore, is a technique that requires careful thought and planning before working. Popular carving materials are hardwoods such as walnut and oak; stone such as limestone, marble, or sandstone; synthetic stones; and aggregates made up of hard particles (vermiculite or brick); plaster of Paris; and even soap. Carving tools include gouges, chisels, mallets, rasps, and sanding and polishing tools.

A third basic technique of sculpture is construction. As the term suggests, almost any material can be used in constructing sculpture. Wood, metal, plastics such as Plexiglas, wire, or cardboard can be sawed, nailed together, welded, riveted, glued, tied, or attached in some way. Sometimes objects are brought together and attached to one another—or assembled—and the result is called an "assemblage." Sometimes the objects are common materials or even discarded materials found by the artist, and the art object created from them is called "found sculpture" or "junk sculpture."

We are accustomed to thinking of sculpture as solid, heavy, and motionless. However, artists have discovered ways to add motion to constructed sculptures, making it possible to look at a work of art over a period of time and see a series of changing relationships or what might be called a number of different sculptures in the same piece. One kind of moving sculpture is the "mobile"

(Figure 39) and is often made of wire and sheet metal, though other materials might be used. Some artists use electric motors to provide motion (kinetic or moving) for their sculpture; some have added noise-making parts so that one can hear as well as see the sculpture. There seems to be no end to the imagination of the artist, and art is exactly the kind of activity that should be thought of as having no end, no point at which one must stop being imaginative.

Relief, half- or part-round sculpture can be modeled, carved, or constructed. Since the parts usually do not extend very far from the surface, no armature is needed. Relief sculpture is seen from one side only, but like sculpture in the round it does depend on shadows cast by the projecting parts for its pattern of dark and light areas.

crafts

The classification of objects known as crafts derives from their earlier name of handicrafts which referred to objects made by hand and requiring a special skill. Painters and sculptors were called craftsmen during the Middle Ages (1000–1400); but by the Renaissance (1400–1500), crafts began to mean handmade objects requiring a special skill but having a practical purpose. Eventually, these items were made by industrial mass-production methods. Dishes, silverware, tools, textiles, furniture, and even jewelry had to be produced in huge quantities and at low costs for expanding populations. Thus, crafts now refer to functional objects made one at a time by special skills.

The crafts include ceramics, jewelry, glass blowing, weaving, enameling, textile design, bookbinding, stitchery (Figure 47, page 21), and objects of metal, leather, and wood. Early in this century the crafts were often called "minor arts" and were looked upon as lesser arts than painting, sculpture, and architecture. Today, however, it is generally recognized that the crafts can be arranged or decorated to provide meanings just as other art forms do.

Ceramics is one of the most ancient of the crafts, and, for that matter, one of the earliest art forms. Originally, and to some extent today, this is the process of making a pot or vessel out of clay; baking it so that it is dry and hard; coating the pot with a substance that will make it usable and watertight; and decorating it and giving it a glasslike surface (Figure 48). The earliest pots were shaped by hand from crude clay dug out of the earth and were dried by the sun and the wind. Later, people learned that clay forms could be made harder and more durable by placing them in a bed of fire—a process called firing. It was also discovered that pots could be shaped with great ease and speed from a mass of clay centered on a horizontal revolving wheel.

The clay used for ceramics is basically earth, and there are many different kinds. Ceramics or pottery is classified in three main types depending on the particular composition of the clay and the temperature at which it is fired. The appearance of each type—earthenware, stoneware, and porcelain—is distinctive. Earthenware is heavy, coarse, and soft, while stoneware is strong and durable and can be much thinner and more delicate. Porcelain has much the same qualities as stoneware, but it fires white or translucent. There are two

48. Ronald Benson, high-fire stoneware, salt glaze, 1969. Courtesy of the artist

main techniques used to create a pot form: hand building and wheel throwing. Working by hand, the potter presses the thumbs firmly but slowly into the center of a ball of clay. As the opening grows larger, the walls of the ball become thinner; and the clay gradually takes the form of a pot.

A mass of clay can also be rolled into a snakelike coil. A number of these coils or one long coil are then stacked in loops or spiraled over a flat clay base. The rounded sides of the coils are flattened and sealed carefully so that the pot wall is built; the longer the coil, the larger the diameter of the pot. The shape of the coils gives the pot its characteristic roundness.

In addition, the potter can shape clay by making slabs like building blocks. The clay is rolled out flat with a round stick or a rolling pin and cut into slabs. These slabs can then be put together end to end or end to side, as in a box, and the meeting edges sealed, or they can be used to make cylindrical objects or to press clay around a form or mold. The process of shaping clay on a potter's wheel is called "throwing." The term was originally used when potters "threw" the clay ball on the already spinning disc or wheel.

There are several types of potter's wheels: those turned by hand; kicked into motion by the foot; and turned by electricity; but the principle is the same in all of them. A flat, solid disc of wood with a wet mass of clay centered on it is kept turning like a phonograph record. As it turns, the clay is shaped with hands and fingers by opening up the center of the clay and gently pulling the walls outward or upward. Since the whole mass is turning around a central axis, it can be kept perfectly round if the potter is skilled in the use of the wheel.

When the ceramic piece is completed and dry, it can be fired by placing it in a special ceramic furnace or oven called a "kiln" where it is heated to the specific temperature required for the type of clay used. Most, though not all, pots are also glazed, that is, covered with a substance which fuses and becomes glasslike when subjected to the heat of the kiln. At this point, the pot can be decorated in a variety of ways. Colored glazes may be applied to the pot, or textures may be cut into or added to its surface. Glazes can be transparent or opaque, shiny or dull, colorless or in varied colors. They present such a wide range of characteristics that the potter's skill includes a knowledge of chemistry and the ability to mix and test the chemical ingredients of glazes.

The potter also forms objects out of clay that are not made to serve any useful function. In this case, it might be said that the potter is working like a sculptor, although the ceramic process is much the same as that used for making pots.

photography

For hundreds of years, people noticed that light from a small opening in one wall of a darkened room (or "camera obscura") would carry the upside-down image of the scene outside. This happens because light (a stream of particles called photons) moves in a straight line. Thus, light streaming from the bottom of a figure through a small hole in a wall will appear on the top of the wall facing that hole. Both our eyes and the camera operate on this same principle.

Unlike the eye, however, a camera is used to capture and fix the image. For this purpose we use a section of film or piece of glass coated with light-sensitive silver compounds, which will change when exposed to light. The brightness of the light controls the change in the film; areas exposed to bright light are changed more than areas exposed to dimmer light. This image is deposited on the film in reverse value; that is, the dark parts are light and light parts dark. The initial film-held image is called a "negative" and appears only when the chemically treated film is developed or placed for appropriate amounts of time in the proper chemical solution. This negative, in turn, must be printed (light is projected through the negative on paper with a coating of light-sensitive silver compounds and the paper is then placed in a chemical bath) so that the final image, in proper values, is fixed on the photographic paper and the still image is captured in an easily seen form. To bring the light in from a preselected spot, we use a light-proof box with a ground-glass lens: the camera. The camera and film are to the photographer what charcoal and paper are to the illustrator or clay and the potter's wheel to the potter.

Photography can and very obviously does serve as an expressive art form (Figure 46), and yet it has so many commercial and practical functions in today's society that it is very much a functional art as well. In fact, we are barraged by photographic images everywhere we go: on television screens in our homes; on billboards on the highways; on the public transportation we use to travel to work or to school; in magazines, newspapers, and books; as well as in museums and movie theaters. Picture-taking with a camera serves a multitude of purposes. It can be used to record an event or scene such as family snapshots or a painting in one stage of development. It can communicate information, as in the case of news photographs and those made for educational purposes. Photographs can be used for advertising goods, services, or political candidates, or for the illustration of stories. High-speed microphotography, x-ray photography, and other special techniques are used to discover information that may be difficult or impossible to obtain in any other way. All these kinds of photography can produce fine works of art, because the photographer is highly skilled and thinks of his work as art, whatever its primary purpose.

The technical aspect of photography is complex, and the expert photographer must know the tools and how to use them. Just as the painter must select from various kinds of paint, the photographer must know about many kinds of cameras, film, and printing papers, in order to select the ones best suited to the particular task. Cameras have now become so much easier to operate and so inexpensive that even small children take both still and motion pictures. In fact, today photography is one of the visual arts taught in our elementary and secondary schools, just as drawing and painting are taught.

At this point, the reader will realize that a good many of the arts we see have been left out of this chapter. Nothing has been said about the making of jewelry and glass objects (Figure 49), weaving, enameling, fabric design, bookbinding, stitchery (Figure 47, page 21), or work in metal, leather, and wood. The reason for this omission is not that they are less important arts or that there

49. Roy Pearson, glass bowl, 5×8″, 1980. Courtesy of the artist

is not as much to say about them as the arts that have been discussed here. The reason is that even a brief technical description—as this has been—of all the many visual-arts processes would have made our chapter far too long. Fortunately, there are books and classes, on many school levels, from which the interested reader can learn about the arts left out of this chapter and more about those which were explored here.

CHAPTER 3

the perception
of art

The title of this chapter identifies the perception of art rather than the broader topic of perception itself. This distinction is a significant one to art teaching and one which has not been attended to as it should have in our theory and literature. Surely there is an intimate and important relationship between perception in general and the perception of art; after all, we cannot respond to an art work until we perceive it. Nevertheless, the perception of art or, more properly, aesthetic perception is a special form of perception, governed (as is all perception) by intention. When we look at and see something for its aesthetic properties, we are looking at it in different ways than when we look at it for its moral or practical implications or consequences. When we look at a chair for its comfort for sitting and then note that it is a handsome object in its visual qualities, we appear to shift mental or attitudinal gears, as it were, and look at it in different ways. Although we do not know enough about the varieties of perception to recognize all of the critical differences, it is reasonable to suggest that they are there and need to be studied. Perhaps the term "perception," or even "aesthetic perception," should, in this context, be replaced by a term such as "negotiation," which more closely describes the reciprocal nature of the activities we are examining. However, the process has been identified with perception for so long that another label may be confusing to the reader.

The first chapter suggested that a work of art is a made object we see that we value for its own sake. But how do we recognize a work of art as art, as a stimulus worthy of provoking aesthetic response in us? Is not this recognition part of the reason we have the responses? We do not seem to have this problem when we deal with aesthetic responses to natural objects. Neither the sunset nor the rock formation has to be recognized as an aesthetic object before we can respond to it. In the case of made objects, however, some form of identification of the object as art appears to initiate the process of response. As chapter 1 reported, the art critic, Harold Rosenberg, once said that art is what is on exhibit in New York City, London, and Paris. When a gallery or museum displays the artist's lunch menu or the contents of the artist's garbage can, these objects become art simply because some agency of the art world—gallery director, art critic, or the artist—has labeled them as art. On the basis of this explanation, it would appear that art is a social construct and that we recognize the occasion for aesthetic response (both positive and negative) by means of some relevant cue. We enter a large building known as a museum of art; or we read a review of an exhibit written by an art critic; or our aesthetic attention is focused on an object of art by hearing someone exclaiming about its handsome (or ugly) qualities.

But what of the object itself; does a work of art have no qualities which can capture our attention and promote an aesthetic posture and response? Perhaps scale is a sound example to consider. Would it be possible to come upon one of the pyramids of Egypt, a Gothic cathedral, or a Boeing 747 without at least a grudging respect, if not outright admiration, for their huge size? Would that be the start of aesthetic attention? Another cue might be skillful contrivance. There are objects so finely made that they seem to attract attention to this quality rather than or more than to any other. It may even be that there are basic, universal, nonculture-bound characteristics of so-called good design which leap out from the object and seize our attention.

The human organism appears to be—in addition to whatever else we believe it to be—a data processing mechanism. Sensory stimuli bombard all our senses constantly; we consciously and unconsciously monitor these data, select those which for one reason or another merit attention, and deal with them. Since the primary business of an organism is survival, we assess the information coming in for any threat or danger, and since good feelings are likely to support survival, we seem also to evaluate these data for pleasantness. Because each of us is not only an individual with a history of experiences, but also a member of a culture, a social structure with a rich and complex social history, we appear to apply all the relevant connections from both these sources to each stimulus or cluster of stimuli which we consider worthy of our concern.

Further, the processes of perceiving art—and anything else, for that matter—are complicated by the involvement of our emotions. Not only do we process the data of the stimuli and attach meaning to those we select as significant, but our feelings seem to be enmeshed in these operations. Perhaps emotions originated as a means of enhancing a physiological alert in the face of some threat. Surely when we move quickly to avoid an oncoming vehicle at an intersection, our fear seems to mobilize all our faculties and speed up our actions. It may be that the fulfillment, satisfaction, excitement, or whatever it is that typifies the aesthetic experience in emotional terms also derives from some such functional source. Suffice it to say that every thought, idea, or perception seems to have some reflection in feeling, some affective reverberation, no matter how slight; and every emotion, its cognitive guidepost even when we are not immediately conscious of its existence or its identity.

All the elements of this complex of physiological and psychological processes appear to be involved in even a simple act of perception. Nor can we, as some claim, separate perception from cognition. As soon as the data we select for our attention leap to our consciousness, or even when we are not completely aware of the stimuli, we attach meaning to them—an act of cognition—and incur some emotive response to them. To talk of percepts as separate from or prior to concepts is to fragment experience into a caricature of itself.

Thus it would seem that the act of looking is a complex affair. Not only do we look (and see, of course) with our brains as well as our eyes, but all that we feel and know affects how we look and what we see. Some investigations indicate that what we see depends partly on what we know about the object or scene we are looking at. For example, to the average passenger, the pilot's cabin of a jet airliner is jammed with a confusing mess of dials, gauges, and levers. To the pilot, however, who knows the purpose and appearance of each and every instrument, the pattern is so clear that one missing dial will immediately be noticed. Other experiments suggest that what we see depends to some extent on what we believe we see or what we want to see.

The act of looking is a combination of many separate processes, though we are not aware of some of them as we look. Looking at a work of art reflects this complexity. The factors involved in looking at a work of art, and how these factors may interrelate, are shown in Figure 50. Each time we look at a work of art, some of these factors are present.

Let us take an ordinary example outside the area of the visual arts to explain the intent of the diagram. If, while waiting at the curb for the traffic signal to change, we see a car going by, we may notice certain features about it even at a glance. Usually, we are not aware of what we have noted; but, if asked about it a few minutes later, we can often provide some information on what we saw—for example, that it was a red Ford Pinto, going north on Maple Street. What we have done in this act of casual looking is to recognize certain visual features and to identify the vehicle. Those of us who know more about automobiles might be able to identify more facts about the car—that it was a 1980 model with four cylinders, the particular model, and the approximate rate of speed. If we like that kind of car and wish we owned one, we might well have thought it an attractive car and enjoyed looking at it. Or, we may have thought —in that moment of looking—how impressed friends might be if we were to drive one.

Similar processes are involved in looking at a work of art. For example, if we know something about Orozco's *Zapatistas* and we come across it in a mu-

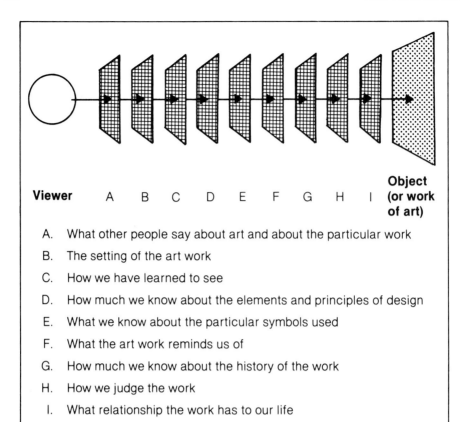

| Viewer | A | B | C | D | E | F | G | H | I | Object (or work of art) |

A. What other people say about art and about the particular work

B. The setting of the art work

C. How we have learned to see

D. How much we know about the elements and principles of design

E. What we know about the particular symbols used

F. What the art work reminds us of

G. How much we know about the history of the work

H. How we judge the work

I. What relationship the work has to our life

50. What we may think of as we look at art

seum or as Figure 51 (page 22) in this book, we will recognize it immediately upon looking at it. In effect, a flood of information will come to mind, usually without our being aware of it. If asked, we might be able to give the title of the painting, the artist who painted it, its present location (The Museum of Modern Art in New York City), the date of its creation (1931), the nationality of the painter (Mexican), other works of his with which we are familiar, as well as other details about the painting, and something about the artist. In other words, we will have "identified" the painting.

These thoughts, and others, appear to be part of what we are thinking about as we look at any object and can have an effect on what we see when we look. We do not know if these are all of the factors involved in our looking or just some of them. But it does seem that what we see is influenced by our knowledge and feelings and that it is difficult to separate the act of looking from the act of responding or having thoughts and feelings about what we look at. When does looking stop and responding take over?

Figure 50 provides one system for understanding how we look at (and respond to) a work of art. There are other possible systems and other factors involved in the process of looking. Further, in looking at a particular work, one of the units of this system (A or C or H) may be far more important than another. Nor do we know in what order we think of these units as we look at art

—whether we think of A before G or F before B. Perhaps the order in which we think of them or the importance of each unit depends upon the particular object we are looking at or how we are feeling at the time. The best way to find out how accurate or how useful the system can be is to try it out in looking at works of art. The advantage of using such a system is to help us to understand more clearly what we are thinking about and what may cause the feelings and ideas we have as we look at the arts we see.

WHAT OTHER PEOPLE SAY ABOUT ART
AND ABOUT THE PARTICULAR WORK (A IN FIGURE 50)

When a costly or important work of art, such as a building, painting, or sculp-ture, is completed and presented to public view, it is usually talked about or written about in newspapers, magazines, radio, or television. Sometimes an art work is controversial because of its style or its politics and attracts greater attention in the news media. More often, however, a work of art is noted and discussed only by a special kind of writer who is called an "art critic." The function of this writer is primarily to explain and to "sell" the art work. The art critic describes it, offers a personal opinion about the quality of the work, may discuss the artist who created it, and may, perhaps, compare it with similar works.

Of course, most people who look at works of art do not read what critics have to say about them. But often they do ask others about the art works they plan to see. Most of us will ask about any event we are planning to attend. This is a sensible practice. If we respect the judgment of the person or persons whose opinions we ask, we may be saved a disappointing experience or, on the other hand, may look forward to what we are going to see with greater eagerness. But we also pick up and carry with us to the work of art some of the ideas and attitudes of the people with whom we talked.

One of the most important pressures that prompts us to seek and accept the attitudes of others is the desire to conform, to belong to the group. It is eas-ier and more comfortable to have the same likes and dislikes as one's friends than to be different. This attitude seems to operate in the way we look at a work of art just as it does in other areas.

How then should one approach a particular work of art? It is easy enough to be critical and to explain that one's attitude comes from what other people say about the work. But what can be done about it? Should we avoid talking or reading about works of art we may see so that there will be no influence on our judgment? Or should we try to find opposing points of view on each work to balance our attitudes? The best answer seems to be that we can and should be aware of any attitudes we pick up about a particular work of art from outside our own thinking and try to make up for it by looking at possible alternatives. For example, if you mention the possibility of going to an exhibit of recent art at a local gallery, a friend may casually comment, "Oh, those people do things like that because they can't draw." It would be difficult, if not impossible, for you to act as if you had never heard that comment. But it is possible to think about alternative ideas. In addition to the possibility that the artists cannot draw, an alternative explanation might be that they can draw but do not choose to do so. Another alternative might be that drawing realistically may not be important in the kind of statements they wish to make. What you can do is to learn about these alternatives, then look for yourself and decide what seems the most reasonable explanation.

Some people talk about having an open mind. This concept does not make too much sense. Probably a truly open mind is an empty one. All of us accumulate many thousands of ideas about everything around us as we grow up. What we are talking about here is a thinking mind in which the ideas and attitudes we already possess are recognized for what they are and all the possible alternatives we can discover are carefully examined. All this is no different from the thinking we do about buying a coat or going to a football game. We can and should approach the work of art in the same way. Furthermore, there are general attitudes toward the visual arts with which each of us grows up. That each of us has a general attitude is easy enough to discover if we honestly weigh our opinions about the arts we see.

We might begin by looking at our national attitude toward the visual arts which should have some influence on personal ideas. Although chapter 1 suggested that the arts we see were very much a part of the civilizations of the past, our own American history reminds us that we as a people have been much less concerned with the fine arts than were many other cultures. Some writers explain this by pointing out that the seemingly endless western frontier occupied much of our attention, energy, and financial investment. In fact, Thomas Jefferson, at the close of the eighteenth century, advised young Americans to study architecture rather than painting or sculpture, since the latter subjects were too expensive for the amount of wealth in the country at the time.

As the continent was settled and the ranks of the wealthy grew larger, Americans became concerned with industry and business to the extent that money became the measure of a man's success. Since we had no feudal families or monasteries to hold and treasure the arts for their own sake or as social graces, the arts were never considered of great importance to any group of Americans. Even today, with private individuals, corporations, and government supporting the arts on a vast scale, most American parents are reluctant to encourage their children to study in the arts, which traditionally do not provide a good income to their practitioners.

In this atmosphere, it is likely that most boys and girls in this country grow up with a suspicion that the fine arts—particularly those we called the expressive arts in chapter 2, such as painting, sculpture, and printmaking—are essentially wasteful enterprises since they do not in most cases bring their creators much financial return. Architects, product and advertising designers, and illustrators appear to be in a different category since these are looked upon as well-paying occupations. One symptom of the attitude that money is the measure of success even in art can be seen in newspaper accounts of the purchases or donations of art works, in which the size of the headline depends on the amount of money spent for the work of art.

We are not only members of the American national community, we are also members of many other smaller groups, called "subcultures" by the sociologist, each of which can have an attitude toward art in general which will affect the individual. First of all, each of us grows up, necessarily, as a girl or a boy, and some expectations of what are feminine or masculine behaviors are taught us by that aspect of grouping. From this point of view, it is clear that generally art has been thought of much more as a girl's activity than that of a boy. Math, science, even language were "solid" subjects, while the arts were by comparison light and perhaps frivolous. The words used to describe these subjects give us some indication of their earlier masculine-feminine distinction.

There is no question that this view of art has changed drastically in the past thirty years. But it still exists in some measure and may come from a second subcultural grouping, that of social-financial class. Here, although income level is certainly not the only measure, it seems the most significant one. Middle- and upper-class youngsters much more than lower-class boys and girls show an interest in fine art either as a profession or as recreation. It may seem distasteful to label young people in this fashion, but these distinctions of social-financial class do exist and have a hand in shaping our attitudes. Furthermore, although we still have much social mobility, or the possibility of moving up (and even down) from one class to another in America, those who do move upward often carry their ideas and attitudes about art with them.

Other subcultures of ethnic (race-religion-national origin) grouping, neighborhood grouping, and family grouping play their parts in influencing our general attitude toward art. However, the first and second of these groupings are so closely related to social-financial class that they do not appear to have as distinct an effect. Today, the poor of all ethnic groups and neighborhoods seem to have more in common with each other than with the well-to-do of their own background. One writer, Oscar Lewis, has called this similarity the "culture of poverty." Oddly enough, the comment, "culture of wealth," might be made about middle- and upper-class groups of various backgrounds.

Before concerning ourselves with the last important group influence, that of family, it must be noted that what has just been said is completely inaccurate when it comes to the popular arts. In fact, it is precisely the opposite. Probably because of what we call the mass media of communication—that is, television, radio, magazines, motion pictures, newspapers, paperback books—youngsters, regardless of sex or class or ethnic origin, and even family, know and enjoy popular music, popular films and television, and popular literature. Forms of visual art that can be classified among the popular arts are comics, clothing, posters, magazine photographs, and advertising art. These seem to be as universally enjoyed by young people as popular music.

The last category of influence on our attitude toward art is that of friends and family. Again, each of us grows up in a group of people from whom we absorb all sorts of ideas on every topic. This is so with regard to religion, politics, food, and habits of dress; and there is no reason why it should not be so with attitudes toward the arts we see. Here, also, social and financial class seems to have much to do with family outlook on art, though many of us know exceptions: middle-class families where the fine arts are ignored and lower-class families where they are important. As in the case of what other people say about a particular work, the general attitude toward art with which we grew up is something we carry with us when viewing an art work. In many instances it keeps us from going to see works of fine art at all. When we do see them, however, we may be prejudiced either for or against them because of our general attitude toward art.

THE SETTING OF THE ART WORK (B IN FIGURE 50)

The setting or the place, time, and other circumstances in which the art work is seen, can be important in influencing the way we view the work. In a play or motion picture or in a museum, the setting is carefully controlled so that we will have the best chance to see what is being shown without interruption or distraction. With many of the arts we see there is no control of this sort and outside factors may distort or help our viewing.

Everything we see is seen in a setting. When we look at a building, that structure is part of an environment, a surrounding; it has a visual relationship to where it is placed. A mountain may be seen through a car window as we drive by; the window will act as a frame. A sculpture in a gallery will be placed in a room and the size of the room or its shape may affect our view of the work. A piece of jewelry is seen as it is worn by its owner. If it is a gold-colored pin, for example, it will be less visible and less striking on a yellow shirt than on a black one. For this reason, art works are displayed with care—appropriately framed, set apart from other work, and well lighted—so that they can be fully enjoyed or appreciated.

Sometimes an ordinary part of the physical setting such as climate can be important to our viewing. The coastline of Maine or Oregon is certainly different on a stormy or cloudy day than it is in brilliant sunshine. Ocean, sandy beach, rocks, trees will look different to us from one setting to the other, even though we know they really are the same. Sometimes it may be that the room in which we see a drawing is too warm for us and our discomfort interrupts our viewing. Or, the way we feel at the time can be a factor. Walking around a large museum can be tiring and sore feet will not help us appreciate a favorite art work. The amount of time we have to look at a work can be important. Driving quickly by a fine old house we may miss much of what the building has to offer us.

The psychological setting can influence us as much as the physical environment. Seeing one of the enormous Mayan pyramids rising up from the dry, rolling jungle of the Yucatan pennisula of southern Mexico adds some shock value to what we see (Figure 33, page 20). The same structure among the mountains of Utah might not be quite so impressive. On the other hand, even the most handsome illustration in our favorite magazine for a breakfast cereal that we do not enjoy eating would hold little interest for us, and we would not see it as an art work.

Sometimes the conventions or rules governing the setting in which we see some art works will influence our view of them. For example, when groups of young school children are taken to visit museums, the repeated warnings of their teachers or museum guides (docents) to be quiet, to stay together, and not to touch are enough to make the youngsters uncomfortable in their view of the works exhibited. Of course, not warning them about these behaviors might cause problems even less to be desired. Looking at the arts we see is not always a simple process.

From time to time, we might even develop what can be called "aesthetic indigestion" from seeing too much serious and important art so that we welcome a change to something light and amusing. Human beings need change as much as they need stability. Further, it is helpful in viewing a painting or a building if we can learn how the ideas for that work developed in the mind of the person who made it. Including the artist's preliminary drawings or notes for the exhibited work, as well as earlier or later works by the same artist, enriches our experience of looking at the particular work. This, too, is an important part of the setting.

HOW WE HAVE LEARNED TO SEE (C IN FIGURE 50)

Learning the mechanics of how we see has an influence on what we understand when we look. There are significant differences among how people see, particularly from one culture to another.

A fascinating illustration of both influence and differences can be found in the inability of isolated, primitive people to follow the sequence of action in a motion picture. One such group was disturbed and confused when a character in a movie moved off the edge of the screen. They wanted to stop the film and find out where he had gone and what had happened to him. For most of us this is not at all a problem since we accept what are called the "conventions" of a stage play or a movie. These are the rules for understanding visual presentations within screen, stage, and picture frames, or the boxes of comic strips. We know very well that there is a world outside that frame as well as inside, yet we are perfectly content to be shown only the events inside.

There are other differences in how we see. About six hundred years ago, during the Renaissance, Western European artists were developing the "convention" of perspective that we are used to in modern times (Figure 52). Long before that, Chinese artists, representing a civilization much more advanced in some ways than that of Europe, were using entirely different conventions to picture the world around them. Figure 53 illustrates one of their conventions which demanded that their feudal lords be painted as large, imposing figures while the attendants standing close by be shown as smaller figures to emphasize their inferior status. Europeans looking at the Chinese painting or Asians looking at the Italian Renaissance painting would be as disturbed by these and other differences in the way they had been trained to see as were the primitive people watching the film mentioned above.

Another type of example can be found in the way perception affects the design or organization of a work of art. The artist uses repetition of lines or col-

(continued on page 94)

52. Paolo Uccello, *The Battle of San Romano*, c. 1456–1458. Courtesy of the Trustees, The National Gallery, London

53. Yen Li-pen (attributed), *The Thirteen Emperors,* handscroll, ink and colors on silk, 51 × 551 cm., China, T'ang period, second half of seventh century. Courtesy of the Museum of Fine Arts, Boston, Denman Waldo Ross Collection

ors or other elements to tie together various parts of the art work. Repetition unifies what we see because our eyes tend to relate or group together like images. For example, if there are three areas of red on a billboard, the eye will see these almost simultaneously within the time it takes to "see"—or "read"—the billboard. The process of seeing any object is so quick that it seems to be almost instantaneous. Psychologists and physiologists tell us that seeing an object is not at all one action, but is, in reality, a process—a series or sequence of activities carried on at great speed.

Psychology, which attempts to investigate human behavior scientifically, is rich in studies of how we see, that is, perception; and we are constantly learning more about these complex processes. That we still know very little is unfortunately true, and not until we learn a great deal more will we be able to understand the role our background in seeing plays in the ways in which we look at the arts we see.

Viewing art is only one special example of seeing, with its own mechanics, some of which we will explore in chapter 4. Imagine a person from the jungles of Borneo or the mountains of Peru suddenly transported to downtown New York City or Chicago. How efficiently would that person be able to "see"; how safely could that person travel around in either city? Then think of yourself exchanging places with the person from Borneo or Peru and ask yourself how long you might survive.

In the meantime, the reader is invited to try a simple experiment that may illustrate some of the problems we have with understanding how we see. As you are reading, close your right eye. You will then be able to see your nose with your left eye. Now close your left eye and you will see your nose with your right eye. Now open both eyes. Can you see your nose? Many hundreds of much more complicated experiments demonstrate that seeing, as well as hearing, smelling, tasting, and feeling are not simple mechanisms and that many of the ways in which we grasp the world we live in are learned as we grow up.

HOW MUCH WE KNOW ABOUT THE ELEMENTS
AND PRINCIPLES OF DESIGN
(D IN FIGURE 50)

That aspect of the way we look at the arts we see which deals with their organization or the way they have been put together—their formal qualities—is the one which has been most often taught in schools. At sometime as we progress through the grades, the art teacher attempts to explain to us some of the rules of visual structure that have been developed over many hundreds of years. Chapter 4 will review these rules in words which may be different from those you have heard before, but which can be applied to a work of art. It makes sense to assume that the amount and clarity of information we have about how works of art are put together will influence how we look at them. In the same way, the knowledge we have about the structure of an automobile engine influences how we look at it. To many of us, as we look at it, an engine is just a mass of puzzling machinery. To the mechanic—who knows which parts are the fuel pump, the carburetor, and the alternator, and how they function in relationship to one another—looking at an engine is in this sense like reading a book.

Some people who write about the visual arts believe that the elements and principles of design, the formal qualities, should be the most important part of our response to a work of art. For these writers, all the other influences we describe in this chapter should be screened out in order that we may have a purely art experience. They would probably argue, based on their ideas, that the important things to look for in both a Rice Pereira (Figure 54) and a David (Figure

54. Irene Rice Pereira, *Rectangles,* oil, 24 × 30", 1940. Courtesy of The University of Arizona Museum of Art, Gift of C. Leonard Pfeiffer

55. Jacques Louis David, *The Death of Socrates*, 1787. Courtesy of The Metropolitan Museum of Art, Wolfe Fund, 1931

55) painting are very much the same, namely the formal qualities or design of the work. That one presents formal relationships by themselves while the other has a story seems to these writers to be an insignificant consideration. Both are patterns of line, shape, value, texture, and color, and these are all-important. The "formalist" might say that when works of art are reduced to these essentials, it is easy to see which ones are most successful as works of art.

One example of the theory that only formal qualities are important to look for in a work of art can be seen in an advertisement for the Metropolitan Museum of Art's home-study book of reproductions and lectures called *Art Seminars in the Home,* published several years ago. Accompanying a reproduction of Leonardo's *Mona Lisa* is the following text:

> Are you one of many who admire the Mona Lisa for the wrong reasons?
> Perhaps, like so many people, you attribute the Mona Lisa's greatness to her enigmatic expression—to the fact that she "begins to smile," if looked at long enough. Or perhaps you are intrigued because her eyes seem to "follow you around the room" through some technique known only to Leonardo. Both of these common reactions are discussed in the very first portfolio of the Metropolitan Museum's Seminars in Art as prime examples of the superficial fashion in which most people look at paintings. As the portfolio points out, anyone who admires a painting solely because of its technical competence or the appeal of its subject matter is probably missing all that the artist is really trying to convey. A surprising number of otherwise cultivated persons have this blind spot when they stand before a famous work of art.

Obviously, to the author of this advertisement, neither "technical competence" nor "subject matter" are part of what we should look for when we look at art; if we note these alone, we are "missing *all* that the artist is *really* trying to convey" (italics mine). The writer of the advertisement would probably suggest that we make an effort to ignore these aspects as much as we can, and concentrate our looking at the structure of the work alone.

Others who write about art speak of it as the expression of feelings or emotions; as an expression of the personality of the artist; as an imitation of nature or life; or as a vivid way of telling about those things we feel to be important. No one as yet has been able to devise a completely satisfactory explanation of what art is, as we saw in chapter 1. In fact, there are those who say this simply cannot be done. But we still try to explain it; and until we have an idea or theory that seems to answer all our questions about art, the definition of art in chapter 1 will, at least, answer most of our questions. According to that interpretation, formal qualities are only one of a number of kinds of meanings one can draw from a work of art. To claim that this is all we should try to get is to eliminate other kinds of meanings which may be enjoyable or exciting. Nevertheless, art works are put together in particular ways that we call design or composition. These arrangements are worth learning about so that we can better understand the art we look at.

WHAT WE KNOW ABOUT
THE PARTICULAR SYMBOLS USED (E IN FIGURE 50)

One device used to convey meanings in a work of art is the symbol. A symbol is a sign, which stands for or represents something else. Any visual form can be a symbol, but there must be some agreement as to what a symbol stands for so that it can be understood, or, in the context of looking at art, so that meanings can be drawn from it.

Mathematical signs ($+$ $-$ $=$) and words are, of course, familiar examples of symbols, but we are talking here about visual symbols. These are around us every day though we may not recognize them as such. For example, a common visual symbol is the dollar sign: $. Without that symbol, a number does not necessarily refer to money; with it, there is no doubt in our minds what the number signifies. However, in England, where the units or pieces of money are different from ours, a few people may not recognize what "$" refers to. In the same way, we may not recognize the symbol "£" which stands for an English unit of money, called a pound (so called because a sum of money—or tax—was paid to the king on each pound of goods imported or exported).

The newspaper comic strip provides another example. When we see spiral lines around Charlie Brown's head in "Peanuts" we know he is dizzy. We need no words to understand the cartoon characters' feelings or condition. Advertising design also makes heavy use of symbols to identify firms or products. We can often recognize a company by its symbol or trademark.

Artists use symbols in the same way. Sometimes they use one or two, and sometimes a great many in the same work. Picasso's *Guernica* is an example of a painting in which several symbols are used. If we look at it (Figure 17) before these symbols are explained to us and then again afterward, it will be easy to see that we can find more meanings in the work with some understanding of the symbols he has used.

Guernica was named after a Spanish town that was bombed by German airplanes during the civil war raging in that country in the 1930s. This was the first time in history in which Europeans had bombed one of their own cities, killing women and children as well as soldiers. The world was shocked and horrified by this barbaric act; and Picasso, who was himself a Spaniard, painted a picture that expressed his own horror. Much of the intent (many of the meanings) in this work can be readily grasped without knowing what the particular symbols stand for; the intent is understood through the formal qualities, that is, the diagonal slashes of line, the jaggedness of forms, and the sharp contrasts of dark and light. Once we know some of the symbols, however, more of the meanings of the painting become clear, even without knowing the history of the particular incident that inspired the artist to paint the picture. For example, to some the bull in the upper left portion is a symbol representing the pride and courage of Spain; the horse in the upper central area stands for the agony of war; the lamp–sun–eye form above the horse is said to be a symbol of a world that is aware of what is happening but does not interfere. The two tortured figures on the extreme left and right look upward and tell us of the terror of death falling from the sky in the form of bombs.

However, not all symbols used by the artist are as precise or as literary—in the sense of providing particular information—as those used by Picasso in *Guernica*. The geometric forms of Kandinsky's painting (Figure 30) can be interpreted as symbols. For instance, the crescent in the upper left might be the moon, symbolizing night, while the spotted globe in the upper right can be the sun standing for daylight. The elongated triangle coming up through the center of the painting might mean the dreams and hopes of humans and the large dark triangular shape at the bottom could mean the evil and struggle in living. Or, they can be looked at without symbolic meanings, simply as shapes.

However, it must be remembered that in order to be useful, symbols must have meanings agreed to by some group of people, such as the dollar sign for Americans or the pound sign for the English. If forms do not have fairly common meanings, they are not really symbols at all. One might interpret special symbols (not commonly understood), such as those in Kandinsky's painting, in many other ways. In other words, not only do we lose meanings placed in a work of art by not knowing about the symbols, but through the same ignorance we can also read meanings into the work that were not intended by the artist. The only way to avoid these problems is to learn as much as we can about artists, their times and ideas, and to be cautious in the interpretations we make of the work. There are those, of course, who claim that such problems are not truly important and that whatever the observer sees in a work of art is not only perfectly permissible but also a gain for the observer even when the artist did not intend these meanings. Although the answers to questions such as these are, for the most part, matters of opinion, it does seem to make some sense to be able to understand what the artist wants to express in the work or what people of his time saw in it, whenever this understanding is at all possible.

WHAT THE ART WORK REMINDS US OF (F IN FIGURE 50)

One of the most common reactions we have to an art work is that it reminds us of something we have seen in the world of art or in everyday living. When I look at Figure 56, for example, I am reminded of the ferryboat I used to take from New York City across the Hudson River to New Jersey to visit my grandmother when I was a child. And since thoughts and memories connect with one another as associations, the painting can remind me of the good times we had as a large family around the big kitchen table, warmed by a coal stove.

In the same way, a sculpture, print, building, or any of the arts we see can serve to remind us of events in our lives, of ideas and feelings we have had, or of other works of art. Often we are aware of these associations and may even express them aloud. "This drawing reminds me of my cat," or "When I look at this advertisement for United Airlines, I remember how I felt when I flew in a jet airplane for the first time." Sometimes associations awakened by the work

56. Louis Bouché, *Ten Cents a Ride,* 1942. Courtesy of The Metropolitan Museum of Art, George A. Hearn Fund, 1950

of art are hidden in our minds and we are not aware of them. We then call these associations "subconscious," or underneath our conscious thinking. This may explain feelings we have when we say something like, "I just don't like that photograph. I don't know what there is about it that bothers me, but I don't like it." We know very little about how these feelings and ideas of association work. We know they happen, but we do not know how or why.

It is difficult to judge how, or how much, these associations affect our responses to the work of art. In some cases it is clear that they would greatly influence how we look at works of art. If much of a painting is done in tones of blue and the blues remind you of the blue sky on a particularly enjoyable day at the beach, it is possible that you will look at the painting for a longer time and with greater sympathy than you might if it were painted in other colors. In the same way, if a sculptured head reminds you of a person you do not like or did not like at one time, that association may "spoil" the work of art for you—that is, you may not wish to look at it again. In any case, it would seem that associations might interfere with your reactions to art works, if you think of an association as something completely outside the experience of art. As we have seen before, some people do believe that any considerations outside of the relationship of line, shape, value, color, and texture are interferences; and some of these, like associations, can keep us from enjoying what a work of art has to offer.

On the other hand, one of the qualities that makes the experience of art a rich one is precisely that it stimulates many kinds of ideas or feelings, and that one of these is our ability to make associations with what we see. Again, we do not have the answers to these questions in any carefully studied or scientific sense. We have only some guesses made by aestheticians, who have thought about these problems for long periods of time and who know a great deal about the arts. These questions are very important, however, since every one of us has reason to wonder about why some things in life seem beautiful or valuable and some do not. In addition to thinking about these problems, the wisest policy is to read what others have to say about them.

HOW MUCH WE KNOW
ABOUT THE HISTORY OF THE WORK
(G IN FIGURE 50)

Another influence on the way in which we look at a work of art is the amount we know about it. We can know its name, the name of the artist, the medium used (oils, watercolors, stone, or film), the date it was created, the place in which it was made, its size, the museum in which it is now shown (if it is in a museum), and any special facts about the work, such as its having been found in the attic of a house in Pennsylvania one hundred years after the death of the artist.

Sometimes, knowing all or some of these facts about a work of art makes a great deal of difference in the way we look at the work. For example, knowing that Figure 52 is a painting by Uccello that was done in the Renaissance period in Italy, we will look at the perspective—that is, the way in which the objects in depth are handled—with more care, since that was a period in which perspective was being studied and developed. Or sometimes, knowing the history of a work of art will help us to see more meanings in it. By knowing the history of the painting *Guernica* and the event (bombing of civilians) that inspired it, we will find more meaning in the work. In other cases, knowing the date and place of origin of a work of art helps us to understand it even if we know nothing about the artist and little about the particular events that influenced the work. Figure 57 is a lithograph called *Brot!* ("Bread!"). Knowing that it was done in 1924 by the German artist Käthe Kollwitz helps us to realize that one of its meanings refers to the hunger of many children in Germany brought about by the ravages of World War I.

As in the case of associations, it is difficult to determine just what effect historical knowledge has on our response to the work of art. It may even be harmful in some instances. For example, if one has not liked some buildings by a particular architect, another one designed by the same person may be viewed with prejudice. Most commonly, however, the more one knows about a work of art—or anything else, for that matter—the better one understands it and, therefore, the better chance one has to make a fair judgment about it. What little we know about how we see things suggests that the more we know, the more we see. To the average person watching a play in a football game, the action may seem like a rapid blur and be hard or impossible to follow. Those who have played or studied the game, can readily distinguish separate events in the play.

Those who gather information about the history of art objects are called "art historians." It is the job of the art historian to discover all that can be learned about the work of art, the person who created it, and the place and time in which it was done. Thus, the art historian collects and records not only events and how people and places looked, but also why the artist and the people of the time acted as they did. In this way, the history of art—or of any human action—is a never-ending task, for there is always more to find out about the past, whether it is yesterday or a thousand years ago. So very much of history is still unknown to us, and the work of art historians is sometimes like that of the storybook detective: from small clues they must reconstruct how artists and the people around them lived.

Art historians usually work in museums or in universities. Most often they need to be near a large library and a place where many works of art are kept, since much of the information they collect comes from books and the art works themselves. We are fortunate to have fine museums in many of our cities. Here one can see works of art at their best, in their original forms. Slides and reproductions of works of art are necessarily only second-best ways of seeing them since important qualities in the work may be distorted in making a slide or reproduction. This is particularly true of color, and, of course, scale or

57. Käthe Kollwitz, *Brot!*, lithograph, 1924. Courtesy of the Grunwald Center for the Graphic Arts, University of California, Los Angeles

size. Sometimes we see a very small work of art, like a piece of jewelry, as a four-by-five-foot slide picture on a screen and lose a sense of what it really looks like when it is only inches in size. A good example of this loss can be made clear to us when we look at the *Guernica* in Figure 17 and realize that the original in the Prado Museum is over eleven feet high and over twenty-five feet wide. The reproduction is very different from the original work of art.

HOW WE JUDGE THE WORK (H IN FIGURE 50)

Another aspect of how we look at a work of art might well be the value we place on it as we look at it. As we saw in some of the preceding sections of this chapter, many influences combine to shape our approach and, therefore, our judgment of an art work. What other people say about a particular work; what friends and family think about art; what we know about the symbols used; our knowledge of the history of the work or the artist; these and other influences tend to make us come to an art work with some idea of what value we will place on it even before we see it. This idea may then turn out to be, or at least to influence, how we judge the work when we look at it for the first time. On the other hand, all of our earlier ideas about it might change when we look at it and we may judge it differently.

We have no way of knowing at what point in time a judgment about what we see is made. Most of the arts we see do not happen over a period of time. A building, a piece of sculpture, a photograph, can be looked at, for the most part, all at one time. Some visual art forms do "take time" to see. Just as in the case of music, the mobile (Figure 39) is an example of a visual art form that "happens" over a period of time. We cannot make a true judgment of it until we have seen it for a while since it is changing the relationships of its parts as we look at it.

However, one sees most art works all together at one time and, it would seem, almost instantaneously. We do know, of course, that we can and usually do look at an art work for much longer periods of time than it takes to see it at one glance. Many art works—complicated ones in particular—need to be studied for a long while in order to see clearly all that they represent in formal relationships or in other meanings. At best, judgment should be made after some careful study of the work, but when it takes place or how one arrives at a judgment is difficult if not impossible for us to know or describe. It may be assumed that whether a judgment is made after careful study and some thought about the work of art, or is made before the work is seen or just as one looks at it for the first time, that judgment will influence how we look at the work from that moment on.

There are many kinds of judgments we can make about a work of art. It may be as simple as: "I like it," or "I don't like it." It may be a judgment that recognizes its value but also includes one's own personal opinion such as: "It may be great art, but I don't like it," or "It may not be art at all, but I like it." Lastly, it may be a critical judgment such as: "I like it (or, I think it's good art) for the following reasons." It is the last of these types of judgment that is the most valuable to make since one must think about and probably look for some time at the work of art in order to make such a judgment. Reasons for judgment can be discussed or debated. One cannot argue with a statement such as: "I like it," or "I don't like it," except to insist that "You should like it," which is not a strong argument. No one can force another person to like or dislike something. But one can argue about reasons for liking or disliking a work of art or anything else. Sometimes when one discusses the reasons for liking or disliking a work of art, one's understanding of the work may change and cause a change in judgment. This is why it is important to talk about and read about works of art. Of course, it is absolutely necessary to see them in order to talk about or read about them. This is why almost all books on art have some or many illustrations. The visual arts are to be looked at just as music is to be listened to.

Another influence on judgment is how we look at other art work that is similar in style or technique or subject, or was done by the same artist. If we see and judge highly one print by Käthe Kollwitz (Figure 57), we may look with greater favor on the next piece of work done by the same artist. Thus, one judgment can influence another. In fact, most of us seem to judge art works, and many other things as well, in sets or classes. We like or rate highly people with brown eyes; or automobiles painted red; or paintings, drawings, carvings, or photographs of dogs. Where the judgment is important, it would probably be wiser to rate each object on its own merits. If the arts we see are important in our lives, they should be judged in this fashion, slowly, individually and with a realization of the reasons for our judgments.

Finally, it is useful to remember that our judgments should be based on what we can find in the work of art. To judge a print or painting as a fine piece of work simply because the artist was good to his family does not make much sense—although you can like it or dislike it for that reason if you wish. That reasoning would make as much sense as condemning a painting by Paul Gauguin as poor work just because that French artist left his family to go to the Pacific Islands to live and work.

WHAT RELATIONSHIP THE WORK HAS TO OUR LIFE
(I IN FIGURE 50)

The last influence to be discussed here is the effect the art work has on other activities in one's life. An obvious example of how this influence works can be seen in the case of a collector of art objects. Since the collector is interested in buying art, the question of the cost of the art work can have considerable effect on how it is seen. Buying it then becomes a business matter, as well as an aesthetic matter.

Even if we are not wealthy collectors of art, the same situation may exist in some way with each of us. Having a large library of popular or classical records can be as much a question of the respect or approval we will have from our friends as it is a question of how much we enjoy or value the recordings themselves. Undoubtedly, fashions in hair style, clothing, dancing, foods, and many other activities in our lives are decided by this need. For those who are interested in the arts we see, the same need can influence how they look at works of art. To look at or to appreciate a certain type of art work becomes "the thing to do" and is, therefore, an influence on how we look at that art.

On the other hand, it is easy enough to think of situations in which the influence of the relationship of the art work to one's life may be wholesome. Take the case of a young couple who are looking for a chair to buy. Even though they may dislike the so-called modern style in furniture, seeing a well built and reasonably priced chair in that style may change their attitude toward the style itself. We might say in such a case that they will look with "new eyes" at the furniture and it will have been precisely the relationship of the chair, which is the art work, to the needs of their present life that brought about the change in attitude.

However, whether the influence of considerations outside the work of art is helpful or harmful to the way you look at it, these considerations do lessen the quality of the experience of art. You will recall that in chapter 1 we described art as objects seen as valuable for their own sakes. The more we are concerned with completely outside considerations, the less we are attending to the work of art itself. Since all of us have aspects of our lives other than art, and these may at times influence how we look at art, we should be aware of these influences so that we may deal with them intelligently.

CHAPTER 4

the structure
of art

One of the most important characteristics of a work of art—to some the most important—is its structure, the way it has been organized or composed or designed. Everything we see is made up of parts, like building blocks. These parts are called the *elements of design: line, shape, value, color,* and *texture.* However, only those objects that are humanmade are deliberately, intentionally organized or designed. The elements are composed in ways the artist or designer believes will most effectively produce the response desired in the viewer or express the kinds of ideas and emotions the designer wishes. The history of the visual arts suggests a development of the ways in which these elements can be put together into a set of rules proven effective through practice. These rules are called the *principles of design.*

Like some other sets of rules, these principles can be ignored in a successful work of art. However, this is usually done either by an artist who is well trained in their use and can compensate in some way for avoiding them or by

children or primitives (those who are untrained), who are substituting innocence for sophistication. Most works of art exhibit these principles in the way
in which they have been arranged or designed, sometimes obviously, sometimes subtly. But we must know something of these principles before we can
recognize them, before we can "read" the work of art to understand how it has
been put together. Once we are able to do this—even on a very simple level—
we can become aware of how the ideas and emotions we have obtained from
the work of art have been enhanced by its composition. We can see more clearly how the meanings we attribute to a work of art have been conveyed to us or
aroused in us.

Those who write about these formal relationships, these elements and
principles of design, use a variety of terms and concepts in describing them;
there is no generally agreed-upon description or terminology. The description
which follows seems the clearest and most accurate. However, other ideas and
other terms will be mentioned and explained when appropriate so that the
reader will be able to follow such discussions in other books.

THE ELEMENTS OF DESIGN

Some writers on composition start their description with the concept of space.
This is, in fact, a legitimate starting point, since all objects, natural or humanmade, inhabit space. Thus the space of a painting may be a 24×36" canvas, with the illusion of depth of several inches or several feet. Or, a building
may be hundreds of feet high, wide, and deep. On the other hand, it can also be
said that the elements (line, shape, value, color, texture) create the space, particularly in the ways in which they are related to one another. It would seem to
make more sense to start with these elements, since the spaces in which they
operate are either given—in the sense that all objects exist in space—or created
by their relationships.

line

The first visual element we shall look at is line. The Swiss artist Paul Klee (1879–
1940) said that a line is a point taking a walk. One might also call a point a very
short line. There are many different kinds of lines: thick, thin, curved, straight,
vertical, horizontal, and diagonal, as can be seen in Figures 58, 59, and 60. As
soon as a line thickens it seems to appear less like a line. Let us take the line in
Figure 58 and thicken it as in Figure 61. Now it looks as much like a shape as a
line. A human or animal hair normally appears to us as a line. However, under
a microscope (Figure 62), it is no longer a line but a shape. Thus, we might say
that a line is really a very narrow shape.

A line or series of lines can make a shape by showing the edge or "outline"
of a form (Figures 63 and 64), or, sometimes, a line can make a shape simply by

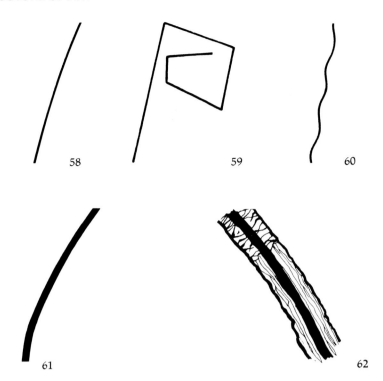

providing some strong suggestions even if it does not completely outline the shape (Figure 65). Since our eyes follow lines, a line will give us a sense of movement inside the space around it. Often this movement, or the direction of the movement, pulling our eyes from one part of the space to another, arouses particular feelings in us as it does so. Figures 66, 67, and 68 illustrate lines creating movements in particular directions. The first two might make us feel alert and energetic; the third, quiet and serene. The artist, being familiar with the effects of line, uses those that promote the kind of feelings he wants to arouse.

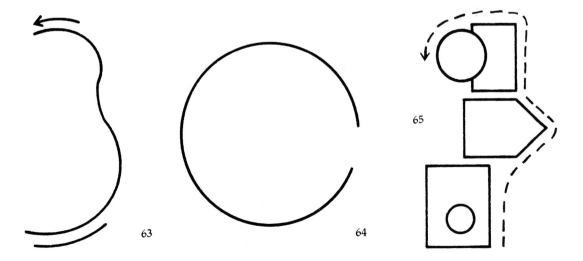

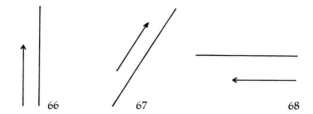

The vertical lines of the Gothic cathedrals, for example (Figure 8), move the eye up toward the heavens, emphasizing and dramatizing the religious meanings in the building, the sculpture, and stained-glass windows.

Line, used as direction, is a concern of the artist as he deals with structure, or how the elements including line are put together. Therefore, we will discuss this aspect of line in the second section of this chapter when we consider the principles of design. There are various qualities of line—that is, thick, thin, harsh, soft, clear, blurred, curved, straight. As with direction of line, the artist will select those lines which will convey the kind of emotional impact or idea required in the work.

shape

The second visual element is shape. It can be made of line, an area of paint, or a piece of paper (Figures 69, 70, and 71). In order to be a shape, it needs an edge, no matter how irregular or indistinct that edge may be, to separate it from what is around it. Everything we see, whether humanmade or natural, is made up of shape or line. Not only is one cloud in a clear sky a shape, but all of the sky around the cloud is a shape as well. The cloud, in the words of the psychologist interested in perception, is the "figure" and the sky around it the "ground." Or, in the words of the artist, the cloud is the "positive" space, of which one is conscious, and the sky around it is the "negative" space, which is just as important in the composition of the work.

There are limitless varieties of shapes: some are huge, others small; some are geometric, others irregular; some appear soft, others hard. Lines and shapes, even without the other visual elements (value, color, texture), cause us to have feelings and ideas and therefore can serve as meaning-carrying devices in a work of art. A shape with real depth (as in the case of a building or a piece of

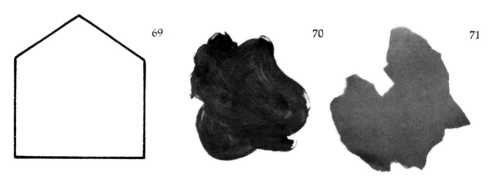

sculpture) or with the illusion of depth (as in the case of a painting or print in which an object gives the appearance of being round) is usually called a *mass*, to account for its three-dimensional quality. Shapes themselves, or their outlines, can create lines and movement as in Figure 65.

There are a variety of ways in which line and shape can create the impression or illusion of depth. One example is the rectangle in Figure 72, which appears to move back into the space within the frame in Figure 73 and, thus, fools us with a feeling of depth even on a flat piece of paper. This provides the artist with space for movement and action going into the paper, canvas, or screen as well as on its surface. It is as if the art work is a box we see from one side, in which the structure is built.

Shapes or masses and the spaces they manipulate create impressions in the viewer of scale or size. Thus, the verticality of the Gothic cathedral exaggerates its height; the wide, horizontal eaves of a ranch house emphasize its width; and the massiveness of one part of a building might make us see it as much deeper than it is. In the same way, masses on a two-dimensional surface can generate impressions of height, width, and depth, even though the masses are, in truth, shapes on a paper or canvas. In the case of depth, these illusions can be provided by modeling or shading a shape (which creates roundness), by overlapping, by placing one shape in front of part of another, or by using perspective. In some of the art of the last fifty to seventy years, artists have chosen to ignore this effect preferring instead to keep their work looking flat, with all the movement and action on the surface.

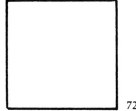
72

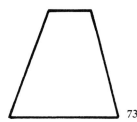
73

value

The third visual element is value, which refers to the darkness of a dark area (line or shape) or the lightness of a light area. A light area has "high" value; a dark area has "low" value. Value usually refers to the lightness or darkness of a color; but where no color is used as in most drawing, printmaking, sculpture, some photographic arts, and some advertising design, it refers to the lightness or darkness of blacks, whites, and grays.

As a visual element, value also plays a specific role in art when it is used to provide varieties of dark and light, that is, the contrasts or degrees of difference between the darkness of a dark area and the lightness of a light area next to it. Figures 74 and 75 show sharp and gradually developed areas of dark and light. Some of the dramatic quality of the David painting (Figure 55) is caused by the sharpness of contrasts between light and dark areas next to one another.

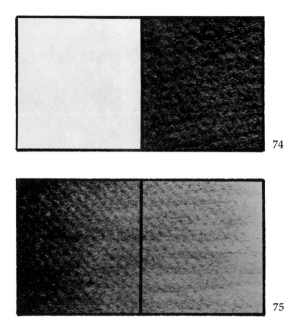

74

75

color

The most obvious of the visual elements is color. We follow directions based on color—stopping at a red light, for example; we associate certain feelings with colors, such as red and danger, blue and sadness; and we often judge objects by color, sometimes selecting the ripe tomato in the market partly by its redness.

As we have seen, there are a number of art forms in which no color is used; some artists prefer working with these forms rather than those with color. Photographers and printmakers, in particular, often enjoy working within the limitations imposed by using black, white, and grays or find that these limitations help to emphasize a specific meaning they wish to convey. However, for the most part, color adds a richness to the visual arts, providing one more visual quality to enjoy. In fact, one word we use to describe a dull or uninteresting person or scene is "colorless."

Color is our response to stimulation of the retina of the eye by light waves reflected from what is around us. Differences in the surfaces of what is around us create differences in the length of the light waves. We see these differences in length as color. All of us have seen a rainbow or a rainbow effect created by light passing through a prism. This range of colors (including other light waves we do not see such as infrared and ultraviolet) is called a spectrum. Black is caused by the complete absorption of light waves, and white by the reflection of all the waves that produce color. Black and white are seldom described as colors.

For the artist who uses pigment, paint, crayon, colored paper, or colored ink, the primary colors of the spectrum are red, yellow, and blue—from which all other colors can be mixed. For the artist who works with colored lights, as in the case of some of the photographic arts and theater design, the primary colors are green, blue-violet, and red-orange. The latter artists are using the light itself rather than light reflected from some surface. "Hue" is the word we use to identify a color of the spectrum. It is the name of the color, such as red, green, or orange. Value, as we saw in the previous section, refers to the amount of lightness or darkness in a color. The term intensity is used to distinguish the strength of brightness of a color.

Like lines, shapes, and values, colors carry meanings or produce effects in us that provoke ideas and feelings. Colors appear to be related to temperature: reds, oranges, and yellows seem warm, blues and greens appear cool. Colors seem to advance or recede. Warm colors generally appear to advance and cool colors recede. Red seems to be an exciting color (perhaps because it is warm and advances) and is, therefore, used on stop signs and other notices which call for alertness and quick response. Furthermore, many colors have particular associations or meanings. White might suggest purity; black, death; purple, royalty; and yellow, cowardice. People in other societies have different associations. In China, for example, white is associated with death and yellow is the color of royalty.

texture

Texture refers to our sensation of touch when we look at a surface. Everything that we touch has some kind of surface quality. Some of the sensation we get when we touch a surface can be felt by looking alone. We recognize a rough sensation when we look, even though we do not touch. The artist may use texture to differentiate the objects in the work, as, for example, the smooth, shiny skin of an apple or the coarse, rough surface of a piece of burlap. Or greater interest can be created on the surface of the work; an architect might use rough brick next to flat stained-wood surfaces for contrast. Texture helps to convey some of the meanings the artist wishes to put into the work. In Figure 22, the shiny texture of the dictator's head seems to make its ugliness even more repellent. The texture used in art may be an actual texture—which you can feel if you touch it—as in the case of a collage, or a piece of sculpture, or a building. Or it may be only visual texture as in Figure 76, created by paint, ink, or photography.

76

THE PRINCIPLES OF DESIGN

Just as the elements described above are the building blocks of all that we see, the principles of design are ways of arranging the elements in works of art. In one sense, everything that we see is arranged, or put together. Even the natural landscape around us—the trees, hills, rocks, and grass—has been arranged by the forces of wind, water, movements of the earth, and the power of growth. An explosion can arrange (perhaps rearrange would be a better word) the parts of a room or a house or a mountain. Or, excavating for the foundation of a building, with bulldozers and steam shovels, is also a way of arranging and is done according to some strict rules. However, when one sets out deliberately to arrange visual elements to convey meanings for their own sake, the process is called design (although the same word can be used for other activities such as machine design or to design a political campaign). The ways of arranging those elements that have been found most successful in expressing the meanings of art, are called the principles of design.

These principles are not and should not be considered strict rules that must be followed. From time to time, artists break these rules and create accepted works of art. In a sense, they create new rules. A most spectacular break of this kind was made by Pop artists (Figure 35), who often ignored all the principles of design. Many artists, however, still choose to remain within the framework of these principles, which helps them to express their meanings. There are many different ways to describe these principles and different terms for each of them. What follows is just one way to describe them and one set of words.

The basic principles of design are *unity* and *contrast*. The artist tries to unify the visual elements being used, to make them hold together within the space of the art work. At the same time, the artist tries to contrast them so that they will pull apart. The more dramatic and exciting the meanings in the work, the greater the contrast. If, on the other hand, a feeling of peace and tranquility is being emphasized, there will be less contrast, or more unity.

All design or composition in art functions within a frame or space. This is easy to see in the rectangle of a painting or photograph and on the screens of films and television. Even where we do not have such an obvious frame, however, as in sculpture, architecture, or industrial design, we tend to create one around the work, and we see the unity and contrast of the elements in relation to that frame or space. As soon as we place a dot or a short line inside a frame, the problem of design—of organizing the elements—has begun. All design is also influenced by scale or relationships of size. It is easy to see, for example, that if we place the wheel of a small compact car beside the axle of a bulldozer or trailer truck, that wheel will look very much smaller. In fact, it will look "out of place." In much the same way, the size of any part of a work of art—or the whole work itself—may be affected by the size or scale of the surrounding space in which it is seen.

For an illustration of the principles of design, we can start with a checkerboard minus its customary color (Figure 77). This design gives us the greatest possible degree of unity—in this case of line, shape, and value—in that it holds together perfectly. We have no unpleasant sensation of falling apart as a result of this image. However, it is uninteresting to look at. If we take the same checkerboard pattern and provide contrast by changing the sizes, shapes, and values of the rectangles (Figure 78), we have a design that is more interesting—less monotonous. If, then, we were to add to or change some of the horizontal and vertical lines to diagonals and curves, we would have even more contrast and, thus, more visual excitement.

77

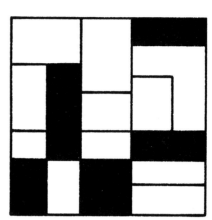
78

The artist achieves unity and contrast with each of the elements: line, shape, value, color, texture. There are specific devices or subprinciples with which to unify and contrast the elements. These are *direction, repetition,* and *gradation* to unify; and *direction, variety,* and *emphasis* to contrast. We will illustrate each of these devices with one of the visual elements, though each device can work with all five.

Since, as we saw in the first section of this chapter, our eyes move along lines inside the space of the frame, the artist uses *direction* of line to pull our eyes back and forth over the surface so that what we see will hold together. Whether working in three dimensions, as in sculpture or architecture, or a flat medium such as a drawing showing depth, the artist will also use direction of line to carry us back in space, but bring us sufficiently forward again so that the work will hold together.

Illustrations of unifying with direction of line can be seen in Figure 79.

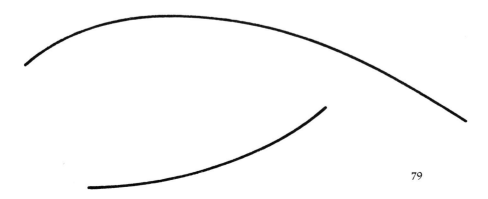
79

Our eyes move over the surface of the paper with the lines in each case, but they do not fall out of the frame. Instead they are brought back by lines placed in directions selected to do just that. When no effort is made by the artist to unify with direction of line, the result can be visually uncomfortable and unpleasant. In Figure 52, Uccello uses direction of line to pull us visually deep into the picture. But he uses the directions of other lines to bring us back near the surface. Figures 80 (page 21) and 81 illustrate direction of line—and shape, value, and texture—as unifying agents in a work of architecture.

The second device the artist uses to unify the elements in his work is *repetition*. The checkerboard we looked at in Figure 77 is an extreme example of repetition of form, which, when carried too far, results in monotony. However, used carefully, repetition of the elements ties together or unifies the image. In Figure 82 shapes are repeated, while in Figure 83 values are repeated. Kandinsky repeats shapes—principally circles and triangles in Figure 30. Colors can be repeated as well to unify the pattern of an art work, since our eyes tend to group the same colors together.

One particular type of repetition is rhythm, which, as in music, refers to a regular accented repetition. Figure 51, José Orozco's *Zapatistas* (page 22), shows rhythm in the regular repetition of the legs, blankets, and hats of the marching men. These shapes are accented not only by repetition but by the

81. Deady Hall, the University of Oregon, Eugene, Oregon, 1886

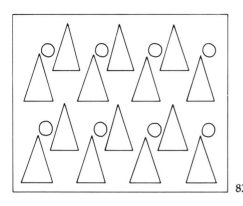 

82   83

sharp difference between the light of each leg area and the dark of the areas surrounding it. In the case of rhythm, repetition is usually obvious and forceful, as the Orozco painting demonstrates. Most repetition in works of art, however, is more subtle, so that it is not easily noticed.

Gradation is the third device used by the artist to unify the elements in the work. It is the gradual change from one color to another, one size of form to another, or one value to another. There seems to be a break or separation on the surface within the frame in both Figures 84 and 85. However, the image in Figures 86 and 87 seems to hold together since there is a gradual change in size

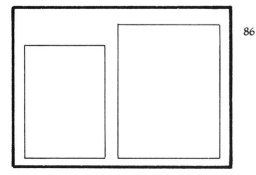 

84   85

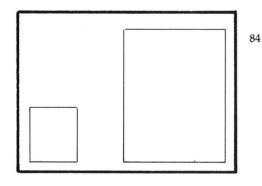 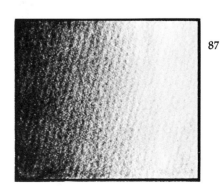

86   87

in the first and in value in the second. Gradation in size is illustrated in Figure 26. The group of four apples on the right seem closer together, more compact, because of the gradual changes in size—as opposed to the sharp changes in size among the group to the left.

Just as the artist used the device of direction to unify the elements, so *direction* can be used to contrast the elements. Figure 51 (page 22) illustrates how direction can be used to contrast lines, in this case the lines of the marching figures and their weapons. The Daumier lithograph in Figure 16 shows even sharper contrasting line direction, pulling the parts of the art work apart and making it exciting and stirring to look at. In this print, the title of which is *Conseil de Guerre* ("Council of War"), the artist uses sharp, opposing diagonal lines, at least in part, to express the violence of his theme. The buildings in Figures 80 (page 21) and 81, on the other hand, are made up of contrasting horizontal and vertical lines, which, being less forceful, give the feeling of stability and repose.

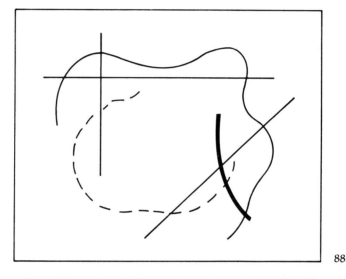

88

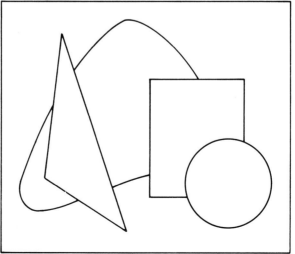

89

90

Another device for contrasting the elements is *variety*, which describes a number of any of the elements differing from one another. Figures 88, 89, and 90 illustrate how three elements—line, shape, and texture—can be varied. Figure 91 shows how subtle varieties can be introduced even using the same form (the repeated face) when the size of that form is changed. On a large scale, the façade of Notre Dame cathedral in Figure 8 has dozens of varied lines, forms, values, and textures which pull our eyes one way and another and produce visual excitement by their contrasts.

The last device, *emphasis*, contrasts the elements by making one portion of an image more important to the eye than the other parts. Socrates in David's *Death of Socrates* (Figure 55) is clearly the point of emphasis where our eyes seem to enter the picture or what is sometimes called the center of interest. The raised arm, the high value (amount of white) of the skin color, as compared to the areas around the figure, the direction of lines of the figures around him, all carry our eyes to the point of emphasis. Sometimes the artist creates more than one center of interest, pulling the eye of the observer from one such center to another.

To summarize, let us look at one work of art in which all these elements and principles of design may be clearly identified. Orozco's *Zapatistas* (Figure 51, page 22), is a painting of the revolutionary peasant army of the Mexican leader, Emiliano Zapata. The emotive meanings of the subject include the powerful surge of a peasant rebellion against the oppression of landowners; the frightening drama of impending bloodshed; and the dignity of men and women fighting for their freedom. The symbols include the many sombreros (a uniquely Mexican hat), the long machete (a specifically peasant knife) worn by some of the marching figures, and the long-robed figures of the women, who, though they will not fight in the battles to come, will care for the wounded and bury the dead.

91. George Tooker, *Government Bureau*, egg tempera on gesso panel, 1956. Courtesy of the Marisa del Re Gallery.

The meanings of the formal relationships discussed in this chapter are easy to grasp once we have some knowledge to guide us. We can see how the movement created by the lines (and shapes, values, colors, and textures) of the rifles, machetes, arms, sombrero crowns, and cartridge bandoleers of the marching and riding men and the faces and robes of the women take our eyes vigorously toward the left. The leftward *direction* of this movement, its strong single *emphasis* and the *variety* of the elements (for example, the sizes and shapes of the forms, the roughness and smoothness of the textures, the sharp differences in value) all combine to promote contrast. This powerful development of contrasts can, in turn, provoke emotions in us of excitement, fear, or anger and thus accentuate the struggle and violence of the story and the symbols of the painting.

At the same time, the *direction*, the *gradation*, and the *repetition* of the elements as seen in the legs and sombrero brims of the marching men, the necks of the horses, the circular hats of the riders, the serapes (blankets), and the neutral tones of the background, all tend to pull our eyes back from the left into the picture, hold it together, and provoke feelings of stability, security, and strength reflecting the artist's recognition of the power and dignity of the peasant masses. Of all the principles, Orozco has used *repetition* in particular in this painting to create the impression of the overwhelming, not-to-be-stopped force of revolutionary purpose. This repetition, like the rhythm of a marching song, batters our senses and supports—by the ideas and emotions it arouses— the meanings Orozco intends us to find in his work.

Even if one does not know the history of Mexico, or cannot identify the symbols used, the formal qualities of the painting alone can provide enough interest to make this a work of art. None of the arts we see, not even paintings, needs to have meanings other than their visual relationships. Nor are all works of art as forceful. Some are, in fact, gentle and delicate, though no less valuable as art. Furthermore, we do not know with any degree of certainty whether Orozco's primary purpose was to create a powerful visual document to celebrate the Mexican revolution or whether, as an artist, he used this theme simply as a vehicle to create a satisfying visual organization. In this case, probably both purposes are involved. For other artists, and in other instances for Orozco himself, one purpose might predominate. It does seem safe to say that if art is anything at all, it is certainly not merely one kind of object nor has it only one kind of purpose.

This chapter has provided a brief introduction to the complicated rules or "grammar" of visual organization. As with any language, this grammar is much more complex than its description here would suggest. Nevertheless, this introduction may be adequate as a starting point. The reader can now go back over the illustrations in the book and apply the same process of analysis to them. These works of art can then be seen by means of their organization and, hopefully, should suggest more of the meanings placed in the work by these formal qualities. The only exceptions, where these formal qualities will be of no help in seeing the work, will be with some of the more recent art such as Figure 35. Here, meanings have to be obtained mostly from symbol or subject content.

An understanding of the formal qualities of art, a knowledge of the symbols and subjects artists have used, together with some insight into how we look at the arts we see, can provide us with the means to greater enjoyment of one part of the world around us. The visual arts are literally all around us and, properly appreciated, add intensity and quality to our lives. If this volume can help the reader gain these benefits—even in some small measure—it will have served its purpose.

CHAPTER 5

two
mass media

This chapter will present basic information about two of the mass media: motion pictures and television. The reader will recall that the distinction made here between mass media such as motion pictures and television and the visual arts, was that the former changed over time, while the latter remained the same even if we looked at them for long periods. In this sense, neither motion pictures nor television can be called visual art forms or instances of the arts we see; they are best understood in a classification by themselves. Nevertheless, despite this important difference, both of these mass media are so close in several other ways to the arts explored in this book, that some consideration of their structure and functions makes sense here and should be of use to the reader.

In its broadest use, the word "media" is the plural of medium and refers to those means through which an effect is produced. The particular media, two of which we will look at in this chapter, are the communications media, which serve as instruments for sending messages. These messages are usually ideas, attitudes, and information which need to be exchanged so that society will function properly or efficiently. Thus, newspapers, radio, magazines, television and, to some extent, motion pictures are called communications media, or, more commonly shortened to "media." Other communications media such as the telephone and telegraph are not usually included in the conception of mass media, probably because they are individual rather than social in their operation. People who work in the visual arts—which we have explored throughout this book—use the word media for the materials of their production, such as paint, clay, or stone. Although this use of the term media is also correct, it is not the usage we will refer to here; we will be talking about the mass media and, specifically, motion pictures and television.

A fortunate aspect of studying the mass media is that all of us know a great deal about them, more, perhaps, than we realize. In fact, it would be difficult, if not impossible, to find anyone growing up and living in a technological society today who is not knowledgeable about these media. They are all around us and highly significant in the formation of our ideas and beliefs about every facet of the world we live in. As a consequence, the mass media have become a primary institution for holding society together, no less important than government, education, and law.

Those of us who live in North America, Western Europe, and Japan tend to think of television and motion pictures as the most widespread mass media forms. However, from a global point of view, it is likely that both radio and newspapers are just as important and even more widespread in the less technologically developed areas of the world. It may be that as many people depend on the latter sources for information and ideas as on the former.

However, we are interested in two of these mass media as art forms, related in some ways to the visual arts. Neither television nor motion pictures were accepted as art forms early in their development, but today most people do recognize them in this way. One reason for this recognition is the quality of some of the work that has been produced over the years: films and television programs of obvious artistry. Another reason may well be the growth in acceptance of the popular arts as objects and events which can provide us with important thoughts and feelings and which can be valued for their own sakes. Whatever the reasons, both of these media are very much a part of our daily lives, give us enjoyment, satisfaction, and value, and should be examined so that we can understand them.

SOME UNIQUE CHARACTERISTICS OF MOTION PICTURES AND TELEVISION

We can begin this examination by noting some unique characteristics of motion pictures and television that give these media their power as particular art forms we watch. Although there are some sharp differences between motion pictures on the one hand and television on the other, the following aspects are common to both. The first characteristic is one we have already noted: both media have sequence. Through a series of images and sounds (including words) they can present us with events, people, and ideas as they change and develop. They are, fundamentally, story-telling devices. In this sense both media are most like literature, that is, stage plays, novels, and short stories and, perhaps, least like the visual arts. Television has the added capability, unlike motion pictures, of showing us events that happened moments ago, or, in some instances, while the events are happening. This ability, helped by satellites that carry picture and word around the surface of the earth, enables us to take part in history immediately, in a way never before possible and can be said to make us all part of what Marshall McLuhan called the "global village."

A second, important aspect of both motion pictures and television is that they are bisensory, involving two of our senses, sight and hearing, at the same time. It is likely that these two senses are the most important ones we have; hearing gives us words with which we can deal with ideas, and sight presents pictures which give us concrete information about objects, people, and places. This audio-visual character by itself is not unique, since dramatic productions such as stage plays and operas do much the same. But combined with some of the other qualities at which we will be looking, the audio-visual nature of these media makes them truly remarkable.

Both motion pictures and television combine in one art form many of the essential features of all the other forms including music, the visual arts, poetry, prose, drama, and dance. Their one defect in this context, of course, is that they are not and cannot be "live"; one cannot be in the same place with the performers, as at a concert or at a play, nor can one see the original painting as one would in a gallery or museum. Undoubtedly, some of the quality of these experiences may well be lost when they come to us second hand, so to speak. Neither film nor videotape can make us feel the thickness of the walls of a medieval cathedral (Figure 8) the way we feel it when we come into the cool interior of the building from the hot sunshine of a summer day and realize how much stone it takes to insulate the structure so effectively. Some other qualities of the other art forms are lost as well, such as accuracy of color and sound, size and scale, and the feeling of closeness we might have to the performer. On the other hand, motion pictures and television give us the chance to see and hear so much that we would not be able to experience without them, that such losses are acceptable, if unfortunate. We should, however, recognize these disadvantages as part of the nature of the media we are dealing with.

In a very real sense, both media completely control time. Even a stage play, which in many ways is similar to them, cannot easily move backward and forward in time and when it tries to do so is awkward and much less believable. With motion pictures and television, flashbacks—jumps backward in time, even of centuries—and flashforwards (in which we see glimpses of the future) are conventions acceptable to us. Even with simple actions, these media control time in a way that makes what they present to us much more intense and dramatic. For example, when a character in a stage play enters from a doorway at the side of the stage, we must follow his progress all the way to the table at center stage. In motion pictures or television he can be shown opening the door, then with a "cut," the next image can show him leaning over the table. We can connect the two events, mentally filling in the part not shown and accepting what is presented as the entire action. In fact, so accustomed are we to this way of handling time, that even this explanation may seem unnecessary.

In both of these media we see events and places of long ago and, when they are well produced, we accept them as real. In science fiction films we see events and places of the future and attend to them as if they were real as well. People age in minutes, places change from scene to scene, and we move from one part of the world to another instantaneously; all these time-controlled sequences of images create screen or movie time as opposed to real time and we accept them without question because we are used to them; they are the rules screened images have developed for telling us stories. Very early motion pictures, in the beginning of this century, were made by setting up a movie camera and having people act out events in front of it just as in a stage play. The next step was to move the camera itself, which gave the moviemaker the new and exciting freedom of showing the action of the story from a variety of viewpoints. After that, the next development was to "cut" or move the scene of the action immediately to another, so that the viewer could see what was happening in two or more places at the same time. At this point, motion pictures achieved complete control of time; unnecessary action could be eliminated by showing only key points of an event and letting the viewer fill in the rest mentally. They could move back and forth as they wished, shortening the real time of the events by presenting them with the unreal but totally comfortable rapidity of screen time.

In much the same way both media control space. We are so accustomed to seeing a character in a story board an airplane in Los Angeles and then seconds later land in New York City or London that we do not question how the camera could move so quickly. We see a long wide shot of a huge desert or city and then, in the very next scene, an intimate close-up of a character's face. The camera can move around an object, above it, or below it. With devices such as a divided screen or one image superimposed upon another, we can even be in two places at the same time. The screen can show us shots of the Empire State Building in New York City, the Eiffel Tower in Paris, and the Houses of Parliament in London one after the other and we will know we have traveled to those countries for the purposes of the story. Literature, in the form of novels and short stories can do this as well, but motion pictures and television control space and time in pictures as well as in words.

Finally, both of these media (perhaps motion pictures even more than television) have an extraordinary ability to get us involved, so that we often forget where we are while we are watching. We can be drawn into the events on the screen almost as if these events replace our consciousness of living; they become a kind of "wrap-around" experience. Whatever the reasons for this unusual power, these media are certainly absorbing art forms and, together with the other characteristics noted above, this power gives them a unique ability to influence our attitudes and ideas about the world. Therefore, we should be careful to examine what these media are telling us, whether we are watching a commercial on television selling us a particular kind of shampoo or a motion picture about war telling us how heroic it is to shoot guns at people.

These five characteristics of motion pictures and television are the results of the technical nature of their production, just as the qualities of a painting—what makes it a handsome and visually exciting object—are the result of the nature of paint and canvas and, of course, the skills of the artist. Thus it is important to look at how these media are produced, just as we briefly explored earlier how lithographs, sculpture, and ceramics are made.

THE TECHNOLOGY OF MOTION PICTURES AND TELEVISION

Although we have been treating these two media together, since their impact on us as viewers is similar in so many ways, the technology of their production is different. The motion picture was developed first, in the early years of the twentieth century, while television did not become a commercial reality until around 1950. Both media are "electric" in that they depend upon the same current, that which we use to heat our homes, cook our food, and light our cities. Beyond this similarity, motion pictures and television have little else in common, even though they are much alike in the ways in which they are used as art forms.

motion pictures

Movies grew out of the technical developments of photography. We noted in chapter 2 that light is captured on film coated with light-sensitive chemicals, the brighter areas of an image changing the areas on the film more than the dimmer areas. The moving picture camera—usually with an electric powered motor—pulls the film past a lens or glass opening, so that the light reflected from an object toward which the lens is pointed is deposited on the film in small segments or pieces of motion. Each of these segments (called a frame) captures one portion of the motion of a moving object, much like a series of individual photographs. When light is beamed through the developed film and projected on a screen at twenty-four frames per second, our eyes see the sequences as a smooth, continuous motion. This is because our eyes keep the same image in sight for some seconds after the image has been removed from our vision (you might test this by shutting your eyes right now to see how long the image of this page remains in sight). Instead of seeing each frame as an individual unit, we tend to overlap them and maintain, with no discomfort, the illusion of motion.

This strange and fortunate capability of the human eye works as readily for slow motion as for normal or faster than normal motion and the moviemaker uses it to make a particular action more dramatic or intense by slowing it down or speeding it up. For contrast or emphasis, a movie or television story may present us with a "freeze-frame," providing a still image on the screen after a series of moving images. We are so accustomed to these gimmicks or tricks that we accept them as part of the rules of the medium and respond to them—when they are competently used—with the reaction appropriate to the story.

A number of film sizes are currently in use: the 8 or Super 8 film size, 16, 35, and 72 and others for wide-screen films. These sizes refer to the width of the film in millimeters: 8 mm. and Super 8 mm. are the usual home movie size, Super 8 being simply a larger image on the same width of film; 16 mm. is the film size most commonly used in those educational films we see in school; 35 mm. is the standard size used in most commercial theaters. Wide-screen sizes such as 72 mm. give us the large panoramas in some motion pictures and the stereo sound coming from the two ends of the screen provide sound which is heard naturally—as, for example, the roar of the engine of an automobile moving from left screen to right, heard from left to right. Some experimental films of recent years have tried three-dimensional screened images, but except for their momentary popular interest these were not successful.

television

The technical process of television or video consists of capturing the brightness and dimness of the light reflected from the parts of an image toward which the video camera is pointed. This camera "reads" or registers these differences in light intensity in a series of back and forth horizontal sweeps of 525 lines and 100,000 details of varying darkness and lightness (with a greater number of lines in some European countries) to make up a single image. To register and project quick movements smoothly, twenty-five to thirty complete pictures per second, built up of 525 horizontal lines each, go through the video camera, are recorded on videotape and then projected on the screen of our television monitor. Since the brain keeps the impression of light for about one-tenth of a second after the light is removed, we do not "see" these images being built up piece by piece or line by line, but, rather, see them as complete pictures and if they show all the parts or segments of a motion, we see them as smoothly moving images in the same way as motion pictures.

Most of us are accustomed to the marvels of this technology through having a television set or monitor in our homes. During the 1970s, complete miniature video systems with a video camera and videotape recorder appeared on the market, along with videotapes of films and television programs, to be handled much like audiotapes of music. Thus we have several different possibilities for television: broadcast television; closed circuit television, in which the picture and sound is sent through a cable; and video recording and playback. In theory at least, we can be our own television producers with access to the third system, just as we can be our own filmmakers with a movie camera. In actuality, both media are expensive, not only because of the cost of the basic equipment—camera and video recorder—but because of the cost of videotape and movie film and developing.

As art forms we watch, motion pictures and television share one special characteristic. Unlike most of the visual arts we looked at in chapter 2, these media are seldom produced or created by individuals, although there are individual video artists and moviemakers who make (understandably enough) short works in those media. Almost all publicly seen movies and television are produced by groups of specialists, ranging from actors to directors to those who operate cameras and lighting equipment, the writers of scripts, costume people, and make-up people. One of the most important of these production details in both media is editing, which is the rearranging of the parts of the film or videotape to make what is seen and heard more appropriate to the story.

In the case of motion pictures, parts of the film may be cut out, discarded, or used elsewhere. In television, editing is done by re-recording parts of the tape in other places, or by the director in the control room of a television studio, who changes what is being shot from one camera to another camera—as for example, from a long shot to a close-up. Obviously in both media editing is a critical factor, since it controls the dramatic quality and the content of what is finally shown on the movie or television screen. Therefore, much more film or videotape is usually shot than is finally shown. In the instance of motion pictures, four to six hours of film is often shot to produce, after editing, a two-hour film.

MOTION PICTURE AND TELEVISION AS ART FORMS

Once we understand the technical aspects of these media, even in the rough, basic way they have been described here, we can concentrate on their uses as art forms. Both media are, perhaps, best recognized as story-telling devices, even though each of them has several other significant and legitimate uses. The motion picture is a common and valuable educational medium, as any student can testify. Both media are also used for advertising, as, for example, in coming film attractions in a theater or in television commercials. In fact, as all of us realize, television is almost completely dependent on the financing of product advertisers and the "TV commercial" is a kind of framework through which we absorb the messages of even the most artistic productions, unless they come to us on an educational or public channel. Television is also used to bring us news and public interest material.

In the sense that these media are story-telling forms, they are most like stage plays and literature, particularly novels and short stories. Since they have the characteristic of occurring over time, they can be used to present events as they develop; people as they perform actions and change; and ideas as they are described and seen to work in the world. There are, of course, other types of motion pictures and television; both media can be used in a "purely" visual way, having no recognizable subject, much like a nonobjective painting. Works such as these experimental films or television do not tell a story, although they do change over time. For the most part, however, both media provide sequences of images and sound which have a beginning, a middle, and an end and present to the viewer a sequence of events.

Both motion pictures and television tell their stories or describe their events in three ways: through the images they present; through the sequence of these images, that is, how images follow one another; and through their sound: natural sounds, dialogue, and music. To start with the last factor, all of us are accustomed to musical accompaniment with the sequences of images we see, although in most cases the music is unrealistic. We know that there is no orchestra present when Sylvester Stallone as Rocky is running through the streets of Philadelphia in training for his fight with the champ. Nevertheless, we accept the convention and the music helps to create the mood of triumph as Rocky gets stronger and more fit for his encounter. Sometimes the music will warn us of the approach of danger to the characters in the story even before we see the danger on the screen. Once in a while the music for a film or television program becomes so popular for its own sake that it sells as a record, as in the case of the sound track from *Star Wars* written by John Williams.

Natural sounds create mood as well as helping us to accept the "reality" of the incidents on the screen. To hear the clicking footsteps of the murderer on a wooden floor as he approaches the hero builds up some anxiety about what is to come. Or, watching an airliner take off from an airport we expect to hear the roar of its jet engines. In the same way, conversation or dialogue is an expected part of both these media. Sometimes, when through technical difficulties the speech and lip movements of the characters are not properly synchronized, we are annoyed by the unnatural quality of the experience. Before movies had sound (roughly before 1930), dialogue was presented as printed words on the screen. We can still see this mechanism in foreign films where translations into English are placed at the bottom of the screened image. The importance of sound in media of this sort is best illustrated, of course, by the radio, which is capable of presenting ideas, information, events, and stories without any visual component at all.

The first two characteristics of motion pictures and television—the visual or image quality and, particularly, the sequence of the shots—give them their unique power and it is in the first aspect that we can most clearly see what these media have inherited from the visual arts. In common with drawings, paintings, and prints, both motion pictures and television are seen within a rectangular frame. Again this framing is a convention in these arts, since we do not naturally see inside a frame. Much of the art of these media is the way in which the visual material to be presented is selected.

If, for example, the story of a small child lost in a city is to be presented, the filmmaker has a variety of alternative pictorial starting points. We can be shown a long shot of a bustling city street with huge buildings looming above the small figure of the lost child. Or, starting from the opposite point of view, we can be shown a close-up of the child's face with a frightened expression, which will also set the mood and begin to tell the story. A third alternative, provided by the sequencing of images, is to show the long-shot street scene and then zoom in to the face of the child. In the case of each of the first two instances, the long shot and the close-up, the visual material which makes up the image is carefully organized or "designed" by the director or cameraperson in much the same way artists or advertising designers compose their visual material. In fact, many filmmakers use small or sometimes even elaborate drawings to plan what they will include in a shot and how these visual materials will be put together. Figure 92 is the actual "storyboard," as these plans are called, for a short film on the life of the American artist, Jacob Lawrence.

Most of the ideas about how visual materials can be organized to create the effects we want to achieve, which we learned about in chapter 4, relate to the design of images in motion pictures and television as well. For example, the long shot of the lost child on the city street can show the child's fright more effectively if the buildings are shown at an angle, creating diagonal lines, rather than if they are presented to us flat, so that the lines of the buildings are simply horizontal and vertical. These diagonal lines present sharper movements to our eyes and, therefore, greater excitement and drama. Thus the first consideration of the film or video image is the organization of the shot or scene.

The second consideration in making filmed images is the camera device. As we saw earlier, filmed media have an almost complete control of space. To use the same story again, it is possible to shoot from almost street level, with the child beside the buildings, so that they appear to loom huge and menacing and, thus, make us more conscious of the child's fright by letting us see the scene the way the child might be seeing it. Or, it is also possible to film almost directly down from the top of a nearby building, so that the smallness of the child and the vastness of the street is exaggerated, producing a similar effect on the viewer. Sometimes the filmmaker will focus the camera on the main character and blur all the other people and objects nearby, or—in the case of our story—the child may be blurred, while the people and objects around the child are clear in focus. This, too, might build up tension. Another device would be to film the child over the shoulders of the people nearby emphasizing again both smallness and being lost. Sometimes we see the events of a film through a window or in a mirror or, even, with several images at once, with a "split screen." Each camera device has its own contribution to the way in which we absorb the story and the device selected for a shot is influenced by developments in the history of the visual arts. For example, while the Dürer engraving (Figure 20) is a balanced composition, presenting most of the important parts of the image fairly evenly to the viewer, the backyard of John Sloan's painting a few hundred years later (Figure 27) seems to show us the view past the corner of the building on the right. This angle of view is similar to a camera device.

Storyboard

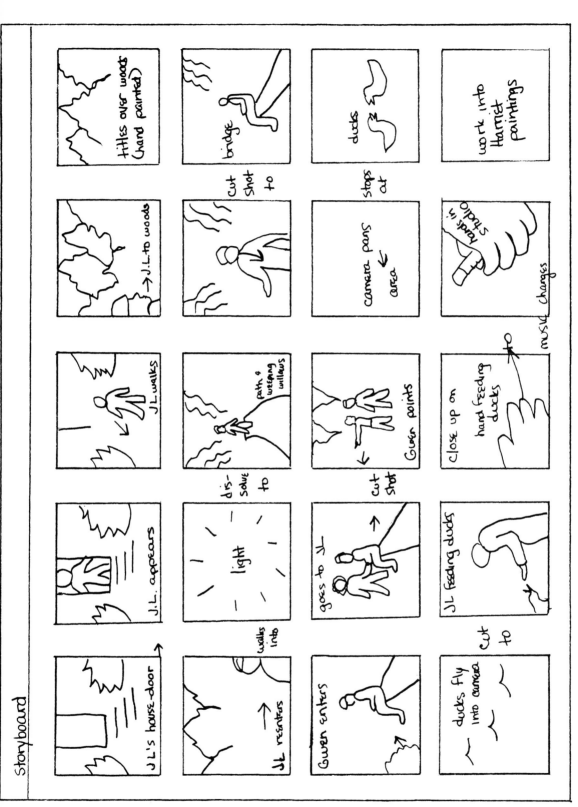

92. Storyboard for film *Jacob Lawrence*, by Paula Rosenblum, 1979. Courtesy of the filmmaker

A third consideration in the filmed image is lighting. We are all accustomed, through watching hundreds of motion pictures and television programs, to the ways in which lighting defines the quality of our viewing experience. Even, all-over bright lighting would help to create one sort of mood—in our illustration of the lost child—while the same scenes shot with sharp contrasts of deep dark areas and bright light areas would help to provide a greater sense of the terror of the child. Hawkeye Pierce's joking comment in the television series M*A*S*H about the "good guys" with the white hats (and the "bad guys" with the dark hats) is only partly humorous. We do tend to be less comfortable in darkness, perhaps because of our ancestral fear of the dangers of night. It is no surprise that many of the horror films made by Hollywood have so many scenes at night or in large houses or buildings with gloomy interiors, although sometimes horror is even more frightening in broad daylight, as in the case of *Jaws*, the film about a killer shark.

Most television situation dramas or comedies are shot in even, all-over bright lighting, because many of the meanings the viewer obtains from the program are conveyed through conversation and dramatic lighting might be distracting. Although it may not always be admitted, it is much easier to film in even bright lights than to take the time and energy to work out careful arrangements of complicated dramatic lighting. Television, unlike motion pictures, demands a tremendous number of productions, since television channels are "on" all day every day and, therefore, are filmed much more quickly. Movies, on the other hand, are filmed over months and sometimes even years, and careful consideration of what the shadows on the face of a character will mean to the viewer is much more a part of the customary process. Again, this does not mean that movies are superior to television as an art form, but only that they are different in their possibilities and impact.

Closely related to lighting and part of the same consideration is color. In both media, the use of color appears to be directed toward making the images as lifelike as possible. Once in a while, the filmmaker uses color as a symbol, as in the case of the yellow and brown desert landscape of Luke Skywalker's home planet in *Star Wars*. These colors tend to emphasize the barren dryness of the landscape around his home. But despite the widespread use of color in today's films, some are still made in black and white. Apparently some filmmakers wish to avoid the tendency of color film to make everything on the screen seem almost unnaturally bright. They prefer black and white for the ideas and feelings they wish to portray, just as printmakers still use the black and white imagery of etchings and lithographs.

All these considerations of the visual image in motion pictures and television, the organization of the image, camera devices and lighting have been influenced by the visual arts. The reader will recall that there are three ways in which the film can tell its story: through sound and through the visual image—both of which we have examined—and through sequence: how images follow one another on the screen. Of these three processes involved in the making of motion pictures and television, the third, sequence, is the one unique to these media. No other medium or art form can control both visual time and space in the same way.

Very early in the development of the movies—in the 1920s—filmmakers recognized that the movement of film from shot to shot, its sequence, could be controlled as completely as space could be controlled by moving the camera. The two film artists best known for this development are the Russian, Sergei Eisenstein and the American, David W. Griffith. In different ways, each of them created movement or sequence which grew out of the dramatic qualities of the story rather than its natural progression of events. For example, if we were to start our film of the lost child with the long shot of the street, followed by the close-up of the child's face, we could then show a rapid sequence of short pieces of film with changing images, all illustrating the terrors which are frightening the child. Such a sequence, which Eisenstein called a "montage," might include a huge truck roaring down toward the camera, a tall building in dark shadow to make it more menacing, a large dog with a fierce bark, and a crowd of adults looking enormous to a small child and hurrying all around but showing no awareness of the child. The speed of the movement from shot to shot, the dramatic unity that comes from the content of the shots—since they all carry the message of menace—all these stimuli would work together to build up our emotional response to the fright of the child.

All our movies and television programs are now built up in this fashion, moving from character to character, object to object, and place to place, in an effort to develop the visual and dramatic interest of the story. We are so accustomed to this process that we take it for granted and accept its rules or conventions, even though we know that the camera cannot be in Darth Vader's command post and in Hans Solo's space ship at almost the same time. This "cutting" or rearrangement of the shots of a film or videotape is usually done by an editor, who is in some ways as vital to the success of what we see on the screen as the author, director, or actors, even though the editor's contribution is not much advertised. Nevertheless, the annual awards given by the Academy of Motion Picture Arts and Sciences include "Oscars" for "best film editing" and those who work in the motion picture and television industries recognize the importance of this member of the production team.

Another effective way to create the feeling of movement and action is to move the camera without cutting or changing shots. This can be done by having the camera roll forward past the action, or back, following the movement of the characters or by moving only the lens of the camera—zooming in on, or away from, the characters. Each of these techniques adds to the ability of filmmakers to influence the ways in which we see the images of the story, following the action almost as if we are part of it. The most common example of devices such as these is their use in chase sequences. The camera rides along with the car, aircraft, or spaceship in a long continuous shot, without a break or change of shot, and we as viewers move with it. Or, sometimes, we see a long shot of a scene and suddenly zoom in to focus on one particular object or person of importance to the story.

So accustomed are we to the use of filming techniques in both motion pictures and television, that we are not conscious of them as devices unless we look at the film as film without involving ourselves in the story. The reader may wish to do that from time to time, so as to become aware of how all these devices are being used. Just as looking at a painting or photograph in this way —analytically—will help us understand and, perhaps, appreciate how our responses are being structured, looking at a movie or television program this way may help us value and enjoy what we are seeing even more. It will also help us to understand the art of these media and why they are recognized as art forms.

The remaining factors which make up the artistic character of these two media are, perhaps, more obvious to us, since we hear more about them. The best known are the actors, who portray the roles in the stories, or bring us the news and weather on television, or narrate the documentaries. In many cases, particularly on television, the actors simply project their own personalities, which we either like or dislike for what they are. Talk show hosts such as Johnny Carson, for example, do not really act a role, nor does John Chancellor on NBC News. On the other hand, it is difficult to conceive of $M*A*S*H$ without the smooth, humorous delivery of funny lines that Alan Alda or Loretta Swit have made so popular, and the Hollywood system of "stars" is a familiar part of all of our lives. So important has the role of the actor become in these media that we often go to see a film or watch a television program because of the actors in it rather than because of the story. All these media personalities, from newscasters and talk show hosts to Burt Reynolds, Jane Fonda, and Clint Eastwood in major films, have specific talents for what they do, thereby making these media exciting and attractive to us.

Another factor in the art of motion pictures and television is the author. Every media presentation, whether it is a news broadcast or a two-hour film at our local theater, must be carefully written out before it can be filmed. Sometimes this is done minutes before a broadcast, as in the case of a news item; sometimes it is done over a period of months before the production. In every case, the quality of what is presented to us is directly dependent upon the abilities of the writers. Despite fine acting and excellent production, many high-budget films and television series do not catch the fancy of the public and in many cases the problem might well be the quality of the writing. Even the highly skilled casts of $M*A*S*H$ or Barney Miller depend on the wit of their writers for the dialogue they speak so well. The importance of the writer is recognized publicly by being listed among the screen credits that usually appear before a movie or a television program.

A third, slightly less known, factor in the production of both of these media is the director. As with actors, we sometimes go to see a film because it was directed by someone whose work we have admired, but this is less likely in the case of television. Directors, particularly in movies, have a recognizable style, like the painter or architect, or, for that matter, like the composer or novelist. Directors have considerable power over the production of the work, changing

—in some cases—the script as it is written; influencing the actors in the ways in which they interpret the roles they play; and devising the organization of the shots, camera devices, lighting, sound, and, in part, the sequence of images. However, all too often the pressures of budget, political or advertising considerations, illness, conflicts of personalities, or pressures of time can interfere with what writers, actors, and directors can do in creating these media productions. The person who is responsible for juggling all these elements is the film or television producer, whose work is often unrecognized.

Like the producer, many others remain behind the scenes in the creation of a media work. Camerapersons, grips who move scenery and props, wardrobe and make-up people, technicians who repair equipment and handle lighting, stand-ins, stunt people, musicians, and sound technicians as well as the editors of film and videotape mentioned before, all of these make up the crews who produce the media we watch. In one sense, they are all artists, all parts of what makes the motion picture and the television program possible and, like some of the arts we see such as buildings, landscaped areas, and magazine advertisements, are all necessary parts in these media that we are accustomed to watching. Except for relatively small numbers of films and videos made by individual artists, most works in these media represent a group art, no less artistic for its group nature.

Nevertheless, both movies and television—in the sense of videotape pieces rather than broadcast television—can be created by individuals. Despite the high costs of cameras, sound and video recording equipment, and film and tape, the materials of production are available to schools and some young people have had the experience of working with these media, just as they do with other art forms. Fortunately, all of us have access to these media as art forms to enjoy and value. With the large number of films now shown on television, even the differences in the way in which we attend to these two media have changed to some extent. Broadcast television, since it comes into our homes, has always been and still is an intimate medium, seen in small spaces like living rooms, with small groups of people—like family and friends—close to the viewer, and enjoyed in casual circumstances where one can talk and move around easily.

Movies, on the other hand, are usually seen in large, darkened theaters, surrounded by strangers whose reactions to what is on the screen might influence our own, and requiring the rather formal circumstances of traveling to the theater, purchasing tickets, finding seats and, often, waiting for the film to begin. Although we have no way, of course, by which to identify or measure the differences in the viewing experiences between these two types of events, it does seem reasonable to suppose that some exist. With the increasing use of movies as television broadcast material, these differences are substantially lessened. The development and popularity of large-screen television images will lessen the differences of screen size. One important advantage of the motion picture does remain, however. The film image has considerably greater clarity and subtler and more authentic color than the television picture. Eventually, that difference will be eliminated by technical advances. In fact, as this book goes to press, it is reported that the Sony Corporation of Japan has developed a marketable television system with a 1,500-line picture (the reader will recall that present U.S. television equipment has a 525-line picture capacity). Such a television system will provide a video image with as much clarity and subtlety of color as motion pictures, perhaps even with a projected television image.

Although we have treated motion pictures and television together in this chapter and emphasized their similarities, their differences should be kept in mind. Furthermore, we have been careful to separate these media from the visual arts, so that the reader can remain aware of the significant differences between these two areas of art forms. It should be remembered, nonetheless, that this separation is not meant to suggest that one art form is superior to another, only that they perform different functions in the many experiences we have and which we value for their own sakes.

Part II ─────────────────────────────

THE TEACHING OF ART

Overview

Just as the first half of this volume describes in concise terms the nature, purposes, range of media, responses of the viewer, and technical language of art, the second half succinctly presents the field of art education as it relates to the elementary school. To this end, this section consists of material applying to theory and practice, the art development of the child, the construction of elementary art curricula, and two specific media and their use in elementary art.

Art education is the study of the teaching of art.[1] As demonstrated by its literature, art education has a specific identity as a body of theory and practice, even though many of its ideas have been borrowed from a variety of disciplines, including in the last decades psychology and the other behavioral sciences. All those who teach art or who concern themselves with its teaching are, in effect, art educators, though the term has come to refer to those who teach or supervise art in kindergarten through the twelfth grade and those who are responsible for art teacher education in colleges and universities.

In addition to a series of books about the teaching of art, the field is represented by a number of periodicals[2] and several professional associations. Of the latter, the National Art Education Association is the largest and publishes the two most widely read journals. While art is certainly not taught as consistently in the schools as its proponents would wish it to be, it does seem to have a place—whatever its form—in the curriculum of most elementary schools and many junior and senior high schools. Aside from the elementary classroom teacher, some districts have art specialists in schools, others have traveling art teachers, and still others have a district-wide art consultant. In recent years—sometimes as a product of federal funds—states, museums, and districts have had traveling art facilities in the form of trailers or buses which contain exhibits of studio or audio-visual materials, usually with a trained person to guide school children in seeing or using them.

Many states and larger school districts have published art guides which provide written and pictorial direction for the elementary art curriculum. Publishers and other commercial firms have a variety of pamphlets, books, slides, films, filmstrips, and studio materials of all types for elementary art, while museums sometimes have prepared materials relating to holdings or exhibits expressly written and organized for elementary children. During the past decade or so, a new orientation toward elementary art—indeed, all art education—has developed in the form of packaged kits, which provide a ready-made curriculum, sometimes including materials. The rationale for these prepackaged materials is that they will support the art program of the classroom teacher who is not knowledgeable about art, in the absence of an art specialist. Also, with federal, state, and some private funds—spearheaded by the National Endowment for the Arts—some districts have instituted an "Artists-in-Schools" (AIS) program, which does precisely what its title implies.

It is appropriate for an overview such as this to provide a broad, general evaluation of the activity at issue. Let us look at the field of elementary art education through the eyes of another author, Laura Chapman.

> Unfortunately, what the majority of our students in elementary school receive in the name of art education is meager, and likely to be presented in a way that inadvertently teaches them art is a frill, instantly produced with minimum effort, and fundamentally useless in life, unless one plans to become an artist. The magnitude of our disservice to children does not seem to have been grasped by the larger community of educators and arts advocates. In order to comprehend the importance of art education in the elementary school and the consequences of its neglect, we must understand that most children have little opportunity to study art beyond elementary school.[3]

CHAPTER 6

theory and practice
in
teaching art

Despite widespread variations in the theory explored by the literature of art education, the teaching of art on every level has remained surprisingly steadfast in practice during its history. Although there have been some minor changes in the media and materials used by the young in the classroom, the primary mode of art behavior is still modeled on that of the artist, and its most important objective is individual psychological development through creative self-expression. Art as a school subject is seen persistently as a productive studio activity providing a means to individual growth in capabilities and qualities not necessarily related to art.

There are several reasons for this narrowness of focus in periods of time of massive social change. Not the least of these reasons has been the dominance of the studio in the educational backgrounds of those who teach art and art education; the majority of them conceive of themselves, at least in part, as artists (hence the term "artist-teacher," popular in the 1950s and again in recent years). A second reason has been the influence of educational psychology. Art educators and psychologists interested in learning, perception, and child development have concentrated their investigations on the art products and studio behavior of children, almost ignoring, for a variety of reasons, children's responses to art. This preoccupation naturally reinforces the classroom teacher's conception of school art as essentially a manipulative studio activity.

A third reason grew out of the continuing tenuous position of art in the school curriculum. Always the last included and the first curtailed, art education has had to find scholastically respectable grounds for its own protection. Growth in competencies and qualities not directly related to art but prompted by art activities was considered a safe and strong rationale with which to protect a curriculum area too often viewed as peripheral in the school. One example of this process occurred during the post-Sputnik era, in the late 1950s and early 1960s. Art educators wrote about and researched the alleged efficacy of art performance to promote a general creativity, which would transfer to creativity in science and engineering, areas high in educational priority at that time.

A fourth reason for the continuing sovereignty of studio activities in art teaching is the considerable recent influence of what might be called an arts bureaucracy, both governmental and private, on present ideas and practices. These groups include: The National Endowment for the Arts, The Kennedy Center for the Performing Arts, The Alliance for Arts Education, The Arts, Education and Americans (supported by David Rockefeller, Jr.), state arts commissions, and literally hundreds of local and regional arts groups. This vast phalanx of arts-interested citizenry represents—for the most part—people who do not produce, teach, criticize, or study art; they manage it. In true managerial fashion, their ideas about art education are not a product of study or of experience in its practice, but rather a small collection of inbred conceptions, often contradictory and sometimes intellectually inadequate. Nonetheless, their generous funding (as compared with that of the art education "establishment") and their access to the media make their conception of what art teaching should be a force to be reckoned with in the schools of the nation.

A further, perhaps minor, influence can be found in the ubiquitous exhibitions of child art. From corridors at Los Angeles International Airport to the prestigious Kennedy Center in Washington, D.C., drawings, paintings, and other art work done by schoolchildren are hung, admired, and analyzed, often with a gravity befitting the Mona Lisa.[1] Naturally, the elementary teacher cannot avoid a sometimes puzzled respect for what is so obviously considered an important part of child behavior. Although most art in the kindergarten through the sixth grade is taught by teachers untrained in art, both the literature on elementary art and most teachers' college course experience have been controlled by those whose background is in fine arts and secondary art education. Thus, elementary art, like junior and senior high school art curriculum, has been and is heavily, if not exclusively, studio based.

In recent years, those who develop theory in the field and write about it seem to have closed ranks around a conception of curriculum quite different from the traditional preoccupation with studio performance and its reputed developmental benefits. Starting in the mid-1960s, a movement identified as "aesthetic education" suggested a widening of the scope of classroom art behaviors to include those patterned after the art historian and the art critic, as well as that of the artist. Also, in the minds of some of its adherents, this conception implied a comprehensive *arts* education, embracing the other arts, such as dance, music, and drama; all the arts would be taught together to some extent, based on their commonalities of purpose and process. It is fair to say that neither aesthetic education nor arts education (in the sense of the term described above) has had a strong impact on classroom art teaching on any school level. Most elementary and secondary art is still dominantly performance in mode and purports to develop (in the minds of the teachers) creativity, self-expression, mental and emotional health, general perceptual skills, and other derivative developmental values.

It is not so much that there is a persistent time lag between theory and practice, though this is probably a significant factor. It is, perhaps, even more that the reasons of the past for this constriction of focus in art teaching are still largely operative. Nevertheless, talking with teacher groups over the last five years or so, the author has noticed some signs of a shift in ideas about classroom art away from an exclusive performance base to some form of aesthetic education.

The conception of the art education professional as to what constitutes the proper domain of art education has slowly but clearly begun to change in recent years. At one time—not too long ago—our concentration, if not our sole concern, was with the teaching and practice of art in the schools. Now we are increasingly aware that we have an obligation not only to the institution of education but to other social activities as well. This expansion of interest includes: the out-of-school adult, the elderly, the media, the museums, the community centers and recreation programs, and the industrial and commercial world. All of these people and agencies are involved not only in art of one kind or another, but they participate in art education or art learning. They are, no less than the school, a part of the province of art teaching.

A review of the highlights of the history of art education will reveal some of the particular historical influences that caused the field to remain stagnant in its curriculum practices during times in which other subjects, such as math and science, made substantial changes in content and procedures. It will also expose an interesting proliferation of concepts of purpose in art developed over the years by a few theoreticians and largely and quietly ignored by practitioners. The emphasis on conceptions of purpose in the teaching of art in the examination of its history has more than just an historical basis. It can be said that all educational enterprise derives from conceptions of purpose, either overtly employed in its shaping or implicit in the nature of the activity. Whether we realize it or not, whatever we do in the school grows out of or can be traced to our beliefs as to what purpose our educational actions will satisfy. Thus, the concentration on purpose here has a logical justification.

A BRIEF HISTORY OF ART EDUCATION

Histories of art education in the United States often start, at least in their chronology, with the appointment of Walter Smith as director of art of the Commonwealth of Massachusetts in 1871. This is not to suggest that nothing had been said or done prior to that time about teaching or learning in art,[2] but that this period in nineteenth-century America manifested the first signs of a belief that art activities should be a legitimate part of the formal education of the young. Earlier art education was limited to the training of artists and to genteel accomplishment for young ladies in finishing schools. In the 1870s school art was used as an adjunct to industrial development. Specifically, school art was to be used to reveal talented youngsters who might be trained as industrial designers in the newly burgeoning factories of the United States, primarily in New England. Also, art activities were to teach future consumers to purchase manufactured goods with greater discrimination, or, at least, with selectivity favoring manufacturers' design tastes.[3] As the nineteenth century progressed, with the Philadelphia and Chicago Expositions in 1876 and 1893, a cultural emphasis developed, albeit primarily reflective of European cultural achievements, and new concepts of value in art activity began to appear in educational literature. The Committee on Drawing of the National Education Association published a report in 1899 which listed as aims of art education: "to develop the creative impulse" and "to develop an appreciation of the beautiful."[4]

At the turn of the century pioneers such as Arthur Wesley Dow saw "creative power as divine gift, the natural endowment of every human soul, showing itself at first in the form that we call appreciation." Dow suggested educating the whole people for appreciation and developed exercises in design to achieve this goal.[5] This was the era of ornamental designs, decorative borders, and scientific content such as color charts and value scales. During most of this time manual training or industrial arts, available in some schools as early as 1866, shared the public identification along with art education. The goals of this eventually separate discipline were practice for skill development with tools and constructive satisfaction.

By the 1920s the child-centered movement in general education, expressionism in painting, and a number of other social forces began to focus attention on self-expression and originality. Austria's Franz Cizek and others influenced American educators to what constituted a newly significant concept of value.[6] Cizek wrote: "Great creative energy exists in every child. This must find outlet in expression or repression will result. Children should be allowed to draw what they wish, what they see in their mind's eye not that which others think they ought to draw."[7] In the 1930s the Owatonna Art Education project, sponsored by the University of Minnesota, added another concept of value to the field. Under a banner labeled "Art, A Way of Life," the project stressed that no differentiation should exist between the fine and the useful arts, that art relates to every aspect of living and that, in the realm of goals, aesthetic discrimination as it affects everyday living should be developed.[8]

The decades of the 1940s and 1950s brought to their highest level and into educational prominence those concepts of art education most influenced by psychology. The art products of children were seen as significant data revealing both their intellectual capabilities and the quality of their adjustment to the problems of living. At the same time, working with art materials—necessarily, of course, in a free, uninfluenced, spontaneous manner—was thought to provide a unique and important means of emotional therapy and creativity in art.

Another psychologically colored objective of that era emphasized personality integration through art. Art educators thought that in art production the emotional, intellectual, and physical aspects of behavior could operate in concert, and thus provide for the individual a pattern of integrated, harmonious functioning. Further, art was seen as a significant means to socialize pupils, to make them understand by practice the procedures and values of democracy. Even this social goal was usually stated in individual, psychological terms.[9]

In addition to these psychological directions, the objectives of the 1940s included using art as training for leisure-time activities, as a means of developing good taste in the selection of personal adornment, and as a subject that could be integrated with several others within the school's curriculum. Other lesser concepts of purpose in art of that period included use of art as a means of gaining insight into human history (as in the instance of learning the history of early Egypt through the study of the pyramids and other ancient artifacts), inculcation of knowledge of right and wrong behavior through the revelation in art of transcendental moral principles, and promotion of international understanding and, ultimately, world peace through art—an understandable concern of the war and post-war years.

Many of these ideas were vigorously promoted and publicized in a series of books written by widely acknowledged leaders in the field, such as Viktor Lowenfeld, Victor D'Amico, and Sir Herbert Read.[10] Notwithstanding a considerable diversity of approach, the dominant focus of these writings embodied belief in the developmental efficacy of self-expressive art activity, serving the ends of creativeness, wholesomeness of personality, and social adjustment. Efland properly labels this period the "child-centered era,"[11] emphasizing its translation into art education terms the concurrent and earlier directions of progressive education, the child-study movement, psychiatry, and educational psychology.

This focus became so powerful that it dominated the thinking of art educators for most of the next thirty years. A study at Stanford University as late as 1974 indicated that from a population of some 200 college students, 74 percent agreed that "the major function of art education is to develop a child's general creativity."[12] The concept of creativity, describable in general terms as behavior characterized by novelty of response, was at first—in the forties, and early fifties—usually limited to an art context. Since the important quality of self-expression in art was for it to be uniquely individual, the term "creativity" and its distinctive coloration neatly encapsulated this direction of thought. The term appeared at least as early as 1899 and was later used by Dow and Cizek. One no longer spoke of an artist but rather of a creative artist, and art materials and activities became creative materials and activities. The enormous amount of empirical research undertaken by art educators and psychologists contributed to the prestige of this concept. As the concept became more popular, particularly as other disciplines seemed to adopt it as a key concern (for example, J. P. Guilford studied creativity in scientists),[13] the idea changed significantly. Instead of a simple vision of promoting creativeness in art, art educators saw appropriate activities in art promoting a general creativity transferable to other behaviors. In 1960 Barkan entitled his textbook on art education *Through Art to Creativity*.[14] In 1961, probably the height of the concept's power, one art educator said about creativity, "The assumption of a transfer of the effects of art experience to other phases of human behavior is unquestionably the most basic tenet of art education, and it is because of the almost universal acceptance of its validity that art education has emerged as a separate academic discipline."[15]

The decade of the sixties brought with it, along with many other social programs of that time, the infusion into art education of a significant amount of federal dollars, principally through the Arts and Humanities branch of the U.S. Office of Education. These funds sponsored a considerable number of conferences and specific researches in art education and although these activities spawned little in the way of new ideas,[16] they did provide a much larger than usual opportunity for dialogue among those interested in the teaching of art. They also conferred a measure of respectability on a professional group badly in need of affirmation. For some, this acceptance by the society at large served as convincing evidence that what they were doing in the field was the best that could be done. For others, the same recognition was a goad to improve their ideas and actions.

By the early sixties art educators began questioning the validity of creativity as a concept and challenging its keystone position in the arch of goals for the field.[17] In place of creativity as the dominant purpose of art education, some writers substituted knowledge of art in the service of enriched aesthetic encounters as a viable objective. The *Guidelines* volume, published in 1970, perhaps most clearly represents this approach called aesthetic education, in which the desirable behavioral models were expanded from that of the artist (the virtually exclusive model of creativity) to include those of the art historian and the art critic.[18] Manuel Barkan, who was the most vigorous proponent of this change of direction in our conception of what constituted school art, explained the idea this way:

> To the detriment of art education . . . we have anchored curriculum almost entirely in relation to the artist, only slightly in relation to the art historian; we have ignored the aesthetician and critic. Art curriculum is faltering, not because of efforts to attend to art history but rather, because we have not learned to use the aesthetician and critic, nor do we properly use the art historian.[19]

It is interesting to note that Barkan's concern for using the model of the aesthetician[20]—in order to include the content of what is usually called aesthetics in the classroom—was quickly forgotten by the field, until it was reintroduced into the literature at a later date.[21]

Another shift in emphasis in the view of purpose in teaching art, which Efland identifies as "social-centered,"[22] was a likely result of the social storms of the sixties and can be seen most clearly in two highly different ideas. Both concepts, however, reflect the conviction that art education should see itself as an instrumental field, using art in the classroom to promote social ends.

The first idea asserts that appropriate art activities can develop sensitivity to the physical environment, particularly to the urban architectual environment and to those cues in those surroundings which affect behavior. Environmental design education—as the idea is called—supports visual literacy in general and, specifically, in the context of the physical environment, culminating in an informed search for those aesthetic alterations which will create more benign surroundings.[23]

The second idea is that the central responsibility of general education is to develop critical consciousness, to promote understanding of the political, economic, and social forces which oppress people, and to explore how one might combat these forces.[24] Art teaching should contribute to the development of these insights primarily through the aesthetic and ideological impact of film and video arts, which more than traditional art media have the special qualities necessary for this task.[25] As described in this paragraph, the concept of social responsibility has been ignored in the literature of art education, except by a few West German art educators.[26]

Further recent conceptions of purpose in school art activities include the potential for art to enrich leisure-time pursuits, particularly in preparation for that period of life when the individual becomes what is euphemistically called a "senior citizen." [27] Some writers in the field suggest that art activities in school enhance the child's ability to learn to read,[28] while others assert that art makes children want to attend school and, thus, serves as general educational motivation.[29] Finally, as a derivative of neurological research in split-brain functioning, which indicates the possibility that the two halves of the brain operate and control different human functions (visual, verbal, logical, intuitive, etc.), some writers claim that school art can develop the right side of the brain—the visual, intuitive side—which is less exercised, as it were, by other classroom content.[30]

Other directions of purpose appear in the recent literature. One such idea, "art therapy," postulates that decision-making during the process of producing original visual designs is important (along with other personality benefits) in promoting a wholesome image of self and independence and confidence in the individual. Art therapy has now grown sufficiently as a specific field to become a discipline separate from art education, with its own academic and practicing personnel and its own distinct literature.[31] A second idea, difficult to categorize, insists on the primacy of immediate sensuous experience within the aesthetic encounter and suggests that this aspect of experience, as opposed to cognitive functioning, is critical in the creation of a natural and open individual. It is somewhat puzzling to envisage a curriculum based on these ideas, that is, a curriculum in the usual sense of the term. However, the ideas exist in our writings and represent a small but vocal group in the field.[32] Finally, one significant strand of the previous psychological orientation persists separately today in the form usually referred to as visual literacy or perceptual efficiency. An outgrowth of concern for and research in creativity, this concept has come to view the visual arts as a communication system much like discursive language and just as important to learn.[33] Also, much like the earlier generalization of creative behavior from art to other areas, visual literacy has been viewed as transferring from art to nonart contexts.[34]

It should be noted again, as it was in the beginning of this chapter, that despite the wealth of scholarly invention in the field (by those who engage and develop theory), art curriculum in elementary and secondary schools has remained almost identical for the last fifty years or more. The artist still serves as the behavioral model of the art room, as in the 1930s, and media and materials are still primarily studio processes. Perhaps the most significant curriculum change has been the virtually universal acceptance of the crafts (ceramics, printmaking, jewelry, textiles, graphic design, and others) as art processes that are as fully honorific as the traditional studio arts of drawing, painting, and sculpture. More recently, some contemporary media such as photography, filmmaking, architectural design, and urban planning are being used in some classrooms. However, even then these media, like the crafts, function, for the most part, as the means to promote artistic behavior. While the literature reveals no empirical study to document this conclusion, the reader can compare curriculum documents of the 1920s and 1930s with recent ones or investigate back issues of popular art education periodicals such as *School Arts* or *Arts and Activities*.[35] One might even refer to the Prang *Textbooks of Art Education* published in 1904[36] and compare these with the elementary art curriculum suggestions in a recent text, for example, the one by Hubbard,[37] or to many state art guides. Such reviews will support the conclusion that practice in art education has remained substantially the same over many years.

PRESENT SCHOOL ART PRACTICES

Unfortunately for our purpose here, no summary statement about elementary art practices can be authoritatively presented since no person or agency has thoroughly surveyed the classrooms of the nation to see what is going on. Neither the national association (National Art Education Association [NAEA]) nor the federal agencies (U.S. Office of Education, The National Endowment for the Arts, National Institute of Education) have been willing to undertake this cumbersome but necessary task. Such surveys as have been made are fragmentary, oriented toward secondary schools, or considerably outdated.[38]

Consequently, those who write about elementary art must depend upon data about present practices taken from the literature on education and art education and upon personal observation and conversation with others who have observed present conditions. It appears to the author on the basis of these sources that the teaching of art in today's elementary schools can be said to fall into four distinctive categories. They are: (1) activities which emphasize expressive, so-called creative concerns, (2) processes primarily concerned with skills and manipulation of materials, such as the crafts, (3) projects which use the visual arts in conjunction with other areas of the curriculum, and (4) experimental activities, which reflect in varied degrees new ideas about elementary art. In current practice these categories prevail; many school situations combine several of them, and extreme variations on them are likely to be so small in number as to warrant neglect.

One significant factor in the current situation is that by far the majority of elementary art activities are taught by the classroom teacher rather than by those who are in one way or another art specialists. As effective as elementary classroom teachers may be in other areas of the curriculum, they tend as a group to lack confidence in their knowledge of art and their ability to guide their pupils in art. This feeling of inadequacy is, in part, justified, since the person untrained in art often knows little technically about the subject, and the one or two courses in art or art education in the traditional teacher preparation program usually do little to promote insight and confidence. On the other hand, much of such a person's concern in this direction might well be caused by the not always appropriate exclusiveness and obscurantism of dialogue—both spoken and written—about art and art education.[39] Nor does the elitist division between the fine arts and those other visual aesthetic experiences accessible to and enjoyed by many, such as the popular and the folk arts, serve to support confidence in those untrained in art.

Although it is impossible to determine with any degree of accuracy just how much art, whatever its nature, is formally experienced by elementary school children across the nation, there is little doubt that the ubiquitous photograph of besmocked seven year olds staring at a paint-dripping easel does represent some portion of the school day for many youngsters. Let us look at the nature of the art education these children are receiving by studying the specific characteristics of our four categories. According to the first—activities that emphasize expressiveness and creativity—classroom practice would include media such as drawing, painting, modeling with clay, collage, wire sculpture, papier mâché, mosaics, photography, printmaking, and construction. The rationale for these media is dependent in one form or another on a belief in the therapeutic benefits of visual free expression and the development of creativity and perceptual skill. The following chapter on child development in art will describe what is surmised from both theory construction and research as to the specifics of growth through expressive visual activities. Suffice it to say for our purposes here that these activities, which provide the products that are displayed in school corridors and that go home to the parents, are for many the present hallmarks of an effective elementary art program. Activities using these media and directed toward these ends are quite often process centered, that is, they focus primarily on the making of the art work rather than on the subject or content of the work, to the extent that such a distinction is viable. For example, second-grade paintings of a class visit to the zoo are done more for the sake of the painting experience itself and the benefits believed to be derived from it than for the amount of learning about animals that might accrue.

Similarly the second type of activity emphasizes process rather than content, but here the benefits and thus the stress are on the actual manipulative procedure. Consequently, this type of project makes heavy use of crafts techniques such as weaving, leather, macrame, jewelry, metalwork, and some ceramics. Generally these media are nonpictorial, that is, they do not involve the making of images, although crafts can sometimes use imagery; on the other hand, activities in the first category can be either pictorial or nonpictorial.

The third category conversely uses any of these media for the purpose of promoting learnings in social studies, language arts, or some other area of the curriculum. A fifth-grade group project in mural painting for example, might stress the facts or ideas serving as the content of the mural, for which the painting activity is primarily a means to that end. It is probable that this kind of activity is at least as common in elementary art programs as the first two types and is likely to reflect the preferences and efforts of classroom teachers who do not consider themselves knowledgeable about art and wish to avoid dealing with art qualities and child art behavior.

The fourth type of activity, the experimental, runs the gamut from analyses similar to art criticism, to the making of films, to the design and construction of architectural structures and represents, for the most part, newer ideas and orientations in the field. Many of these newer activities such as photography, filmmaking, or city planning can easily be and are often used in the classroom to attain the traditional ends of personality development or artistic skills. For example, the "Artists-in-Schools" program, which is itself an experimental idea in the scope in which it is being used, claims as its rationale performance skills and artistic perception. Chapter 8 in this book will review three selected curriculum ideas of an experimental nature.

While there is probably no typical elementary art program, these four categories identify the range of activities as they presently exist. Again, it is plausible that many programs consist of combinations of these types. Much of the nature of the art curriculum, of course, depends on the existence—or more likely, the absence—of an art specialist in or available to the school or the district. Perhaps the most valid generalization one can make about elementary art is the one with which this chapter was introduced—that art in kindergarten through sixth grade is a manipulative studio activity with a variety of materials thought to provide several kinds of individual, psychological developments.

What this review of theory and practice, both historical and contemporary, does not reveal, however, are the assumptions upon which theories about art education and practices derived from them are based and, particularly, the fragility of those assumptions. To identify these assumptions and question their validity might provide firmer grounds for developing a theory of art education from which more sturdy elementary art curricula might be built.

A QUESTIONING OF BASIC ASSUMPTIONS

Although numerous questions have been raised about the validity of aesthetic and art concepts—primarily, of course, by aestheticians, whose business it is to examine such ideas—it appears that few have challenged those basic assumptions which provide a foundation for theories about the teaching of art. This situation is less surprising than it might seem at first glance. Much of what all of us take for granted in art education would be open to serious question if these assumptions are any less stable than we believe. Nonetheless, such analysis is necessary, if not essential, if we are to conceive of art teaching theories and practices that reflect a progressive view of the field. There are at least four of these assumptions.

1. *The arts are the highest achievement of human civilization and engaging in the arts (usually by producing them) is fundamental and central to human growth. Thus, the arts deserve a place in the core of education.* Bluntly put as it is here, the idea seems overstated. Nevertheless, it can be found repeatedly in literature about art and education. Here is one such pronouncement.

> Technology without human understanding is like an answer without a question. *True human understanding is only possible through the arts.* If education is learning to grow, learning to choose, to provide a medium of self-awareness and communication, then the integral role of the arts in the learning process is neither contrived nor tangential.[40] (italics mine)

One of the concluding recommendations of the Rockefeller Commission Report presents this claim:

> The fundamental goals of American education can be realized only when the arts become central to the individual's learning experience, in or out of school and at every stage of life.[41]

The second chapter of the 1977 NAEA Commission Report expands the previous point:

> Art education, the commission believes, can be regarded as *the most fundamental aspect* of a child's intellectual development, a development concerned with moral as well as academic values. For example, the sense of proportion, harmony, beauty, and rightness that work in art makes possible not only provides the basis of what we know, but also of what we value. The conceptual aspects of art help to form the initial realization, and the expressive aspects cultivate a respect for the quality of action. Neither knowledge nor morality can exist without them.[42] (italics mine)

Another author explains:

> *We must be able to point with insistence to those historical and social antecedents which designate the central place of the arts during the millennia of significant human development.*[43]

The authors cited and others who write similarly about the centrality and humanizing qualities of art seem to have overlooked the testimony of history.

It is not that the arts—the visual arts in our examination here—are of no importance in history, but, rather, that economics, philosophy, science, religion, and politics can be said to have as much to do with human culture. Nor does history tell us that artists, who are the closest of all persons to art, or those surrounded by the finest arts are any more capable of true human understanding than others. Instead, the story of the human race is peopled with dozens of revered artists who have worked for and even supported the most repressive of rulers and institutions and with numbers of Cesare Borgias and Hermann Goerings whose undeniable love of art was coupled with brutal callousness.

Quarrels in the professional and popular press about whether or not art is basic to the curriculum of the school have resulted in the yellow button and bumper sticker bearing the legend "You Gotta Have Art," issued by the NAEA, a volume of essays on the subject,[44] and a program of advocacy based on the rationale expressed in Figure 93. It does not seem to be enough for art educators to assert that the visual arts are one portion of the culture of our society and as such deserve to be explored with some care by the young. Instead, we seem intent on maintaining that art is *more* important than other activities in the curriculum—a claim that is dubious at best, and one which is not likely to persuade our colleagues in other disciplines. Jacques Barzun has called these exaggerated claims "educational inflation."[45] It should be unnecessary to suggest that if we were more modest—and, indeed, accurate—in our claims, we might be more convincing and, hence, less vulnerable.

2.   *Aesthetic response can be generated only by the "fine arts" and requires special and unique human qualities. All other responses to objects are substantively and qualitatively different.* This concept protects the fine arts from contamination by the folk arts, the popular arts, and the mass media (with a few exotic exceptions) and supports the feelings of superiority to the mass of citizenry with which some in our society comfort themselves. If it were not true, the art experiences most of us enjoy would define the boundaries of what is accepted as art, rather than the preconceptions of an educated and, usually, wealthy elite. Figure 94 is an unfortunate (if amusing) illustration of this assumption. Although this is a newspaper advertisement and can be construed as journalistic jesting, some serious scholars writing about the teaching of art take much the same position, as the following paragraph indicates.

> The quality of life is measured by the repertory of feeling which pervades it. Life is rich if the repertory of feelings is large and the discrimination among them fine. Life is coarse, brutish and violent when the repertory is meager and undifferentiated. Aesthetic education's role in enlightened cherishing is to enlarge and refine the repertory of feeling.[46]

The same narrow definition of aesthetic response, limited (perhaps unwittingly) to the fine arts, informs the statement that follows on page 155.

Art in the Mainstream: A Statement of Value and Commitment

Edmund Burke Feldman

For much of recent history, art has been regarded as an educational extra, a valuable subject but not an essential. We believe it belongs at the core. We believe it should be in the mainstream of every educational effort at every educational level. Why? Because art means three things that everyone wants and needs.

Art means work. Beyond the qualities of creativity, self-expression, and communication, art is a type of work. This is what art has been from the beginning. This is what art is from childhood to old age. Through art, our students learn the meaning of joy of work—work done to the best of one's ability, for its own sake, for the satisfaction of a job well done. There is a desperate need in our society for a revival of the idea of good work. Work for personal fulfillment; work for social recognition; work for economic development. Work is one of the noblest expressions of the human spirit, and art is the visible evidence of work carried to the highest possible level. Today we hear much about productivity and workmanship. Both of these ideas are strengthened each time we commit ourselves to the endeavor of art. We are dedicated to the idea that art is the best way for every young person to learn the value of work.

Art means language. Art is a language of visual images that everyone must learn to read. In art classes, we make visual images, and we study visual images. Increasingly, these images affect our needs, our daily behavior, our hopes, our opinions, and our ultimate ideals. That is why the individual who cannot understand or read images is incompletely educated. Complete literacy includes the ability to understand, respond to, and talk about visual images. Therefore, to carry out its total mission, art education stimulates language—spoken and written—about visual images. As art teachers we work continuously on the development of critical skills. This is our way of encouraging linguistic skills. By teaching pupils to describe, analyze, and interpret visual images, we enhance their powers of verbal expression. That is no educational frill.

Art means values. You cannot touch art without touching values: Values about home and family, work and play, the individual and society, nature and the environment, war and peace, beauty and ugliness, violence and love. The great art of the past and the present deals with these durable human concerns. As art teachers we do not indoctrinate. But when we study the art of many lands and peoples, we expose our students to the expression of a wide range of human values and concerns. We sensitize students to the fact that values shape all human efforts, and that visual images can affect their personal value choices. All of them should be given the opportunity to see how art can express the highest aspirations of the human spirit. From that foundation we believe they will be in a better position to choose what is right and good. ∎

"... art means three things that everyone wants and needs."

93. NAEA's "AIM" statement is a rationale that illustrates art education's frequent overcompensation for its relative weakness in the school curriculum. Reprinted by permission of the National Art Education, 1916 Association Drive, Reston, Virginia 22091

BEFORE
*This is me before I started listening to
KFAC. Overweight, poor, unhappy and alone.*

AFTER
*This is I after 16 short years as a
KFAC listener. Rich, trim and sexy.*

How classical music changed my life.

The other day at Ma Maison, as I was waiting for the attendant to retrieve my chocolate brown 450 SLC, the Saudi prince I'd been noshing with said, "Say, Bill, how did an unassuming guy like yourself come to be so rich, so trim, so...sexy?"

My eyes grew misty. "It wasn't always this way, Ahmed, old buddy..."

My mind raced back to the Bad Time, before the investment tips, the real estate empire, before Dino bought my screenplay and I bought my Columbia 50...

Once I was a lot like you.

Working at a nowhere job, hitting the singles bars, watching situation comedies in my free time. I tipped the scales at a hefty 232, but my bank balance couldn't have tipped the bus boy at the Midnight Mission.

Finally, I hit bottom...picked up by the Castaic police for barreling my old heap the wrong way over some parking lot spikes.

My last friend in this lonely world, Hardy Gustavsen, set me straight while he was driving me back to L.A.

"Bill, get hold of yourself! Start listening to KFAC!"

"Gosh, Hardy, don't they play classical music? I'm not sure I cotton to that high brow stuff!"

Aside from a couple of summers at Tanglewood and Aspen, and one semester in Casals' Master Class...

I knew absolutely nothing about classical music.

"Bill, who would be wrong if you got better?"

Looking into his steely blue eyes, I realized Hardy was right. I resolved to give KFAC a shot.

At first, it was quite painful. Listening to all those 100-piece groups was confusing—I was used to having the drums on the right and the bass on the left and the singer in the middle. All those semidemihemiquavers made my head spin.

But I started to feel the beneficial effects of classical music listening in just one short week.

In no time, I was using napkins with every meal, I switched from Bourbon to an unpretentious Montrachet and I became able to hear sirens even with my car windows rolled up.

Soon I was spending every night with KFAC and a good book, like Aquinas' *Summa Theologica.*

I realized that some of the wealthiest, most famous people in this world listened to classical music—Napoleon, Bismark, George Washington, Beethoven...and many others who are yet alive today.

Then I met Marlene. The first girl who knew there was more to *Also Sprach Zarathustra* than the theme from *2001.* And I fell in love.

Today, I'm on top of the world with a wonderful wife, close friends in high places and a promising career in foreign currency manipulation.

Can classical music do for you what it did for me?

A few years back, scientific studies showed that when dairy cows are played classical music the quantity and quality of their milk dramatically improves.

Now if it can do that for plain old moo cows, imagine what it can do for you!

You might use it to control disgusting personal habits and make fun new friends. The possibilities are endless!

Can you afford KFAC?

Is lox kosher?

Even though marketing surveys show that KFAC's audience is the most affluent assemblage of nice people in Southern California, yes, you *can* afford KFAC! Thanks to their Special Introductory Offer, you can listen FREE OF CHARGE for *as many hours as you like* without obligation!

Begin the KFAC habit today.

Remember, the longest journey begins by getting dressed. Don't let this opportunity slip through your fingers. Tune to KFAC right NOW, while you're thinking about it.

And get ready for a spectacular improvement in your life.

Warn your family and friends that you may start dressing for dinner.

You may lose your taste for beer nuts.

And the next time you're on the freeway thinking about playing with your nose, you'll find yourself asking:

"Really. Would a KFAC listener do this?"

94. This newspaper advertisement has some unfortunate social implications. Created by and used with the permission of KFAC, Inc., Los Angeles, California

In general, the contemporary environment does not value aesthetic experience. Consequently, most people do not have an interest in making objects for aesthetic experience, nor do they have an interest in viewing them. Lacking that fundamental attitude, they do not attend to the sources from which artistically relevant knowledge is obtained. . . . Teachers of art must do all they can to teach their students the value of aesthetic experience.[47]

It is a short step from these assertions to Dwight MacDonald's "Law of Raspberry Jam" in which the wider you spread it (in this case, the arts), the thinner it becomes.

Not only is this concept based on a possible misunderstanding of the nature of aesthetic experience, but it serves to isolate the fine arts from the historical experiences of most of humankind. No culture we know seems to have been without some form of visual enrichment, be it embellishments on tools or pots or carefully designed structures or pictorial images and statuary. Even contemporary American society, despite the disparagements of some critics, pays a high priority of attention to the visual richness of clothing, advertising, photography, film, and buildings. It is not that all these popular arts and mass media are "well designed" or "artfully" done—whatever the relevant criteria might be—but, rather, that as a society we attend consistently to the visual aesthetic qualities around us. Art critics may disdain the yellow arc of McDonald's golden arches, but it is also clear that most of us recognize that there is some issue beyond the food they advertise involved in viewing them.

Describing aesthetic experience in similarly broad terms, John Dewey wrote:

In order to *understand* the esthetic in its ultimate and approved forms, one must begin with it in the raw; in the events and scenes that hold the attentive eye and ear of man, arousing his interest and affording him enjoyment as he looks and listens: the sights that hold the crowd—the fire-engine rushing by; the machines excavating enormous holes in the earth; the human-fly climbing the steeple-side; the men perched high in air on girders, throwing and catching red-hot bolts. The sources of art in human experience will be learned by him who sees how the tense grace of the ball-player infects the onlooking crowd; who notes the delight of the housewife in tending her plants, and the intent interest of her goodman in tending the patch of green in front of the house; the zest of the spectator in poking the wood burning on the hearth and in watching the darting flames and crumbling coals. These people, if questioned as to the reason for their actions, would doubtless return reasonable answers. The man who poked the sticks of burning wood would say he did it to make the fire burn better; but he is none the less fascinated by the colorful drama of change enacted before his eyes and imaginatively partakes in it. He does not remain a cold spectator. What Coleridge said of the reader of poetry is true in its way of all who are happily absorbed in their activities of mind and body: "The reader should be carried forward, not merely or chiefly by the mechanical impulse of curiosity, not by a restless desire to arrive at the final solution, but by the pleasurable activity of the journey itself.[48]

Another writer maintains that in terms of aesthetic value to the individual, all visual stimuli sustain a kind of equality and fraternity. Herbert Gans, a sociologist, writes:

> I would argue, therefore, that if people seek aesthetic gratification and that if their cultural choices express their own values and taste standards, they are equally valid and desirable whether the culture is high or low. A person from a high culture public may choose abstract expressionist paintings while one from a low culture public selects calendar art, but both choose from content related to their standards and educational level. Moreover, both derive emotional and intellectual rewards from their choices, and both may add new ideas, feelings, and insights to their lives as a result. The rewards may differ because their *educational backgrounds and previous experiences differ, but the choices of both individuals result in additions to that experience.* The evaluation of people's choices cannot depend only on the content they choose but must compare what might be called the *incremental aesthetic reward* that results from their choices: the extent to which each person's choice adds something to his or her previous experience and his or her effort toward self-realization. This incremental reward can be as great for a member of a low culture public as for a high culture one, for the reward has nothing to do with the quality of the cultural content; instead it judges the person's progress beyond his or her own past experience.[49]

Using these descriptions as a basis, one might say that aesthetic response is a general reaction to a large variety of objects and events, both humble and sophisticated, common to all of us. Aesthetic response to art objects—identified as art by society—is a special instance of aesthetic response. It may require more learning; it may deal with different qualities; it might even be more worthwhile. But it is not absolutely different in kind from aesthetic responses to other than art stimuli. Once we accept this more tenable position, its implications delineate a very different picture of the arts we see; one in which folk arts, popular arts, and mass media are properly part of the visual arts and one in which every child participates in art experiences and has done so long before arriving in the school.

3.   *The making or viewing of art provokes in the personality of the participant certain changes, which have historically included becoming creative, generally perceptually efficient, independent, emotionally healthy, socially aware, sensitive to the quality of experience, and the like.* These are, of course, the developmental values mentioned (and abundantly documented) earlier and have been the mainstay of our rationale for teaching art over the years. Rarely are these individual developments conceived or stated in terms of growth in art but, rather, as general psychological gains, with art as the means to ends not related to art.

The simplest and most effective criticism of this assumption is to repeat that if it were true, then artists and art lovers as a group would demonstrate a higher level of these qualities: they would have better mental health, greater sensitivity to all the qualities of experience, a higher level of general creativity, and greater general perceptual skill. However, it is unlikely that such is the case. The more plausible assumption is that activity in art promotes perceptual competence in art and (to the extent that creativity has integrity as a psychological concept) creativity or imaginativeness in art. It would be healthier and more reasonable for art education to view art as the end of our efforts, rather than as a means to ends outside of art, no matter how valuable these other ends might be. The generalizing of art benefits to other behavior outside of art has been called "developmental" and, later, "contextualist," while viewing the benefits of art as related to art has been called "intrinsic" and, later, "essentialist."[50] Developmental conceptions of the value (hence, the purpose) of art activities are dangerous. If it can be shown that other curriculum areas provide the same benefits in adequate measure (benefits such as creativity, perceptual competence, humaneness, and right brain development), the need for art in the school will have been weakened or eliminated. Despite this rather obvious hazard, art education writings continue to include developmental conceptions of purpose where they do not emphasize them.

The generalizing of art-specific skills can lead to some unknowingly arrogant attitudes. For example, writings about perceptual development in art education often confuse perceiving art with perceiving other aspects of what is around us, or perception in general. The distinction is perhaps best illustrated by the following anecdote. A graduate student returning from two years in the Peace Corps reported that much to her sorrow the people she lived and worked with—to use her own words—were "visually illiterate." When asked how she arrived at this conclusion, she explained that they could not distinguish the outline of a leaf held against a hand. She did not seem to realize that they could negotiate their forest environment with ease and relative safety, while she would almost literally not "see" the dangers around her.

It is this kind of error of basic reasoning that has resulted in some art educators taking perceptual tests to urban or rural slums, testing the so-called disadvantaged young, and pronouncing them as defective in perception. If the children of the poor are indeed inadequate in perception, it is only middle-class art they do not "see" as well as they might. In truth, the vision-based survival rate of such children in their own environments is just as high as that of most art educators in their own familiar surroundings. Furthermore, the children see their own art forms with verve and vigor.

Efland neatly summarizes the argument against relying on developmental or instrumental values as a rationale for art in the schools when he writes, "On further examination, the claim that 'art has value because it saves society' leads to other difficulties. It implies that art is *good for what it does, not for what it is!* Art is good because it is good to want to save society. Thus, [Sir Herbert] Read's passionate pleas for art have within them a curious denial of the inherent value of art itself."[51] This book supports as art education theory the recognition that art is good (in the school) for *what it is* rather than for *what it does*, instead of the traditional developmental ideas.

4.   *The fashioning of visual statements is a necessary activity for all persons.* So pervasive and powerful is this idea that its validity has rarely been

questioned. For example, the 1977 NAEA Commission Report (what might be called a position paper on the field by the field) states unequivocally:

> Art education programs have a unique contribution to make to children by providing them with opportunities to encounter content absent in other areas of the curriculum and by eliciting thinking processes that are free from the constraints of logic and strictly defined rules. Take as an example the opportunity to work with a three-dimensional form—say a sculpture made of clay. Consider also the child's *need* to express an idea, image, or feeling he or she has had through this material. Somehow the child must formulate a conception that can be not only rendered public, but rendered public within the child's conception of the limits and opportunities provided by the clay. Artistic problems seldom post a single route that one must tread. The forms one can use, the techniques one might apply, the scale, the style are open. Furthermore, the criteria for determining when one is finished is a matter of making a judgment rather than applying a standard. An equation is solved when certain rules are applied; art forms have no such analog.[52] (italics mine)

A more reasonable approach toward this issue is to suggest that neither children nor adults *need* to create visual statements. There are dozens of other ways in which people express or make public their ideas and feelings, in other art forms and outside the arts as well. It is quite another matter to assert that everyone should have the *opportunity* for expression in visual form, or should be motivated or assisted to do so, but to exaggerate this function to the level of a need is to distort both education and life.

What people in the visual arts do not seem able to realize is that the need for visual expression they themselves feel is not a universal requirement. Just as artists and art educators have no need to express their ideas and feelings in musical or dramatic or poetic form, the rest of humankind can fully exploit their formal schooling and their lives without *necessarily* creating visual forms. We will return later in this chapter to this issue, which has rather startling curriculum implications, since the different viewpoint offered here permits a far greater concern for other, nonperformance means of learning in art activities. Making a point somewhat similar to ours, Feldman puts it this way:

> A great deal of the literature in art education endeavors to bring the mass of pupils up to the artistic level of that gifted minority. To be sure, this effort is carried out under the banner of enlarging the creative powers of *all* children. Alas, it often succeeds in convincing many of them that they are inadequate as *performers*. But their tremendous creative potentials as intelligent viewers, perceptive critics, and sensitive interpreters of the arts are left largely untapped.[53]

Chapman is even clearer and more adamant on this issue when she writes:

> Educators have long claimed that every child benefits from making art. Indeed, educators have been so extravagant in their claims about the value of art activities in childhood that one would think that making art is all children need to do—a solution to almost every educational problem. For example, art activities

have been proposed as a remedy for low achievement scores, emotional distress, lack of creativity, juvenile delinquency, dropping out of school, and lack of a positive self-concept, among many other problems. What we forget is that these and other possible values that may be realized from making art very likely could be achieved by other paths, and perhaps with greater success.

If we are genuinely interested in basic education in art, there are two main reasons for engaging children and youths in the process of making art: 1) to teach them how art can be made, or 2) to use the art-making experience as a stimulus for discussions about the kind of work artists do. In teaching art, studio activities should have essentially the same role that laboratory work has in teaching science. In teaching science, laboratory work is intended to cultivate general skills and attitudes that will be of equal use to the few who will pursue science as a career and to the many who will deal with science as citizens, not as scientists.[54]

In recent years an occasional article in art education periodicals has raised questions about one or another of these assumptions.[55] In the main, however, the ideology defined by these beliefs is so powerful as to defy any substantial criticism. What we have seen instead is the usual functional compromise which accommodates a broad range of viewpoints among theoreticians and practitioners. Heavily influenced by an ever-growing arts bureaucracy on the federal, state, and local levels, current art teaching theory is fragmented at least as much as, if not more than, it has ever been. The theoretical stance dominant in the literature, aesthetic education, has a wider variety of definitions than its supporters might wish, and none of these conceptions is widely represented in classroom practice, particularly on the elementary level.

Perhaps the least heartening symptom of all in both theory and practice is the almost unchanging elitism of the art and art education establishment, a reflection of the second assumption described in this chapter. When surveys by state art commissions or other pollsters glowingly report a surge of interest in the arts among Americans, they have in mind only those "respectable" arts of the museum, gallery, legitimate theater, art film, dance recital. This distortion of the view of sources for aesthetic experience is likely to continue to have an unfortunate impact on children's understandings about the arts, especially since such insights and attitudes are so closely interwoven with economic and class status. For those pupils whose family orientation is middle class, a comfortable but unhealthy superiority with respect to art is reinforced. For pupils who are the children of the poor, a climate fostering alienation from those arts is difficult to avoid. The reader may recall the "bringing the symphony to the ghetto" mentality of the 1960s when the welfare of the poor and of minorities was much more of a public issue than it is today.

Fortunately our society also provides a counterforce to the pressures maintaining this aspect of the status quo. For example, in the adult lifetime of the author, ceramics has moved from an "inferior" craft taught most often in an industrial arts context to a highly respected fine art. Photography, film, folk arts, and industrial design now appear in some secondary school art curricula, and museums—and consequently art teachers—accept quilts, macrame, and batik as legitimate arts. It is hoped that this broadening of what is accepted as art will continue until all of the folk arts, popular arts, and mass media are included in this category. This volume vigorously supports such a development, the effects of which can be highly significant to and eminently healthy for the field of art education.

A further issue among present trends in art education theory is the movement toward a "comprehensive arts" or multi-arts teaching format. Often associated with, but not necessarily related to, aesthetic education, this approach asserts that the high degree of commonalities among the arts (i.e., music, drama, poetry, dance, visual arts, etc.) makes it desirable to study them together.

This idea, of course, is by no means a new one. For many years we have had, mostly on the college and university level, courses identified as "humanities," in which several art forms were studied in combinations of various sorts. Early supporters of this idea in the literature of art education had, in addition to ideological conviction, the realization that future federal funding would be available only or primarily for combined arts programs. In fact, some of the last several projects funded by the Department of Health, Education and Welfare or the National Endowment for the Arts, such as IMPACT and AIS, often followed a format that was oriented toward the comprehensive arts. As an example, IMPACT involved music, dance, drama, and visual arts, and although these arts were not always studied together, both pupils and teachers were conscious that they were related and planning was done in combined groups. Although no theoretical pattern has been developed which purports to structure the collective teaching of several arts, published materials suggest with little doubt that this is a favored direction for many in the education of the various arts and, in particular, those who presently speak for federal funding agencies.

The idea of a comprehensive arts curriculum, which is a superficially attractive approach, suffers from some serious drawbacks. On the theoretical level, it can clearly be argued that the differences between the visual and other arts are significant enough to warrant serious consideration. Chief among these differences is the fact that the visual arts are inherently spatial while the other arts are basically temporal. Except for some more recent arts forms specifically designed to circumvent this characteristic, such as mobiles, other moving sculpture, and happenings, works of visual art do not change or "occur" over a period of time (films and video are fundamentally dramatic arts, even though they are apprehended visually). One can and does, of course, look at a work of art over time, and one can find new cues in it and generate new responses to it; but the work of art itself does not change. The artistic and educational possibilities of an art form that derive from a temporal, sequential character simply do not exist in the visual arts. This is perhaps why one of them (architecture) has been called "frozen music."

This does not mean that the visual arts are less worthy than other arts, only that they are different in this and other ways. To the extent that theoretical differences such as this one might be ignored or minimized in a comprehensive approach, some danger of inadequate aesthetic insight exists in that approach. The position of this volume is that those who deal with the teaching of art should consider such an idea with caution before embracing it.

In summary, present art education theory and the practice that supports it can be said to conceive of school art as the activity of making objects with art materials, objects cast in the mold of the fine arts of museum and gallery. This activity not only is touted as the most important in the curriculum, but is purported to develop all kinds of highly desirable capabilities in the individual, from general perceptual competence to humaneness. A much smaller, but growing, segment of art education belief rests on the conception that art education should deal with the area of art as a discipline, with content to be learned, so that the pupil will be a more competent consumer. The distinctions between the two points of view are clear and sharp and easily recognized in the partisan rhetoric on each side. Obviously, this volume embraces the second position.

REDIRECTING THEORY IN ART EDUCATION

In order to develop a sound conceptual base for a theory of teaching art, it would seem reasonable to examine how we negotiate aesthetic experience, an issue already briefly explored in the first chapter. To summarize the conclusions proposed there, it was suggested that valuation theory, which characterized the aesthetic as that response unconcerned with consequences beyond itself, was the most authentic available explanation.

From the viewpoint of this theoretical position, we went on to suggest that a work of art was a made object that we value for its own sake. Although these are admittedly inadequate descriptions of aesthetic experience and of art, they are the most satisfactory and the most useful in the context of education. What follows from these descriptions is that aesthetic experience is the general and universal human behavior, of which response to works of art is one particular instance. It is not that there are no special qualities to one's responses to works of art, but that to understand these special qualities properly requires a clear view of all aesthetic experience.

A theory of purpose in art teaching compatible with this view is the development of aesthetic literacy, knowledge of how we respond to the objects we see, and, in particular, to those objects we identify as works of art in the broadest sense. Graduates of our schools should have had access to adequate knowledge about all the visual arts available, both past and present, including those art forms they enjoyed before coming to school and those they now enjoy in extracurricular experiences. They should be able to talk about and read about the various arts we see, so that they can (when they wish to) learn more about a form of art or a specific work of art. Only when these conditions are fulfilled is an individual aesthetically literate.

None of the four assumptions challenged earlier is included in this statement of purpose. Art is not seen as the primary source of learning and understanding but, rather, one of the good things of life, among many. Response to art is not viewed as unique among human responses but, rather, as one of a wide range of inherent responses. Our rationale for art education does not include nonart personality changes, though if one or more of these should result, so much the better. No part of this statement of purpose requires that young people produce art of any kind, though if it can be shown that a studio activity enhances some portion of this purpose, there is no reason not to use it.

Further, this concept of purpose drastically alters the practice of art teaching in the elementary classroom, when its implications are examined. Nevertheless, it must be carefully noted that even an egalitarianism as thorough as that of Gans (quoted previously), need not imply that we limit the scope of visual materials studied in art activities to one segment of the arts alone or to what is already enjoyed by the learners. Indeed, the effect of expanding and intensifying response to art is precisely to develop educated access to as much of what is available in terms of visual objects and events as possible. All youngsters do not have to like Rembrandt or crazy quilts or "Hill Street Blues." But they all should learn enough about the arts we see and how they affect us to be able to choose what they prefer from among all the available visual arts.

Thus, it becomes necessary in our curricula to attend to the broadest possible range of objects and events, both historical and current, capable of provoking aesthetic response. It would be just as inappropriate to this system of ideas to neglect Renaissance painting, contemporary sculpture, or architectural design as it would be to omit the folk arts or mass media from the content of school art experience. Whether one or a group of these is in some way superior to others in our own personal or group predilections is not as important as that they all receive adequate examination as potential sources of aesthetic response. Let the learner choose—as long as choice is based on sufficient knowledge rather than ignorance.

There is a further, strategic reason why the scope of art content considered in school curricula should be widened to include more than the largely "high art" museums and galleries deal with today. Young people in our present society respond to and appreciate the popular visual arts and the mass media, such as film, television, comics, clothes, advertising, and posters, far more commonly than they do the fine arts. Certainly it makes sense to start enlarging their visual aesthetic horizons by using those familiar and presently enjoyed arts as a point of departure. A music educator writing about his subject area says:

> Many music educators throughout the United States are looking at popular music styles with a new respect as they realize the central role that music plays in the cultural patterns of American youth. They understand the necessity of becoming conversant with popular musical styles before they can adequately develop music curricula that seriously take into account the cultural backgrounds of their students.[56]

The curricular suggestions in chapter 8 of this volume follow the direction pointed to here.

The impact of these ideas on the present predominantly studio curriculum, based as it is on custom and the concept of "behaving like an artist," is considerable. Obviously studio curricula require specific materials and some special knowledge and skills on the part of the teacher and an investment of school time and money often unwillingly supported by the community. Furthermore, it is far from certain that behaving like an artist is for the child anything like what it is for the mature artist. The hallmark of the artist's behavior—the one which most clearly distinguishes artist from nonartist—is the recognition, if not the command, of the formal problems involved in arranging visual elements. Although this competence is not always productive of success, it is a characteristic quality of the artist's process. On the other hand, the most notable characteristic of the child's output with art materials is often called innocence or spontaneity, referring, with justification, to precisely the lack of either recognition or command just noted in the instance of the artist. The art products of those who fall somewhere in the middle ground between artist and child, such as folk artists or street artists, often betray a middle-ground awareness of the formal problems of art.

It is also unclear on the basis of present knowledge how much appreciation of art can be engendered by studio activities. Nevertheless, working with art materials is one way of engaging art, and since it is already a firmly established portion of the curriculum of the elementary school, the teacher might use it as one base for developing the educated consumer of art.

Furthermore, although there is no need for people or children to produce art, it is possible that working with art materials (even though it is questionable that children are behaving like artists when they do this) might at least promote some sense of how works of art are put together and why they are created. This insight, in turn, might serve to heighten one's capacity to "read" the art work and thus intensify one's response to it. It can be argued that the degree of knowledge of how art is put together, its design or technology, so to speak, has been exaggerated as a prerequisite for aesthetic enjoyment. Using music as the art form, one advertisement claims:

> Classic music, to borrow a Madison Avenue term, had a bad image. Vast numbers of people believe it is only to be enjoyed by those who have been initiated into its mysteries; others are faintly uncomfortable in the society-page setting of symphony hall or opera house . . . It really needn't be that way . . . You don't have to know that the Beatles' "Norwegian Wood" is in the mixolydian mode to enjoy it, do you? Then why . . . should it be necessary to know the structure of the sonata form in order to understand Beethoven?[57]

Unless it is assumed—as some contemporary art critics do—that the design qualities of an art work are their only or most significant aesthetic characteristics, the quotation above does have some credibility. Nevertheless, knowing how a ceramic piece is thrown on a potter's wheel or how the shapes and texture of a building can be balanced is likely to add to our understanding of that work. In general, the position of this volume is that the more one brings to an aesthetic transaction in terms of information and relevant past experience, the more value one can obtain from it. The contrasting argument, stressing ignorance as it does, is not as convincing, except in extreme examples. Certainly, the entire thrust of education is away from naivete and toward sophistication. After all, though it may make little difference to one's enjoyment to know that the piece of music is in the mixolydian mode, even the simple act of identifying "Norwegian Wood" as the work of the Beatles does provide a rich associational ground on which one can build further responses.

Another related issue and source of considerable confusion among art educators is the arbitrary division of aesthetic response into so-called cognitive and affective factors. While such a distinction is perfectly proper for analytical purposes, it does seem to neglect the fact that both types of response patterns must, after all, take place within the same person and that there is the strong likelihood that each type influences the other. Thus, the kind of curriculum proposed here need not dilute the affective or emotive intensity of response to art. Our assumption is that the greater our cognitive grasp of an art work—the more we know about it—the richer the affective possibilities. In the same way, the more we prize a work of art, the greater our desire to know about it. Certainly talking and reading about works of art does not replace the affective experience of it, but can provide more cues with which to enrich that experience.

By now the reader has been able to substitute the beliefs about the teaching of art proposed by this volume in place of the four assumptions currently structuring much of our practice. These newer ideas can be summarized:

1.   The most important benefit we can provide for young people is aesthetic literacy, that is, we can enhance their access to objects they experience aesthetically. So important is this conception of the purpose of school art that it can stand alone as our justification.

2.   All people, including children, already enjoy visual aesthetic experiences in a wide variety of contexts. What art education can and should do is to expand these horizons. All the art ever made belongs to all of us.

3.   All the visual arts, including folk arts, popular arts, mass media, and the fine arts, are capable of arousing legitimate aesthetic responses and should be dealt with in the classroom.

4.   The curriculum of the art program should be an examination of the characteristics of aesthetic response to objects in the world around us. Producing objects of art should be an available option in the school, but not a part of the required program, except where it is found to provide the learnings noted more effectively than other means.

Collectively these assumptions move art teaching *beyond* aesthetic education to a conception of its purpose and process appropriate to the end of the twentieth century. Aesthetic literacy correctly applies the description of the valuational view of aesthetic experience. If aesthetic response is the general behavior of which response to works of art is one particular instance, then it is this general response which should be studied first in the art program. Once pupils have learned how and why they respond to stimuli which can be identified as aesthetic, and the various natural and social objects in which these stimuli have already been found, the area of the fine arts of museum and gallery becomes a logical extension for study. This conception of art teaching is what aesthetic education should be but is not, and it is the conception that Manuel Barkan demanded in 1962 (see page 146).

It should not be difficult to anticipate that these ideas suggest an important distinction in the responsibilities of the elementary staff. A resident specialist trained in art and art education will be better able than the multi-subject classroom teacher to help children take advantage of those benefits available through the making of art objects. The resident specialist will ensure that pupils understand how works of art are put together and how the artist functions. Thus, this volume supports the development of positions of special art teachers where they do not exist and the institution of a special elementary-art credential where local conditions require it.[58]

The existence of a special art teacher who can effectively guide studio activities and special art learnings leaves the classroom teacher free to develop those curricula which promote understanding of aesthetic response, survey the visual arts available in past and present cultures, and impart some knowledge of how to apply critical dialogue to these arts at a level appropriate to the age of the pupils. Since these latter skills are primarily verbal, that is, they do not depend upon studio skills and knowledge, classroom teachers may be adequately trained in their undergraduate certification work in a realistic minimum of college courses. This is in contrast to present requirements which make it necessary that elementary art education courses provide for some degree of learning in studio skills, history, and criticism. Instead, such courses, by closely relating the traditional and contemporary fine arts to the broader everyday aesthetic and art experience of the teacher candidate, would generate a kind of comfort with the visual arts which is presently difficult to do. It is one thing to be expected to perform in art, but quite another to learn about it by looking at it, talking about it, and reading about it.

In the absence of a trained special art teacher, because of local funding problems or the lack of a state special credential, the preparatory college course or courses in art education will continue to cover all of the requirements for the classroom teacher. Also, that teacher will have to teach all aspects of art content. A philosophy of art teaching that legitimizes a continuity between the teacher's everyday visual aesthetic experiences on the one hand and the exclusive, esoteric superiority with which the fine arts are so often and so unhappily viewed on the other ought to help make that task easier. The thrust of this volume is to assure the elementary classroom teacher or teacher candidate that a considerable and important part of what should be done in art for children is well within the grasp of a teacher untrained in art and does not require a great deal of specialized art study and performance skills. The most critical facet of our redirection in art education theory and the change that makes this thrust possible is to think of the goal of school art as educating children to be aesthetically literate consumers rather than creative, perceptive, or humane individuals who must *create* art in order to benefit from its values. The curriculum implications of this redirection will be explored in chapter 8.

CHAPTER 7

art and
child development

Traditionally, this is the chapter in elementary art education textbooks in which numbers of drawings, paintings, and three-dimensional constructions by children provide explosions of immature shapes and vivid colors. We will try here to avoid the extremes of such display. The history of art education is filled with an intense and often misplaced concentration on the studio production of children, ignoring, in contrast, their legitimate development as consumers of the visual arts, their aesthetic literacy.

There are some significant reasons why this volume adopts such a reluctant posture. First of all, it is to be regretted that the word we use for the objects fashioned by children, that is, "art," is precisely the same word we use for objects made by mature individual artists, who study and work for numbers of years to learn to produce them. This attitude is not meant to demean the possible aesthetic value of objects made by children, for those objects, like all other visual materials, are no less capable of provoking aesthetic encounters than the products of artists. It simply recognizes that children cannot confront and deal with the same intricate problems that artists grapple with in their works, or bring to them similar skills, even when the children's solutions are more appealing. The art work of the artist is not superior to or better than that of the child; it is different—valuable, when it is, for different reasons.

This approach to children's art also does not imply that the more complicated the problem, the more meritorious the art; nor does it suggest that there is some easily visible line of demarcation with the artist on one side and the nonartist on the other. The nature of the behavior, at least as far as we can observe it and speculate about it, is significantly different at either end of the scale. When grandmother sewed that quilt, she was aware of the problems she faced and could bring a lifetime of skills to bear on them at a point somewhere between the second-grade child and the architect.

On the other hand, this identification of the product of consistent sophistication with that of spontaneous innocence leaves the general public with the thoroughly false impression that the work of artists is uninformed, expressive play, not to be compared to serious activities such as science, math, history, or music. Hence, one of the most vehement professional complaints of art educators—that our discipline is looked upon as a frill and not as a "hard" subject —is, at least in part, self-inflicted.

Secondly, it is apparent that as children grow into adults, they use art, for the most part, as consumers rather than as producers. Nor is there any compelling reason why the converse should be mandatory or even desirable. There are, after all, numbers of legitimate activities that people can and do use as media to express themselves, enjoy the benefits of therapy, become creative (whatever that might signify), learn intense concentration, develop imagination, enhance the quality of their lives, and so on, in addition to the visual arts. There are other arts of poetry, prose, drama, dance, video, film, and music, as well as math, science, social studies, sports, gardening, and even some forms of work for pay. Almost every human activity is a clear alternative to making art for the purposes art educators have traditionally cited; conversely, there is no alternative to studying art if our purpose is to learn about it.

Thirdly, restricting the art curriculum to studio production or unduly emphasizing that aspect reinforces in the mind of the student the ill-conceived notion that significant visual aesthetic experiences are limited to special encounters with objects made with paint or clay. Such curricula also might suggest that art experience is mysterious, esoteric, and reserved for special people such as artists and patrons of museums and galleries. There are excellent arguments for maintaining that neither proposition is the case at all and that there are grounds for assuming strong commonalities among aesthetic experiences of a visual nature, only one of which is the encounter with the fine arts of the museum or gallery. Furthermore, the relationship between making art and learning to respond to it knowledgeably is by no means clearly established, either by theory or by research. Although there might be far less influence from the former behavior to the latter than our school practices assume, there might be enough carry-over to legitimize some classroom art production.

The character and force of these reservations notwithstanding, art education involves a long history of studio activity in the classroom and, consequently, concern in both the literature and research about the relationship between child development and the producing of art. This chapter will explore the ideas which this literature and research have generated, as well as some ideas about the nature and growth of the child as consumer. If the reader understands the bias of this volume and the reasons behind it, this chapter will serve to describe art and child development.

The intellectual pressures which prompt concern with child art production, both its study and its support in the curriculum of the school, seem to arise from two rather obvious observations. One is that the work of children with art materials appears to be similar in some significant ways to the art works of early "primitive" people. Both can be said to be direct, unself-conscious, and almost playful. The second observation is that children manifest changes in the ways in which they create forms in a line of development describable as stages and that these stages appear in some ways to transcend differences in era as well as differences in culture. Given these characteristics and given, further, a climate of support from a long tradition of productive activities in the classroom, art educators and psychologists have studied and theorized about child art in order to understand its nature and its relevance to schooling.

However, it is readily apparent, if one reads the literature in this area with some care, that these two groups, that is, art educators and psychologists, possess (and very properly so) two highly different motivations for their efforts. In one case, Howard Gardner, a psychologist, states clearly, "Participation in the arts is so natural and integral a part of human growth that an understanding of this process should provide important clues to many pivotal questions of human development. . . . In a sense, then, I am writing about the arts because they enable me most cogently to express my notions about development."[1] Assuming this attitude to be general, of course, in no way denies or demeans the contributions of the psychologists. What it does, on the other hand, is to place their descriptions in perspective; it warns us not to translate directly to classroom practice prescriptions from their accumulated observations. Also, it should provide us with some rudimentary caution in reading their work, a caution the best of them will endorse. The behavioral scientist who studies the child and/or art work is more than likely to be carrying on that study in a context or contexts quite separate from and dissimilar to the arena of the classroom.

As a result of this plausible and significant distinction, this chapter will separate the theory and research of those in the behavioral sciences from the writings about the same issues done by those whose primary concern is the teaching of art in some kind of classroom situation, even though, ultimately, the conclusions of the first group might be or may become more relevant to education than those of the second group.

WHAT CHILDREN MAKE WITH ART MATERIALS

Before we examine the writings of psychologists and art educators in the area of child development and art, it would be well to devote some attention to just what it is that children fashion when they work with art materials. Fortunately, thousands of children's drawings, paintings, and constructions have been collected since at least the 1930s;[2] these form the basis for most of the interpretations to be described in this chapter. It would be simplest and clearest, however, to provide the reader with a verbal and pictorial description of the most common and, therefore, most generalizable evidence in this category, a baseline, so to speak, of the character of children's production.

At some point in the growth of the very young child, he or she will begin to grasp objects or implements which when rubbed on a surface leave discernible marks. Even before that, children seem to be able to manipulate and are very interested in handling a variety of malleable materials in a seemingly haphazard rather than purposive manner. For example, when not admonished by the parent, the child delightedly smears food such as cereal on the table surface or mud on a pavement or floor. Whether this seemingly instinctive testing of the impact of bodily movement on the environment is in any sense a rudimentary form of creation is, of course, impossible to determine. Still, it seems to predate the making of marks and to constitute a kind of rough practice for that activity.

The earliest marks, made with a tight-fisted clumsy grasp of the drawing implement, appear to be lines (Figure 95), which give way in time to curved lines, ovals, and circles (Figure 96). This chronological segment of the child's output has been called the scribble or manipulative stage and is considered by many to be the first stage of fashioning behavior. Those who write about the art of children place boundaries of age on its appearance and eventual displacement depending on their particular views. It is safe to say, without adopting a partisan position, that these manipulative activities appear at some point between the first and third year of the child's growth and continue in a relatively repetitive fashion.

Next the child begins to name the scribbles, to identify them as things in the environment or in fantasy or in combinations of both sources. The child also discovers that marks made on the surface can, in fact, depict or "stand for" elements in the world around him or her and moves to what is called the second stage of growth. Since there is considerable variance in both the starting age and the age at which this recognition is achieved, greater specificity should be avoided at this point. Nor are we in any sense certain what forces impose this variance or other differences among children that will be described in this section. Nevertheless, this second kind of fashioning behavior appears at some time between the child's second and fifth year and consists of the rendering of what might be called shorthand signs or "symbols" which provide at least a temporarily satisfactory depiction of the desired objects. Tadpole forms symbolize people (Figures 97, 98, and 99), lollipop forms stand for flowers and

(continued on page 173)

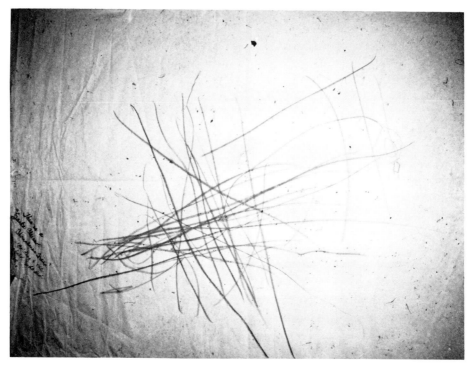

95. A crayon scribble by a two year old

96. A monoprint scribble consisting of lines, ovals, and circles by a two year old

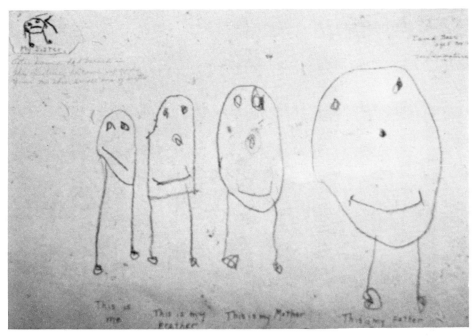

97. A tadpole crayon drawing of people by a three year old

98. *Two Heads,* a crayon drawing by a four year old

99. A tadpole crayon drawing by a five year old

100. A crayon drawing of a house and trees by a three year old

trees (Figure 100), boxes with triangular tops represent houses (Figure 100), and circles with lines like rays mean the sun. All of these develop rather quickly once the child becomes aware that marks can stand for these parts of the surrounding world. It seems as if the child discovers a language system of visual notations and expresses ideas and feelings in this notation without apparent concern for its lack of accuracy.

Gardner provides us with a delightful anecdote illustrating this issue.

> When my daughter Kay was six, she, like many other children, insisted on drawing arms in such a way that they extended horizontally from the middle of the torso. One day I asked her where arms leave the body and she immediately assured me that they emanated from the shoulder. I then asked her if she could draw them in that way and she readily complied. I assumed that we had negotiated a developmental milestone: now that her knowledge was aligned with her graphic repertoire, there surely could be no reason for her to insist on locating arms at the center of the torso. But I was wrong. Kay immediately drew another person, with the arms once again coming out of the center of the body. "I know that's not the way you want to do it, Dad," she said sympathetically, "but that's the way I like to do it, at least for now," . . . In deciding how to render her "person," Kay was exercising a choice, one that made sense to her in terms of criteria of simplicity, symmetry, or some other set of personal standards.[3]

The first and most frequent object to be rendered during this stage is the human figure. Early in this period of symbolism, each object drawn or painted appears to be unrelated spatially to the other objects around it, though they may be related in subject, as in the case of several animals in the zoo. The animals are shown and their cages may be shown, but the animals are not necessarily placed in the cages. Frequently, the sizes of objects or parts of objects are exaggerated. A child's hand grasping an apple may be several times life-size. Our assumption in explaining this, for which there does not seem to be enough striking evidence, is that the part enlarged is of more importance psychologically—just as in some periods in the history of adult art, those of noble birth were rendered larger in size than the peasants or servants around them (Figure 53). Sometimes colors are used in an unrealistic manner; a cow may be painted green while the tree next to it is red. Also, objects may be placed on the paper in such a way as to suggest that the child turned the paper from side to side, rather than attempting to keep to one baseline. The arrangement of objects would seem haphazard and the self-requirement of naturalism relatively meager. These observations seem to be even more pertinent to three-dimensional work, possibly because it is even harder to render figures realistically in clay or other kinds of construction materials.

Sometime during this symbolic period, the child begins to place the objects fashioned on a baseline, either the bottom of the paper itself or one drawn or painted in. The lower part of the paper becomes the ground and the top the sky, often shown by a simple band or stripe of blue. As the child matures during this period, details in every object become greater in number and specificity, colors more naturalistic, and spatial relationships between one element and another more accurate. X-ray drawings and paintings appear (Figure 101) with people inside an automobile or a baby inside the mother. Sometimes children make pictures which show the top and the sides of an object at the same time. For example, the surface of a table is shown from above, with all four legs in a row protruding from one edge. Still another mechanism the child employs at this stage is to show several events which occur over time in a sequence, at the same time in the same picture.

Eventually many children adopt a double or even multiple baseline (Figure 102) and what is called "folding over." The latter technique involves drawing a scene with the bottom edge of the paper as the baseline or groundline, then turning the paper either upside down or to one of the two other sides and using that edge as another baseline. Thus, if we fold over the paper, we will have two scenes perpendicular to each other or with one scene upside down like a reflection in a pool. At this time, children begin to develop perspective by making objects in the distance smaller and closer objects larger; by overlapping, that is, having closer objects cover and hide the objects behind them; and, sometimes, even by crude sorts of linear perspective, in which parallel lines move closer together as they recede into the picture.

In general, as the child nears puberty, rendering becomes increasingly natural or realistic and, at a final point, unsatisfactory. For many children, this third stage is the point at which their expectations exceed what they deem to be their competence and thus their attitude toward picturemaking might well be called inhibited. Some writers identify this third stage as the stage of artistic decision, signifying that the child is aware of natural requirements and, also, of the need to arrange what is fashioned so that it will be coherent and pleasing to the eye. This is, perhaps, an overly august title for this final stage of development. On the other hand, this stage can be looked at as characterizing the approach of the vast majority of the adult population. Almost without exception, everyone seems to reach this point, and, indeed, very few of us progress beyond it without some sort of formal instruction.

While this description of child art production effectively suggests three stages or identifiable developmental plateaus, it has been deliberately ambiguous about assigning age levels to these stages. The position of this volume on the matter is succinctly summarized in a statement made by Brent and Marjorie Wilson.

Perhaps the most problematic aspect of the stages is that, although a drawing which falls quite clearly in the middle may be easily classified using the stage accounts, beyond those central examples there is no way to classify those that fall somewhere between the stages. We must state flatly that the most widely used accounts of development are not only inadequate and incomplete but they seriously misinform; indeed, they tend to obscure more than they reveal about children's drawings. They are equally inadequate as guides for informing prospective teachers about children's artistic development as they have always been as scales for the use of researchers in charting that same development.[4]

101. *A Turtle*, an x-ray monoprint by a four year old

102. A multiple baseline crayon etching by a nine year old

INTERPRETATIONS OF CHILDREN'S ARTISTIC BEHAVIOR BY PSYCHOLOGISTS

Three broad avenues of psychological orientation can be detected in theories about child development and art. While these three schools are far from mutually exclusive, they do possess in each case a clearly defined and reasonably unique explanatory system, an ideology of developmental style and structure. The first of these orientations is *psychoanalytic* in its disposition. It suggests that much human behavior, both in its motivation and in its expression, originates in the unconscious or subconscious mind. Hence, art, for both the child and to a lesser extent the adult artist, is a product of unconscious expression in visible form. The "tadpole" figure, for example, which is fundamentally a circle with only rudimentary features and lines to represent arms and legs, is seen here as an unconscious symbol arising from that inner level of mental activity which dictates visual form to the overt and conscious behavior of the child.

As the child matures, more and more conscious control is exerted on these powerful surges of unconscious expression, so that a more realistic and accurate rendering of the external world can be developed. Indeed, mature and sophisticated artists often attempt to recapture this ease of movement from the unconscious to artistic expression, in order to effect what they (and many others) conceive to be a more primitive power to their work. Although there is a body of writings which employs this orientation with respect to art and, particularly, to artists, the greatest import of the position for us lies in the influence it seems to have had on portions of the thinking of others who do not represent psychoanalytic thought. Except in this sense, the relevance of the position to the classroom is somewhat muted.

The second orientation of consequence is that of the *Gestalt* psychologists, who postulate that we see images according to structural patterns imposed by the brain on the visual data it receives. Patterning such as closure, regularity, and figure-ground relationships determines the ways in which the visual information the eyes transmit is processed by the brain, and since these patterns are biological requirements, they are in a gross sense the same for all of us.

However, there is, reasons the Gestaltist, a gap between the raw data of vision and the coherent picture one perceives. Thus the mental picture is to a greater or lesser extent a distortion of the image seen; for the small child the distortion is greater, while subsequent maturation narrows the gap and lessens the incongruence. When we move one step further to the act of drawing or working with other art materials, it is not unreasonable to suggest that the same sort of process operates in the opposite direction and the child (when conscious of the need for representational accuracy) becomes dissatisfied with a consistent inability to make the product correspond to the perception. To the Gestaltist, the tadpole figure is not an unconsciously derived symbol, but an unsuccessful approximation of what the child knows is visually present in the image. It is, however, an approximation without which the desired product would simply never be completed. To that end it becomes acceptable and habitual. This accounts for the maintenance of child art forms like the tadpole over a period of time until the next developmental stage.

In its simplest terms, the position of the Gestaltist is that the child draws what he or she sees or, more accurately, what he or she perceives. The particular character of child art is determined by immature or inadequate or childlike perception. Support for and explanation of this approach can be found in the work of Rudolf Arnheim[5] as well as what would seem to be rough, common-sense observation. If children are, in fact, not fully developed physically, intellectually, or linguistically, there is no reason to assume that they are fully developed perceptually and that their visions, however they are expressed, are derived from some extra, complex source. In the absence of overwhelming evidence for another point of view, the simplest explanation is likely to be the correct one or, at least, the most adequate one.

Cognitive psychology approaches these problems from a very different viewpoint. In effect, this position suggests that the child represents what he or she knows rather than what he or she sees. The character of child art is, therefore, the product of immature conceptual development, of inadequate knowledge of the proper contours and relationships of the real world. As the child grows and accumulates more accurate knowledge, this increasing conceptual competence is reflected in more accurate and elaborate images. In this view, symbols like the tadpole are somewhat primitive abstractions, shorthand versions in pictorial form of the concepts which structure the way the child thinks about the world, and constitute gross parallels of the child's verbal development.

Perhaps the most fully developed and most influential example of the cognitive viewpoint among psychologists is that of Jean Piaget.[6] The work of this Swiss psychologist suggests that the character of art work made by children is dependent upon the development of visual concepts. Built upon previous experience, a continually evolving series of ideas (spatial ideas, in particular) about the world governs the structure and the nature of the images the child creates. The sequential levels of this development reflect the growth of the ability to think itself, following much the same pattern. Piaget proposes these levels or stages: the sensorimotor period from birth to age two, the concrete operations period from age two to eleven, and the formal operations period from age eleven to fifteen. Each of these stages represents a step in the progression of the child's expanding awareness of the distinctions between a unique personal point of view and other aspects of the same object.

The vigor of Piaget's insight into intellectual development propelled one writer, Suzi Gablik, into suggesting that the history of style in art itself parallels and reflects that pattern of growth.[7] Thus her position interprets the lack of spatial sophistication of pre-Renaissance art as a product of its having reached only a preoperational stage in conceptual spatial development. Once the artists of that period conquered the visual problems of depicting perspective and drew from a single viewpoint, they were able to present the world in their art much the way it looked. It was not until roughly the twentieth century that artists began to present multiple viewpoints in a geometrical analysis—as in the work of the Cubists—and that the stage of formal operations can be said to have been reached. In this system, no matter how fanciful it may appear, there is a serious attempt (if not an exaggerated one) to apply the cognitive position to social phenomena such as art and to employ knowledge gained from the art work of children to understandings in a much broader context.

Another psychologist researching this area and taking much the same kind of position as that of Piaget is Dale Harris.[8] Revising the original Good-enough Draw-A-Man test (a nonverbal intelligence test based on the number, quality, and location of elements of a drawn human figure), Harris supports the principle that conceptual development structures the changes in the way the child depicts the world. Conversely, of course, drawings will reveal the level of complexity of the child's concepts and can thus be used as a test of intellectual maturity.

These are the three main psychological orientations used to explain child development in art. There is a fourth, the British-American tradition of psychological investigation (as opposed to the continental European origins of the psychoanalytic, Gestalt, and cognitive schools), which recognizes the importance of experiential, social, and educational influences on human behavior. However, research reflecting this posture is considerably smaller in quantity with respect to child development and art and more commonly represented by the work of art educators than by psychologists. For example, although behaviorists such as B. F. Skinner[9] have had significant influence on education, they have had very little concern with art education and even less effect on its thinking. This preference for contextual over clinical emphasis among educators is understandable in light of their direct interest in and responsibility to classroom practice. In any case, no substantial body of theory and research in the area we are looking at can be attributed to the British-American tradition.

CONTRIBUTIONS OF ART EDUCATORS

In addition to the investigations and theories of psychologists, professional art educators—most of them college teachers with the time, inclination, and training for scholarly study—have attempted to examine the implications of what the child creates with art materials. Although the vigor and number of such researches have diminished somewhat since the forties and fifties, there is still considerable interest in the area of child development and art. It is likely that at least part of this interest stems from the influence of earlier writers, both in psychology and in art education itself, rather than from a direct concern for curricular needs in the school today.

A pioneer in generating, investigating, and popularizing conceptions of age and maturation related to art production was the head of the art education department at Pennsylvania State University, Viktor Lowenfeld. While Lowenfeld almost singlehandedly made scientific research in the visual arts respectable at a time when it was far from acceptable, he also imposed on child development in art a rigidity of structure from which it still suffers in some of its thinking and writing. Since he was a man of tremendous personal charm and authority, Lowenfeld successfully carried his message about child art all over the nation. His major written work, *Creative and Mental Growth*,[10] has appeared in eight editions and to this day is used in some universities as the class text in elementary art education courses.

In 1947 Lowenfeld proposed the following pattern in which children develop in art production: scribbling, preschematic forms, schematic forms, dawning realism, and pseudo-realism. These stages were tied, in what is viewed today as alarming and inappropriate precision, to chronological age. Despite attempts by followers and students of Lowenfeld to soften these maturational imperatives, the inheritance of his age-related art development is still very much part of the ideology of the field, more a tribute to the power of his personality than to the reliability of his insight.

In more than one sense, Lowenfeld continued and amplified an existing tradition of viewing the relationship of children and art, that of earlier pioneers such as Arthur Wesley Dow and Franz Cizek. This view emphasized the idea that the child possessed a viable and inherent capability to see the world in fresh and satisfying ways (and could express these visions in the media of the arts) that were contaminated and repressed by the imposition of adult visions and standards. The child's creativity, which Lowenfeld saw as transferring from art activity to general behavior, was a given, what one writer has called "the unfolding of a genetic program"[11] which ought not to be constrained but, rather, ought to be nurtured, in the primary interest not necessarily of better art expression, but in the interest of a more wholesome and emotionally healthy individual.

Lowenfeld's researches prompted two derivative positions which might inform our understanding and structure our teaching in art. The first was that most individuals can be categorized as perceiving the world—and expressing their perception of it—in two distinctly different modes: visual and haptic. Visual people, child or adult, concentrate on visible, objective forms, while haptics see and describe in pictorial terms what they experience emotionally and kinesthetically. These two genetically inherent ways of perceiving are observable in the art work of children and, further, can serve to influence the ways in which we teach them; thus, for example, pressing the visual child to produce in a haptic manner is seen as similar to pushing the left-handed child to draw and write with the right hand.

The second derivative position suggested that the factors which cumulatively defined the creative individual (at that time increasingly attended to by researchers in the general area of psychology) could be carefully supported by art teaching. By this strategy, art education could participate in what was seen as a critical social need, the requirement that our national interests be enhanced by so-called creative individuals in the sciences and engineering. The reader will recall that this was the era of the cold war and of the initial conquest of space by the USSR, and many Americans were concerned with what was thought to be our lagging national competence in industrial development. The discovery that psychologists such as J. P. Guilford were working on factors of creative behavior, discernible among scientists, was a tremendous incentive to justify and expand art education's preoccupation with the idea of creativity and to reinforce the conviction that what had been proposed in connection with the concept be implemented in the classroom, particularly in art teaching.

The popularity of these ideas in the United States was even further supported by the writings of Sir Herbert Read in England.[12] A man of letters rather than an empirical researcher, Read brought a cosmopolitan scholarship to the literature of art education. He postulated that the arts provided the most adequate means whereby the individual might confront the universal and transcendental harmonies which describe good and evil and become a whole individual. This confrontation can be guaranteed by educational activities which train the child's senses and which support the child's subconscious inclination to reach through the medium of art to those universals embodied in archetypal visual forms, the residuals carried by the mind of a common "collective unconscious."

Read's colorful if fanciful ideas still maintain a healthy measure of influence in much of the world where art education is an issue of some consequence, perhaps most of all in England and the continent. A symbol of this influence can be seen in the name of the sole world organization of art educators, the International Society for Education Through Art, the substantive portion of whose title coincides with the title of Read's most influential book in regard to art teaching.

The reader who is familiar with psychological literature will recognize that Read's ideas have their parentage in the writings of Freud and in the work of Carl Jung. Lowenfeld's ideas are, on the other hand, built upon the concepts of the Gestalt and cognitive psychologists, at least insofar as his structuring of developmental stages is concerned.

Another, perhaps less influential, interpreter of child art of roughly the same period of the 1940s was Henry Schaefer-Simmern.[13] His position in this area was that the progression of natural growth in drawing is independent of cognitive development; its potential is inherent in the child, when the child is free of societal influences on drawing skills. In its emphasis on perception, the viewpoint is nicely consonant with much of the work of the Gestalt psychologists and with Arnheim's writings. A somewhat later follower of this tradition is June McFee, whose perception-delineation theory suggests that in order to understand the development of child art one must take into account those social and psychological factors which structure the level at which the child sees and creates art. These factors include: (1) physical, intellectual, and perceptual readiness; (2) the psychological environment of support or its opposite; (3) the child's ability for information handling; and (4) the child's delineation skills or manipulative and design ability.[14]

While it is easy to be unimpressed by and even negative about this confusing accumulation of theories and research about children's expressions with art materials, it is also important to realize that these issues and questions arise from some real and sometimes significant behaviors. One newspaper columnist, writing about a trip to rural, impoverished America, describes this experience.

During the weekend when I was there, it poured incessantly and the longer it rained, the better nature looked and the worse this man and his fellows—damp, cursing, and manipulating tin cans under the larger leaks in their jerry-built houses.

Before I left the place, I talked to a pale girl, about 12, who stood, more or less soaked by the rain, and who was apparently indifferent to being wet; do not ask me why. What interested me most about her, since our conversation was generally undistinguished, was a drawing that she had done in some kind of blue indelible ink on the back of her left hand.

She had drawn three plain, rectangular gravestones, with flowers in front of each one, and on each stone, there were initials.

I pointed to the drawing and asked, "What is that?" She ran her tongue around her lips once or twice, apparently deciding whether she would answer the question.

Then she smiled a little, for the first time during our talk, and said, "Those are people I don't like. Stuck-up people." And she walked off slowly into the rain, not looking back, but stopping once to stamp in a puddle with her muddy bare legs.[15]

CHILDREN'S AESTHETIC RESPONSES

In contrast to the considerable literature on the productive behavior of the child with art materials, exploration of the way the child functions as a viewer or responder is relatively scanty. There are several reasons for this restriction. One is that productive activity is much more revealing of the child's general development, which is the important purpose of most psychological study. Another is that studio or manipulative activities have been the primary focus of most school art, and serious concern for the child as a consumer or viewer is a recent phenomenon. A third reason is that the activity of viewing objects aesthetically has been confused with the act of perception per se, or viewing all things, regardless of the attitude or posture from which they are seen.

A fourth reason is derived from a misunderstanding of the nature of aesthetic response. One reads repeatedly in books on art education that children grow into capability for aesthetic experiences sometime during their developmental stages, as if only the fine or "serious" arts can occasion such response.[16] These attitudes discourage careful study of the aesthetic reactions of the young child and influence the art curriculum of the elementary school to emphasize or be limited to manipulative activities. As a result, there are no theories of children's aesthetic response in the same sense that there are theories of children's productive development. Instead we are forced to rely, for the most part, on gross descriptions drawn from personal observation and the writings of others who rely on the same sort of experience.

The most general and perhaps most important statement in this context is that children from the earliest age appear to have some sense of aesthetic preference, no matter how rudimentary. Even infants in the crib might be said to make an aesthetic selection when they reach for the most brightly colored element in a mobile swinging over the crib. Receptivity to aesthetic experience may well be a "given" in the human repertoire of responses to the world around us, a part of our genetic inheritance. Without becoming too highly theoretical, it is likely that the aesthetic posture is a complex result of a more fundamental gratification with an aspect of the environment which is nonthreatening or benign to the organism. While there may be no direct evidence of such a mechanism, it is, in the absence of other evidence, an economical and thus plausible supposition.

If some such basic human operation describes the origins of aesthetic functioning, it would be appropriate to conclude that response precedes production in the life of the child and that the child may come to work with art materials with more than a little experience of visual values. This principle is particularly important when one realizes the wealth of influences from the human environment which structure all of our early conceptions of value, from overt statements about what is "nice" made by parents, to covert indications such as pictures on the walls of rooms in which infants sleep. However, it is unnecessary to be speculative in this context. Suffice it to say that small children manifest selectivity or preference with visual objects and that this preference can be recognized as some sort of primitive evaluation on an aesthetic basis. They seem to prefer bright colors, sharp contrasts, and obvious textures. They are much more attracted to images which emphasize representational qualities; the cow that looks like a cow seems to be preferred to an abstraction of a cow. As soon as the naming portion of the scribbling stage commences, or even earlier, the child is able to elaborate imaginative stories in response to visual stimuli, whether it is the child's own work or some other object.

As children develop their ability to render space, figures, and objects in their own creations, they also grow in their interest in aspects of the visual arts in the world around them (Figures 103, 104, 105, and 106). Being less contaminated as yet in some of the biases from which adults suffer, they are perfectly willing to react favorably to the vernacular arts—cartoons, comics, and visual "stories" of all kinds—in much the same way that adults respond to the fine arts. They prefer direct and simple visual images, like comics, and respect and recognize skill in craftsmanship. They are very conscious of what they conceive to be the hierarchy of rank in drawing ability. This author remembers that in a sixth-grade class he taught, the children habitually crowded around the desk of one of the pupils with exclamations of awe and delight each time that child drew his unbelievably detailed x-ray creations. Angelo was the class "artist," and no amount of praise from the teacher for the work of other children lessened the sovereignty of Angelo's position. In truth, the drawings were amazing and quite as much admired by myself as teacher as by the class, though surreptitiously.

Existing specific researches in this area are limited to those which deal with aesthetic preferences, such as Irvin Child[17] and Harold McWhinnie,[18] and those concerned with children's verbal and nonverbal reactions to art works or the making of art, such as Diana Korzenik[19] and Barry Moore.[20] Research by psychologists in this area of child development includes a series of related studies undertaken by Gardner and his associates at Harvard University as part of

103. *Dinosaur,* a monoprint by a nine year old

104. *Horses,* a tempera painting by a five year old

105. *Helicopter,* a crayon drawing by a seven year old

106. *Picking Apples,* a crayon drawing by an eight year old

"Project Zero." These studies investigated children's sensitivity to painting style, conceptions about the arts, development of critical judgment, and perceptual responses to texture. Despite some interesting indications revealed by these studies, the series suffers from a number of conceptual flaws often common to researchers untrained in art.[21]

As laudable as these pioneer efforts may be, they hardly constitute grounds for informed curriculum building. It would seem that we need to accumulate much more data on the basis of which theories can be developed and tested.

The tendency to be interested in the subject of the work and to value realism in rendering remains throughout the elementary years. Since there is very little evidence as to the results of consistent teaching of other characteristics of the visual arts, we can only guess whether these attitudes might be enlarged and enriched by instructional efforts. There would seem to be no logical or developmental reason why we could not do this, but it does not seem to have been done long enough or well enough as yet so that such evidence can be accumulated. Nevertheless, that this should be done and how it might be done is —more than anything else—the prescription of this volume.

IMPLICATIONS OF THE STUDY OF CHILD DEVELOPMENT FOR THE CLASSROOM

Significant conclusions about child development and art can be summarized in the following observations. When given the opportunity and often even spontaneously (as in the case of pictorial graffiti), children, adolescents, and adults will create objects which appear to represent the results of motivations similar to those of practicing artists. They will form or fashion materials ranging from images scribbled on telephone pads to elaborate, if naive, plans for residential buildings. Some of these objects are careful constructions reflecting a significant degree of intellectual effort. Others seem to be highly emotive expressions pictorializing some important response to the experiences of living. Still others are attempts, no matter how innocent, to take part in the social world of the visual arts, whether they are paint-by-number kits or the products of evening art classes in community centers. All people, including children, seem to enjoy to whatever degree some form of participation in making art, no matter how momentary or unsuccessful the activity.

The vast majority of people accept the assumption that this participation is an inconsequential aspect of their lives, even if it becomes an enjoyable and absorbing recreation at some point. If they, indeed, share a "need" to express themselves (whatever the psychological ramifications of such a proposition), they discover ways other than visual expression to satisfy this requirement— through political activity, parenthood, paid work, or hobbies. There are no verifiable data which clearly suggest that such redirection of attention away from working with visual materials seriously deprives the great majority of the population of any significant or irreplaceable experience. Being unable or unwilling to work with art materials is no more serious a loss than not creating poetry or literary prose or music or dance or dramatic events. It might be nice to do so, but it is in no sense critical to successful living. Hence, concentration on understanding child development in art for the purpose of preparing better functioning adults—those who can satisfy a need to express themselves in visual form—is not germane to art teaching. It is, at best, the proper province of psychologists who wish to inquire into all aspects of human behavior, including art behavior, in order to understand it.

Further, a considerable history of empirical research and sometimes fascinating speculation has left us without enough firm data which we can authoritatively use to explain the origins of childrens' growth in image-making or from which we can extrapolate prescriptions about the curriculum of elementary school art. What we presently do in the classroom is as much, if not more, a function of tradition or habit as it is a product of documented art teaching theory. We do not even know, nor can we be reasonably confident, that many of the activities we provide in art in the school support and promote those ends of general education all of us salute: responsible citizenship, intellectual power, and knowledge of the past and present of the world around us. As long as our curricula emphasize required manipulative activities and studio production, we run the risk of significant misdirection of child learning.

It would not do to close this chapter without two highly significant statements on child development and art, one from a psychologist who has carefully investigated that area and written widely about it and one from an art educator whose credentials in the field cannot be improved upon. Howard Gardner, the present director of Project Zero at Harvard University, writes:

> A grown individual has evolved in a way the child cannot have: he has undergone experiences, crises, and satisfactions which the younger individual cannot even fathom. Hence his drawings can reflect a depth of emotional life and a sense of a person behind that life that remain impossible for even the most precocious child. . . . We can be delighted, charmed, even thrilled by the drawings of young children, but it is difficult to fathom how we can be deeply moved or profoundly awakened by a work of art from an individual yet to enter his adult years.[22]

The reader will recognize that Gardner's statement raises questions about child behavior with art materials which in some ways parallel the attitudes in this volume.

The second quotation is from the writings of Edmund Feldman, author of one of the standard texts in art education, who has achieved the rank of president of the National Art Education Association.

> Because of a convincing theory of child art, a teacher may be persuaded to entrap children into creating images because it is supposed to be good for them. In practice, we often *force* a child to create art in the absence of any compelling reason *of his own* to do so. The work that emerges may reflect the characteristic imagery of children. But it rarely reflects an authentic, a *genuinely felt occasion* for artistic expression. As a result, children use materials and create images under the auspices of the elementary school largely because they have to.[23]

CHAPTER 8

the elementary art curriculum

One might with some gravity call the curriculum proposed or endorsed by any educational document its "moment of truth." Whatever is said, eloquently or passionately, about any other aspect of education, curricular statements define—potentially at least—the actual actions of pupils and teachers and, thus, constitute the heart of the educational enterprise. In fact, one can find in educational writings occasional discrepancies between objectives and methodology on the one hand, the curriculum proposed to implement them on the other.

The origin of the word "curriculum" means a course or track, and in education it is that track of behaviors along which the student travels in order to attain the goals seen as the appropriate and valuable benefits of that track. By tradition, a curriculum includes the implication of a preplanned series of events, though in practice some of what happens in a classroom has an ad hoc or spontaneous character. Curricula can be planned by any element of the educational equation: the pupils, the teacher, the school district or state, community groups, or even the author of an educational text—or two or more of these in concert. Since there are fewer institutionally mandated curricula prepared by state or local agencies in the visual arts than in most other subject areas, both teachers and, theoretically, pupils, have more leeway in selecting and organizing art activities. In effect, however, traditional activities learned by the teacher from other teachers, college coursework, and books and magazines appear to form the bulk of what is actually done in the elementary classroom. It is interesting to note that much the same curriculum in elementary art has been used over the last several decades to support a considerable diversity of goals, as noted in our discussion in chapter 6.

CONSIDERATIONS IN THE ORGANIZATION OF THE CURRICULUM

The simplest organization of the mechanics of building curricula suggests that the curriculum builder select the activities of a curriculum, the "what," as it were, on the basis of at least three other relevant factors: the group of pupils for whom the curriculum is being designed, the "who"; the learning benefits envisioned in the activity, the "why"; and the techniques by which the content is brought to the pupils, the methodology or the "how." Curriculum designers sometimes add a fifth ingredient to these, the "how well," that is, the means whereby the effectiveness of the curriculum can be evaluated.[1] Until recently, with the advent of behavioral objectives and competency-based education, the importance of evaluation had been minimized in art education.

At this point, our analysis of curriculum construction raises three pertinent questions. The first is to what extent the nature of the learner or group of learners, the "who," affects the goals or ends toward which the curriculum is directed. It is, perhaps, educationally obvious that one cannot design a curriculum for all the pupils of a nation, state, or community on one grade level without some regard for differences of background, interests, expectations of parents, or anticipations of the pupils themselves. Thus, there is no basic curriculum for all children. On the other hand, it is just as convincing to assert that children and adults are more alike than they are dissimilar and that certain preeminent goals in art teaching assume priority and relate to all children at roughly the same age or grade level. Earlier educational writings differentiated between these two viable necessities by preparing both "general" and "specific" objectives. This volume will do somewhat the same by proposing general objectives for which the theoretical groundwork has been developed in chapter 6 and by presenting concepts here by which specific objectives can be considered and employed by the curriculum designer.

The second question is to assess the now frequent use of behavioral objectives and competency-based education as they pertain to elementary art education. These ideas can be summarized as demanding that the ends of the curriculum or track be defined as measurable behavior of the pupils and that these measurements be made consistently and reported. Although this approach does impose much needed care and exactitude on the way in which goal statements are conceived and written, it also constrains art teaching into a more mechanistic process than is presently appropriate to its structure.

There is no question that stating an art education goal in behavioral terms is an asset to a field that has been more than a little vague in its descriptions of ends; for example, "interesting the pupil in independently visiting exhibits of visual materials" is a worthwhile objective. It becomes obvious, however, that in this example any careful, and by implication quantitative, measurement of the achievement of the objective, independent visits, would be almost fruitless. The reader can see that beyond simply counting the number of such visits, problems such as equating visits to the county fair with visits to the county art museum would make the process ludicrous.

However, while it is easy for a college textbook to assume a casual or critical position toward an educational movement as we are doing here, it is highly difficult if not impossible for the teacher to ignore the legitimate dictates of educational authority in the form of the school district or state. Therefore, we will adopt the viewpoint here that we can, in fact, describe the consequences of the aesthetic encounter in behavioral terms, as long as the inherent criterion of precise measurement of the benefits of that behavior is somewhat relaxed.

The third question, which is, of course, broader than the art aspect of the curriculum, is the extent to which pupils can or should participate in planning or organizing classroom activities. While it is tempting and has been fashionable to suggest in absolute terms varying degrees of curricular freedom for children,[2] current educational theory, with which this volume concurs, supports a balance between the legitimate learning expectations of society and the wishes of the pupils. On the one hand, a repressive teacher-dominated classroom can discourage learning and inflame unwholesome social tendencies. On the other hand, minimizing structure in the curriculum to any appreciable extent encourages a disregard for intellectual activity and the capabilities necessary to negotiate a complex society.

Deciding upon the level and character of pupil participation in planning and selecting curriculum is dependent upon a number of factors such as the subject matter context, the maturity of the pupils, and the educational orientation of the community, the school, and the individual teacher. A reasonable generalization might be to develop the greatest amount of freedom for children consonant with important necessary learnings. This very difficult balance must be decided by each teacher in terms of a specific school context; no textbook can stipulate particulars. Nevertheless, the old educational term "teacher-pupil planning" is quite appropriate here. At the very least, the teacher should consult with the pupils as to what they anticipate and desire from the learning experience under consideration. A very simple "What do we think we can learn, what do we want to learn about art, and how best can we learn it?" can be a starting point. The rest of the planning can be negotiated.

This approach is by no means as simple as it sounds, as any beginning teacher quickly realizes; nor do we wish to belittle its complexity. Neither does it help to suggest that it is a broad educational problem rather than one centered in art teaching. Just as the teacher must decide the proper balance, a textbook must maintain a reasonable equity between detailed prescription and the independent integrity of the teacher. We are saying to the reader, in effect, "you decide" within the boundaries noted.

aesthetic literacy as the basis for organizing the curriculum

These three issues partially resolved, we can now turn to concepts appropriate to the construction of curricula according to the redirections in theory recommended in chapter 6. The reader will recall that these alterations of basic viewpoint emphasized that the main obligation of school art is to help the pupils expand and intensify their available aesthetic experiences, particularly in those realms to which they do not yet have informed access. For most American boys and girls this is the area of the honorific fine arts. Clearly then, this idea, aesthetic literacy, is a general objective in the sense described earlier in the chapter. Independent of age level, geographical location, or economic or social origin, this is what art education should do for *all* our children. It is not that there are no other goals worth working toward, nor that this main objective in itself may not dictate different content for different groups or even individuals. It does mean that this is the one irreducible end-in-view of our efforts, whatever else art in the elementary school does or does not accomplish.

Further, chapter 6 asserted the continuity between interaction with the fine arts and interaction with nature, folk arts, popular arts, and mass media. These are all legitimate areas of available aesthetic value for us; in this sense no one of them as a type is more valuable than another. In addition, the paths to intensifying and broadening one's capacity for aesthetic experience depend on the extent to which one understands the processes and contents of aesthetic encounters. To be educated is to know how the individual and the world works and how to exert greater personal and collective control over that world. Finally, what these ideas imply is that the curricular means employed in art activities must be several rather than singular, that the aesthetically literate individual is not the result simply of working with art materials or watching adult artists at work. In terms of the customary classroom art activities available for our task, a strong elementary art curriculum should include studio production, art history, art criticism, and dialogue clarifying the process of aesthetic experience to the extent that present theories are adequate to do so.

Now we can easily visualize the answers to all of our basic curriculum questions. Once we have determined the predominant "why" of our efforts, the primary general objective, we can sensibly select particular goals for specific groups of children, the "who" question of our curriculum design format. For example, if a second-grade class represents for the most part children whose home backgrounds include some familiarity with the fine arts—books and magazines in the home, museum and gallery visits, and dinner-table conversation—the "specific" objectives for that group will include an understanding of the other accessible arts or a further analysis of how those arts they already respond to provoke that response. Similarly, the "how" question is answered by stipulating a multiplicity of methodologies: looking at, talking about, reading about, and making. Given all these answers then, we can assert that the proper "what" to be engaged, the content of the elementary art curriculum, should be made up of all the sources of aesthetic transactions around us and all the relevant information we have about them. Thus, the discussion of what factors might account for the success (in aesthetic terms) of a particular television commercial, the explanation of how a pot is thrown on a potter's wheel, the description by viewing, reading about, and talking of the cave paintings in Altamira, or the experience of photographing the school building are all examples of the types of processes that constitute the art curriculum.

It is possible to combine all of these operations into one definitive curriculum principle, which we can call "canalization."[3] In communications theory, canalization refers to beaming a signal or message compatible with the comprehension level of the audience at which it is aimed. In our terms canalization will mean orienting the content of the art curriculum toward those art experiences the children we are teaching already appreciate, as a starting point, so that we can expand that appreciation. In curriculum terms, this principle is much like the idea of "starting where the children are" and not only is theoretically sound but also has a rough common-sense appeal. By analogy, it is similar to basing mathematics concepts in the practical operations of buying, selling, measuring, and counting in "real life" situations. Properly conceived and organized in a sensible curriculum, art is no less a part of our everyday lives than math or language or science.

A canalized curriculum demands content that progressively widens the areas of art a child sees as viable sources of aesthetic experience and that promotes increasing insight into how we obtain such experience. However, it is important to note that this progressive widening and increasing insight do not presuppose a developmental movement from simple to complex, in the same sense as math or science or language. In recent years art education has sought desperately to construct just such sequential patterns of development. An example can be found in the curriculum guide for California, *Art Education Framework*.[4] The position of this volume is that there is no presently determined inherent pattern in art content directed toward developing the educated consumer; there are no simple skills which must be assimilated before more complex skills can be tackled. Much of this concept of sequence has grown out of a preoccupation with art performance skills and may be appropriate to that end. If we do not concentrate on performance, but rather on response, the need for a structured developmental curriculum is substantially lessened.

The canalized curriculum supports a structure that is lateral rather than vertical or hierarchical. The educated consumer cannot be helped to develop by tightly sequenced prescriptions of what to do on each grade level. The alternative suggested here, possible only if we assume an equity among the various visual arts in terms of human use, is to move in ever widening circles around the core of pupil response, which is made up of what the particular group of children already appreciate. Our contention is that one cannot broaden and deepen appreciation with mechanistic, graded sequences of activities that inevitably lead to age or grade expectations, in turn intimidating both pupil and teacher rather than liberating them. This process is analogous to the kind of rigidity of expectations growing out of hypothesizing age levels in child art development that concentrated almost solely on performance (see chapter 7). The Ohio State elementary art guide puts it this way:

> There are few clues in the content of art to suggest a "proper" sequence for art activities to follow. Most ideas of sequence come from traditions of teaching practice inherited from the nineteenth century. For example, some teachers believe that drawing skill should be mastered before children learn to paint, or that the elements and principles of design should be mastered before children are permitted freedom of expression, or that studio studies should come before critical and historical study. There is little inherent in art or in the patterns of child growth and development either to affirm or deny these ideas.[5]

A happy result of this newer view of art curriculum is the renewed respect it accords to the classroom teacher. In contrast with carrying out the prescriptive dictates of a mechanically articulated sequence of so-called developmental activities, teachers are freed to weave imaginatively a fabric of exercises appropriate to the specific group of children and to the kinds of learnings about art most useful to that group. However, this concept of curriculum is not a license for encouraging a random string of art activities allowed to occur at the whim of pupils or teachers or both in conjunction. Indeed, such a series of unrelated behaviors would require no curriculum at all, since they would be unplanned at best. What a canalized curriculum suggests is that the teacher involve his or her aesthetic life outside the classroom in the popular arts, mass media, and folk arts as well as the fine arts in planning art content. Thus, the breadth of the average teacher's and teacher candidate's concept of worthwhile art experience becomes an asset rather than a liability. The elementary classroom teacher need no longer apologetically confess a lack of familiarity with the honorific masterpieces of museum art or the esoteria of complex performance skills, if such is presently the case.

The author vividly recalls his own early efforts as an elementary classroom teacher. In music, the predominantly performance curriculum necessitated his singing or playing the piano in front of the class—an ordeal eliciting a high level of terror. Consequently, the music program was restricted to releasing interested pupils (usually from middle-class homes) to go to the music specialist, who taught them to play a musical instrument. Had the idea of the canalized curriculum been available in the literature of music education or in the lone "methods" course (more accurately, the portion of a course) taken in teacher training, the same teacher might have tried to relate the range of music extending from the rich vein of popular music available in every home via the radio to those exalted selections of the Masters, as we are recommending here be done in the visual arts.

Before we can turn to specific suggestions as to just how the elementary teacher can weave that imaginative web of appropriate curriculum activities mentioned previously, we must confront the difficult question of evaluation. It is a significant aspect of curriculum construction for most authors in the field of education, equivalent in power to the who, why, how, and what indicated earlier. It could well be added to these four as a "how well," and we have no intention here of slighting it.

The process of evaluation in education can be said to have at least three basic components: judgment, measurement, and reporting. One can assess the merits of an educational enterprise in a variety of reasonable ways, usually reflecting some degree of interpretation by the assessor. Or one can measure the degree of success or failure according to specific tests of some sort, usually suggesting quantification and some precision of means. Either judgment or measurement or both can be reported, often in our schools by way of a letter or number grade or by a verbal description. There is no question that the teacher and others in the school need to have some sense of how well learning is going on in the classroom; nor is it improper for parents to wish to have some basis for viewing the growth of their children. Even the strictures of competency-based education (CBE), which require precision in describing learnings in terms of pupil behavior, are reasonable, as we noted earlier in this chapter. What is irksome to most art educators, however, is that aspect of CBE that requires objective measurement in art just as in other subject areas. It is not that there are no behavioral goals, but that these, for the most part, cannot be precisely measured and reported; they can only be judged and interpreted.

For example, we can easily and properly submit that the educated consumer we wish to foster is one who: (1) talks comfortably and knowledgeably about why art works of all kinds affect him or her as they do, (2) independently visits exhibits of visual materials, (3) reads more than assigned book, magazine, or newspaper writings on art, (4) collects some form of art—for example, posters, jewelry, reproductions—for his or her own use, (5) explains clearly how a particular physical environment can be made to be more functional or pleasing in appearance, or (6) describes the technical processes, the design of an art work, with reasonable accuracy. These are all behaviorally and carefully stated objectives, but they invariably defy any precise measurement. They can be assessed or interpreted and reported, but they cannot be measured in any way we have developed at present. Thus the conception of evaluation endorsed here is to support the judgment of the teacher reported in a verbal description.

Art educators also seem to be fond of suggesting that art appreciation is an attitudinal behavior composed of primarily affective or emotive factors and for this reason not amenable to CBE types of language or ideas. Others are willing to accept verbal responses to works of art as legitimate indications of levels of aesthetic knowledge, while still others are reluctant to consider these verbal responses as "authentic." The position of this volume is that precise measurements of aesthetic growth are problematical in any form at the present time, whatever the reasons. It may be that at some time in the future, more exact techniques for such measurement will be developed.[6]

A final caution is in order. Despite our reluctance to endorse any sequence or structure in art content, there is no question that there are significant differences which must be attended to in the capabilities of children at the various ages or grade levels of the elementary school. Obviously, a second- and a sixth-grade pupil cannot negotiate the same demands of knowledge or skill in performance or dialogue. While rigidity of expectations, which often act as self-fulfilling prophecies, should be avoided, curricular plans must be framed to reflect broad levels of maturity. What is critical to realize is that only the teacher can accurately gauge the capabilities of a particular pupil or class. It is unrealistic for the authors of textbooks or curriculum planners in state capital or school district offices to stipulate such levels in the absence of a working knowledge of the children in question. The only appropriate generalization is to observe that—in art education, at least—authors and planners seem consistently to underrate the sophistication of our youth. Indeed, if education can be characterized as growth, some stretching of the pupil's capabilities to a higher level of insight is an inherent obligation of the classroom process.

Some years ago, the author had the opportunity to observe a group of art educators preparing a chart of suggested audio-visual units for art in kindergarten through twelfth grade. The group had used as representative content for the two ends of the grade range the following items: the study of the design or patterning of a leaf for kindergarten and Rembrandt's *Night Watch* for twelfth graders. The author's comment that perhaps the units might be reversed and that kindergarten children could more effectively negotiate the Dutch painting and, indeed find it more interesting, while twelfth-grade pupils could better handle the deceptive simplicity of the leaf, was met with a cool silence. Nevertheless, this kind of assumption, that young children cannot deal with the factors or cues of a complex art work, may well be faulty. Or such an assumption may be the result of supposing that only formal aesthetic factors such as color and line are significant and that the story, mood, background materials, and associations are unimportant in the experience of art. All of these elements, formal and informal, are equally relevant to response to art, and even kindergarten children can be helped to articulate and better understand how they are responding and the objects they are responding to. The reader will understand, of course, that we are not recommending that Rembrandt necessarily be the starting point of the kindergarten curriculum.

THE STRUCTURE OF THE CURRICULUM

Curriculum planners have traditionally prepared lessons and units of instruction (a unit being a series of several lessons usually connected by a common concept) according to a format or outline which requires identifying the elements to be considered. There is no question that planning demands some sort of format and the simple plan form in Figure 107 is recommended here.

"Time" in this plan form refers to the number of class hours the planner envisions being devoted to the lesson. The "materials" category is a space in

107. Sample format for a lesson plan

GRADE _____   TIME _____

SUBJECT

OBJECTIVES

MATERIALS

MOTIVATION

ACTIVITY

EVALUATION

---

which the planner could list those tools, expendable materials, books, magazines, films, slides, and so forth, required for the activity. "Motivation," where such a concern is appropriate, directs the planner's attention to the item or items to be used to arouse the interest of the pupils in the activity. Ideally such an entry is unnecessary, since the activity should be one which is itself inherently stimulating. When this is not the case, the teacher should have some devices available for promoting interest.

This plan form accurately reflects the elements of curriculum design described in the previous section, namely: Who (grade), Why (objectives), What (activity), How (materials), and How well (evaluation). The strictly proper starting point for filling in the plan form in a canalized curriculum is to locate the span of objects and events which seem to be worthwhile to look at in the day-to-day activities, both in and outside school, of the children of the particular class for whom the plan is being written; however, it is only realistic to assume that much curricular planning will have to be done before the teacher meets the class. Identifying the specific interests and differences among the students in a particular class once school is under way will help to modify preplanned lessons and units. Differences among youngsters in areas such as economic backgrounds, rural-urban origins, ethnic groupings, and breadth of exposure to various art forms, once ascertained by the teacher early in the year, can be useful in altering activities or motivation or the materials to be used in the class units. It should be noted that the teacher does not need a complex educational mechanism or a battery of psychological tests to discover the interests of the children. A simple assignment to bring in an object of art, or the description of such an object, or a class discussion identifying such objects for younger children may well be adequate.

In this case, the lesson and unit plans will involve the general application of the canalization principle to planning. A useful way to present the possibilities is to examine several sample lesson plans and refer to the larger units of which they might be parts. Figure 108, for example, is one possible program of content sources for the elementary grades. Each content source, in turn, provides sample art forms or subjects which might serve as themes for either a single lesson or an entire unit. Figure 109 presents a sample lesson plan describing student activities in greater detail. While the program's progression through the grades is far from sequential or developmental, it does—as is obvious—move from the immediate environment of younger children to wider domains for the older ones.

Much the same kind of program can be devised on the basis of other kinds of classifications of the visual arts, as long as the curriculum planner applies the principle of canalization, that is, using the pupil's present interests as the starting point. For example, each grade might study a form of art: architecture, fabrics, ceramics, painting, film and video, and so forth. Or each grade might work with a function of art that can serve as a subject area: advertising, home design, television, public monuments (buildings, sculpture, and paintings), product design, and so forth. The particular arrangement of the art content is far less critical than the necessity for including *all* of the visual arts in the curriculum. (Some specific curriculum ideas will be provided in the next chapter on pages 224–30.)

Also, it should not be difficult to see how specific individual differences among children in one class or regional, ethnic, economic, or cultural differences among classes can be respected and, indeed, exploited within such planning. For example, when kindergarten youngsters are asked to bring in examples of quilting or other types of linens made or decorated by members of the family, all of the various types offered by the children must be accepted and recognized as worthy of discussion by the teacher. Or when a fourth-grade pupil uses themes in drawing that appear to be derived from the pupil's own ethnic heritage, the teacher should capitalize on the situation to explore with the class the relevant artistic high points of that culture.

Since the emphasis of this type of elementary art curriculum is on knowledge about works of art as much as on making them, the visual and verbal re-

108. Sample elementary program

GRADE	CONTENT SOURCE	SUBJECT	LOOKING	TALKING	MAKING	READING
Kindergarten	The Home	Quilts Old Photos Dishes Paintings				
First	The School	Furniture Films Plays Photography				
Second	The Community	Buildings Parks Monuments Transportation				
Third	The Nation	Museums Television Advertising Fabrics				
Fourth	Other Cultures	Mexico Scandinavia Japan Africa				
Fifth	Historical Cultures	Egypt Greece Early U.S.A. Renaissance				
Sixth	The Future	Cities Video Clothing Transportation				

109. Sample lesson plan

GRADE   Kindergarten   **TIME** 3-5 days

SUBJECT   Quilt-making

OBJECTIVES   To talk knowledgeably about the function, design, and construction of quilts.

MATERIALS   1. Swatches of fabric
2. Needle and thread
3. Quilt examples from children's homes
4. Book: Robert Bishop, New Discoveries in American Quilts, E. P. Dutton, 1975

MOTIVATION   Looking at and talking about quilts that pupils bring from home, along with photos, slides of quilts.

ACTIVITY   Discussion of function, design, and construction of quilts.

In groups of 3 or 4 pupils, plan and sew quilts of various kinds.

EVALUATION   Completed quilts are exhibited in school hallways and explained by groups of pupils to visitors. Teacher notes (by memory or by recording) the degree to which children appear to have accumulated information on the subject.

sources available to the teacher are extremely important. An art specialist, either resident or itinerant, can be highly useful in bringing such resources to the attention of the classroom teacher. However, many schools and districts do not have art specialists and some source of reference for slides, films, books, and magazines would be of value to the prospective or in-service teacher. An almost invariably helpful agency for this sort of assistance is the district or county instructional media center, especially with regard to film and video materials. The bibliography in this volume provides the names of books and journals appropriate to the area of elementary art education. Further resources of potential aid of this sort are the National Art Education Association (1916 Association Drive, Reston, Virginia 22091), the art education faculty of a local or state college or university, and the state professional association of art teachers affiliated with the NAEA.

SOME ART CURRICULUM EXAMPLES

A textbook is obligated to present the ideas and curriculum suggestions of other writers and agencies in its field. The following pages provide a short review of three selected proposals for elementary art curriculum, along with an assessment of each of them from the point of view of this volume. The first is a state art guide from 1970, the second is a book written by an individual in 1974, and the third is the curricular material developed at the Southwest Regional Educational Laboratory (SWRL) in Los Alamitos, California, one of the two regional educational laboratories dealing with the visual arts (the other is the Central Midwestern Educational Research Laboratory in St. Louis, Missouri).

All three curriculum plans reflect what is presently called aesthetic education, in that the content to be taught extends the activities of the pupils beyond simply the making of art to the historical and critical areas as well. After our review of the history and current ideas and practices in the field in chapter 6, it should come as no surprise to the reader that these curricular recommendations are quite different from what happens in art in most classrooms today.

The 1970 Ohio State Department of Education elementary art guide is still in use in that state. Its ideological orientation is evident in the introduction with the words:

> For both of these groups, it presents a model for planning effective art programs by describing types of content and suggests a broad range of children's activities for study in the visual arts. While activities involving the making of art are accorded the central place in elementary school art instruction, activities such as looking, interpreting, judging, and explaining works of art are also featured and related to studio activities.[7]

In order to carry out this concept the guide arranges the selection of art program objectives as shown in Figure 110. The reader might note the considerable emphasis on concepts about art, the so-called historical and critical aspects.

Appropriate content in the form of sample units and sample lessons are then provided with very careful and thorough references as to visual and written material to assist both the teacher and the pupils. One unit outline (Figure 111) and one sample lesson from that unit (Figure 112) are presented here in complete form so that the reader can obtain some substantial sense of this guide's approach.

As the quotation alluding to the central position of making art indicates, the Ohio art guide seems concerned with one of the assumptions we have criticized, that *the fashioning of visual statements is a necessary activity for all persons.* (See page 157.) However, a careful reading of even the few examples presented here reveals that there is far more "looking, talking, and reading" about art than the disclaimer in the introduction would suggest. Thus, the Ohio guide

(continued on page 203)

110. Art program objectives from the *Guidelines*

Objectives for Art Activities

I. Personal Fulfillment Through Art	II. Awareness of Art in Society	III. Awareness of the Artistic Heritage
Objectives for Personal Expression to help children: • find sources of subjects and themes in their personal experiences with objects and events in the natural and man-made environment. • use their inner feelings, beliefs, and personal concerns about the past, present, and future as sources of subjects and themes. • interpret their ideas and feelings by studying different ways of presenting them in visual form. • compare planned and improvised ways of working as means for helping ideas unfold. • explore various qualities of media to make appropriate selections for expressing ideas. • develop control of various media to enable them to produce intended effects.	**Objectives for Understanding How Societies Use Art Expression** to help children: • understand how societies communicate beliefs by developing visual symbols in their art forms. • understand the various ways that different social groups express their ideas through the things they make. • understand that changes in the art styles of a society usually reflect changes in social conditions and beliefs. • compare and contrast styles of art produced by people in different cultures. • understand some of the conditions that influence the physical shape of man-made environments. • study the different ways men have planned their environment.	**Objectives for Understanding How Artists Achieve Expression** to help children: • understand the different sources that artists draw upon for their ideas. • compare the sources of ideas used by artists with those they use in their own personal expression. • understand that artists interpret their ideas by developing different ways of presenting them in visual form. • compare the ways artists interpret their ideas with those in their own personal expression. • understand how artists explore various qualities of their media and make appropriate selections for expressing their ideas. • compare ways artists achieve control with various media with those they themselves use for achieving control.
Objectives for Personal Response to help children: • develop their powers of perception by taking note of visual qualities in works of art and the environment. • voice descriptions of the qualities they see in works of art and the environment. • account for their feelings about works of art and the environment in terms of the visual qualities they find. • interpret works of art from more than a single point of view. • judge and explain the personal significance of works of art in their own lives. • develop or identify criteria for judging works of art and the environment.	**Objectives for Understanding How Societies Respond to Art** to help children: • understand how people in social groups respond to visual symbols in the arts. • study different systems of visual communication developed by various societies. • understand that people in a social group will often interpret the same symbol in different ways. • understand that a person's choice of a particular product may result from the design of a given package. • understand that different social groups have their own ways of judging their arts. • compare the criteria by which so-called serious art is judged with those used to judge the popular arts.	**Objectives for Understanding How Critics and Historians Respond to Art** to help children: • understand that art critics and historians help people to perceive qualities in works of art. • compare some of the differences in viewpoints held by critics and historians and how these influence their perception of art. • understand that critics try to account for their feelings about works of art in terms of the qualities they have perceived. • compare some of the differences in points of view about art held by critics and historians and how these views influence their interpretations. • understand that critics and historians judge and explain works of art making use of various criteria. • compare the differences in judgments that result when different criteria are employed.

Note. From *State of Ohio, Department of Education, Guidelines: Guidelines for Planning Art Instruction in the Elementary Schools of Ohio* (1970), p. 27. Reprinted by permission.

111. Unit outline *from the* Guidelines

Unit Theme: Expressing Feelings in Art
Objectives of the Unit
Grades 4-6

I. Personal Fulfillment	II. Awareness of Art in Society	III. Awareness of the Artistic Heritage
Expression to help children: 1. find sources of subject and themes in their personal experiences with objects and events in the natural and man-made environment. 2. use their inner feelings as sources of subjects and themes. 3. interpret their feelings by studying different ways of presenting them in visual form. 4. develop control of various media to enable them to produce intended effects.	Expression to help children: 1. compare and contrast styles of art produced by people in different cultures.	Expression to help children: 1. understand the different sources that artists draw upon for their ideas. 2. understand that artists interpret their feelings by developing different ways of presenting them in visual form.
Response to help children: 1. voice descriptions of the qualities they see in works of art and the environment. 2. account for their feelings about works of art and the environment in terms of the visual qualities they find. 3. interpret works of art from more than a single point of view.		Response to help children: 1. understand that art critics and historians help people to perceive qualities in works of art. 2. understand that critics try to account for their feelings about works of art in terms of the qualities they have perceived. 3. compare some of the differences in view points held by critics and historians and how these influence their perception of art.

Note: From State of Ohio Department of Education, Guidelines, p. 68. Reprinted by permission.

Unit Theme: Expressing Feelings in Art
LESSON 6: Non-Representational Art
Grades 4–6
Depth

OBJECTIVES OF THE LESSON
to help children:

1. understand that artists interpret their feelings through non-representational forms.
2. understand that art critics and historians help people to perceive qualities in works of art.
3. interpret their feelings by studying ways of presenting them in nonrepresentational forms.
4. voice descriptions of the qualities they see in works of art.

ACTIVITIES

Explain to the children that some artists, in order to express their feelings, paint pictures in which there is no realistic subject matter and that these are referred to as non-representational paintings.

Prepare a display of non-representational paintings. Encourage the children to study the paintings to sense the feelings they see in the paintings. Ask them to compare paintings which have decidedly different feelings such as Franz Kline's *New York* and Ellsworth Kelly's *Red Blue*. Help them create simple descriptions of the paintings' qualities such as this one by a fourth grade child, "One painting has smooth and clean shapes. The other has ragged and rough shapes."

To help children increase their awareness of how the language which art critics use can lead them to see the qualities in a work of art more sensitively, ask them to read (or read to them) the writings of art critics. One critic who could be read is Rachael Baker. Her description of Stuart Davis' painting, *Owh! In San Pao* can lead children to see how feelings are created by shapes and colors in a non-representational painting. Direct their attention to her use of "qualitative language" consisting of suggestive analogies and well chosen adjectives and adverbs.

She says, "The modern American painter Stuart Davis catches the excitement of a moment of jazz in the vivid painting that is called tantalizingly *Owh! In San Pao.*

"This is a painting of startling contrasts. We see contrasts of shape, size, direction, light and dark, and dazzling contrasts of color.

"Circles are contrasted with squares. Triangles are contrasted with rectangles. Shapes point up, down, sideways, in every direction. Planes tilt at all angles, interestingly, excitingly.

"Light shapes contrasted with dark shapes, and dark shapes contrasted with light shapes seem to move restlessly, incessantly before our eyes.

"Vivid, intense color contrasts startle us, bright yellow, brilliant blue, intense green, burning orange, hot glaring violet purple.

"Unexpected shades jolt us, a circle slashed, a rectangle flaring strangely, a bite taken out of a triangle. No matter where we look, the eye has no rest. We feel change and excitement.

"Though this painting pictures no girls in beaded dress, no couples dancing the Charleston, though it portrays no wail of saxophones, no hot heat of drums still with shapes alone it makes us feel the excitement in some nameless night spot, of a thrilling moment of jazz."*

Invite the children to create their own non-representational paintings as ways to express their feelings.

Encourage them to use "qualitative language" to share with one another the feelings they see in their own work.

VISUAL MATERIALS

Brooks, James. *Rasalus.* Oil. 1959. Whitney Museum of American Art, New York.
Davis, Stuart. *Owh! In San Pao.* Whitney Museum of American Art, New York.
Kelly, Ellsworth. *Red Blue.* Cleveland Museum of Art, Cleveland, Ohio.
Kline, Franz. *New York.* Albright Knox Art Gallery, Buffalo, New York.
Vasarely, Victor. *Composition.* Columbus Gallery of Fine Arts.

---

*Baker, Rachael. "Shapes That Say Owh! In San Pao," *Artist Jr.*, Vol. 7, No. 3, Jan., 1966.

Note: From State of Ohio Department of Education, *Guidelines*, pp. 80–81. Reprinted by permission.

is closer to the orientation we recommend here than most of the other materials on elementary art curriculum currently available. However, the Ohio guide does fairly consistently limit the domain of the visual arts to be explored by children to the museum fine arts and is in that sense a very different format for elementary art than the approach taken in this book.

The 1974 publication by Gordon Plummer entitled *Children's Art Judgment* is subtitled *A Curriculum for Elementary Art Appreciation*. Early in the volume Plummer identifies his work as clearly within the boundaries of the aesthetic education movement when he writes, "What is *still lacking* is a marriage of the two disciplines: *the making* of art with the *criticising, appreciation, and judging* of it."[8] In order to consummate the marriage, he reviews recent writings on ways to implement aesthetic education, empirical researches in art judgment and preference, and some of the other experimental programs in elementary art. He then surveys in chapters the elements of design (line, value, color, etc.), the principles of design (rhythm, balance, etc.) and some of the areas in which pupils might look for art, such as drawing, painting, stained glass, printmaking, sculpture, and photography. Finally, he deals with criticism, suggesting that it must be based on "know-how" and briefly examines some recent styles in art from "abstract composition" to Surrealism.

In each chapter he closes with a suggested "syllabus" for grades one through six, each of which is, in effect, a sample unit plan. Here, for example, is Plummer's unit for grade three from the final chapter on what he calls the affective domain.

Grade 3

Behavioral Objective.   To encourage ideas from master works to be used in the student's own work. To develop individual interpretations. To develop awareness of locations of these original master works where they may be seen.

Presentation.   Show a short film on some famous paintings in a particular museum. Display some famous paintings in reproduction and call attention to them from time to time. Not more than one art period a week should be taken for this activity in the third grade. Appreciation deals with media other than drawing and painting. Show some examples but do not emphasize facts alone. In the work the children are doing, try to relate this to master works on display. Make sure that the works displayed are those seen in the movie film.

Discussion.   Talk about the appreciation of art in everyday life, using the following types of questions: Where can one see some of these master works? Do they have any influence on our life? Should one know about good paintings? Why? Where do you see a master work or a copy of one everyday?

Summation.   Value any move the student makes to correlate his work with the works on display. Do not condemn the student for what seems to be a copy of a master work; rather, encourage this. However, if the student is discouraged when comparing his copy, encourage another, more "derived" attempt (a less literal one).[9]

Plummer's volume is an attempt to implement a combination of art behaviors usually called aesthetic education. However one reacts to his curriculum ideas, it is important to note that the volume clearly illustrates at least one of the traditional attitudes we attempted to identify in chapter 5. There is little doubt that the material supports an elitist approach, a belief that "aesthetic response can be generated only by the fine arts and requires special and unique human qualities."

Plummer states this viewpoint in the following passage from the first chapter:

> Teachers have a responsibility, therefore, to guide the development of taste. Some may be disturbed by the thought that this may be a process of indoctrination of young and highly impressionable minds. Since, however, all education is a process of presenting material that has been chosen by specialists, it is indeed an indoctrination. Teachers present facts for examination by the children who, in turn, form value judgments. The same is true for art objects, and even if the teacher were to refrain from all comment, the children would still conclude something as to quality. The educational process can include the *learning* of what is or is not good art. Certainly this kind of taste is not an inherited trait; rather, it is caused by environmental factors. . . . I do not believe that such learnings could be considered a harmful influence upon the impressionable young mind. Indoctrination, in this sense, *is* valid as an educational process.[10]

This would seem to be the very opposite of the canalized curriculum recommended here, and therefore represents a difference in basic attitude toward both art and the teaching of art.

The Southwest Regional Educational Laboratory elementary art curriculum is a carefully organized, clearly and simply presented sequence of art activities, which can serve as the art program of a school or school district. The ideological premise of the material is that the subject of art, like other school subjects, is a discipline, with significant content which merits instruction no less rigorous than other school subject matter. This viewpoint, which is the attitude structuring the position of much aesthetic education, is easily and quickly apparent in the text of the program.

> The program is based on the premise that all elementary school age children can develop proficiency in these areas. The aim of the program is to build a base of knowledge and skills that will enable children to produce increasingly well-constructed art works of individual character. Beginning with simple techniques, children learn to work with a variety of art materials to create their own individual art works. By observing and analyzing objects and illustrations of objects in the environment, students learn to attend to visual characteristics of the subject matter that can be represented and manipulated in their own work. Students also observe and discuss the works of mature artists and begin to acquire the means to analyze and evaluate works and place them in their appropriate cultural and historical context. More advanced techniques are introduced as the students become more sophisticated in their artistic experience and control, and are able to deal with increasingly subtle and complex ideas and images.[11]

The SWRL program is arranged in a series of eight instructional blocks, each consisting of four units. These blocks, though ungraded, roughly parallel the progress of the pupil through eight school grades. Each activity, several of which make up each unit of instruction, purports to develop a particular skill serving as the focus of that unit. Thus, "A unit consists of a sequence of instructional activities centering on the creation of an art work in a particular medium."[12] There are three types of activities:

> As an *artist*, the child learns basic artistic techniques and concepts and applies them in producing works of art in a variety of media.
>
> As an *art critic*, the child learns to make informed judgments about art works, based on a developing sensitivity to both natural and man-made beauty.
>
> As an *art historian*, the child learns to place art works in their appropriate cultural and historical contexts.[13]

Each unit in the curriculum kit has an accompanying filmstrip with appropriate visuals and extensive supporting text materials. Thus, the elementary teacher has easily available information about the aesthetic qualities and the cultural and historical background of the particular image being viewed and relevant, step-by-step visual and verbal guidance on how to produce the object in question. Figure 113 illustrates one of the activities.

The SWRL art program now being marketed by Phi Delta Kappa's Center for Dissemination of Innovative Programs was developed by a group coordinated by Dwaine Greer. Although the laboratory initially operated with federal funds, part of its original charge was to locate and contract with agencies of the private sector for the marketing of the curriculum materials prepared by the lab, a procedure duplicated in the other federally supported educational labs. Present plans are to continue this series with blocks nine through fourteen and to broaden the venue of the curriculum to include the other arts of music, dance, and drama for a comprehensive arts program.

This program has several unusual virtues or advantages for the elementary school. It is simply and concisely organized. It pays careful attention to pupil behaviors of a critical and historical nature, in addition to production of art. It takes art as a school subject seriously, treating it as a discipline with a body of important content to be learned. It contains in its kit form relevant and illustrative visuals in the form of filmstrips, thus removing from the classroom teacher the burden of locating and bringing the necessary pictorial material into the classroom. It has been used and tested in elementary classrooms, and the results of the testing have been applied to the materials as feedback. It includes historical supporting data for the teacher untrained in art. All of these advantages make this program unusually appealing and highly welcome on the art education scene.

From the theoretical position already established in this volume, the SWRL program also manifests some disadvantages. First, the backbone of the curriculum remains the traditional act of producing art objects. This emphasis is apparent in the definition of a unit, which was quoted previously. It can also be observed in the text of the program under the heading of the purpose of the program filmstrips (see Figure 114). Ultimately, the impact of such an empha-

(continued on page 208)

MODE	*Painting*		
SUBJECT	*Vegetation and Scenes*	UNIT	2
STYLE	*Imaginative*	ACTIVITY	2

TITLE   Colossal Crests

EMPHASIS   The wet chalk technique is used to draw imaginary mountains. Overlapping shapes and changes in color are introduced as means to portray depth.

VOCABULARY	MEDIA SKILLS	VISUALS
Foreground Shade	Chalk: wet chalk on wet paper	Filmstrip

MATERIALS FOR TEACHER	MATERIALS FOR EACH CHILD
1 sheet of 9″ × 12″ manila or white drawing paper Chalk (warm colors: yellows, reds, oranges, browns) Sponge Container of water Wet paper towels Smock (optional)	1 sheet of 9″ × 12″ manila or white drawing paper Sponge Wet paper towels Smock (optional)
	MATERIALS FOR TABLE
	Boxes of chalk (warm colors: yellows, reds, oranges, browns) Containers of water (one for every two children) Covering for work surfaces

PREPARATION

- Set up necessary materials for wet chalk drawing.
- Refill boxes of chalk (see Management Hints).

- Cut paper to size.
- Prepare a place to dry wet papers.
- Cover work tables.

ORIENTATION

Show the Visual Analysis filmstrip pictures of mountains seen at a distance. You may also wish to show children any photographs of mountain ranges you have collected. Remind children that distant objects (in this case mountains) appear higher on the picture plane than those closer to the viewer. Point out the following in the pictures: distant mountains appear "fuzzier" (less distinct) and lighter in color than those closer to the viewer; mountains closer to the viewer appear darker and more distinct than those farther away; the FOREGROUND is that part of the landscape nearest to the viewer. Explain to children that artists often draw mountains in an imaginary way by simplifying or exaggerating the shapes, or by the use of arbitrary colors. Tell them that you will show them how to draw imaginary mountains using wet chalk in warm colors.

DEMONSTRATION

Draw one wet chalk picture in arbitrary warm colors to demonstrate how to make imaginary mountains and foreground giving the illusion of depth. You may wish to draw other mountain shapes on the board using ideas presented in this section.

1. Hold paper either vertically or horizontally.
2. Wet both surfaces of the paper with a sponge before beginning to draw with chalk.
3. Use the side of a light color of chalk to fill the top third of the paper to represent sky. Leave the bottom two-thirds of the paper for representing mountains and foreground.
4. Choose three shades of one color (e.g., a light, a medium and a dark red), or three colors of different shades (e.g., light color, yellow; medium color, orange; dark color, violet) to draw mountains. Define SHADE as the degree of darkness of a color.
5. Use the lightest shade to draw the farthest distant mountains overlapping the bottom edge of the sky color and covering the center third of the paper. Mountains can be jagged, rounded, pyramid, rectangular or other exaggerated or simplified shapes.
6. Use a medium shade to draw the middle range of mountains overlapping parts of the farthest range, with their base a bit farther down the paper.
7. Use the darkest shade to draw the nearest range of mountains. Overlap parts of both the middle range and farthest distant mountains leaving one third to one fourth of the paper for flat foreground. Blend medium and light shades to represent the foreground.

Save demonstration picture for reference in Activity 4.

3
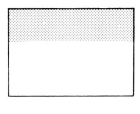 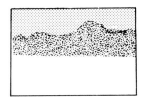

5
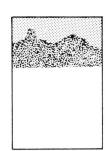 

6
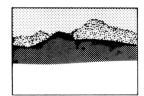

7

(continued)

Figure 113 *(continued)*

ACTIVITY

Have children make their own imaginary mountain drawings, using variations and combinations of shapes presented. Encourage variety in portrayal of mountains. Tell children that in the finished picture most or all of the paper should be covered with chalk. Save children's drawings for reference in Activity 4.

GUIDANCE

Remind children to keep paper and/or chalk wet during drawing, but to avoid scrubbing the paper with the sponge. Check to see that changes of color and overlapping of shapes occur to give the illusion of depth.

EVALUATION

1. Simplified or exaggerated shapes are used to portray imaginary mountains.
2. Arbitrary warm colors are used.
3. Mountain shapes are overlapped to give the illusion of depth.
4. Color changes are used on mountain shapes to give the illusion of depth.
5. The picture plane is divided so that part of the area represents sky, and part represents mountains and foreground.
6. The drawing is done with the wet chalk technique.
7. Most or all of the paper is covered with chalk.

Note: From Greer, *SWRL Elementary Art Program*, p. 18. Reprinted by permission of the Southwest Regional Educational Laboratory.

sis on the pupil is to reinforce the view of art as a special and "precious" activity, performed with special materials by special people known as artists. The inclusion of natural objects in the purview of worthwhile visual experiences, while a healthy step, does not go as far as it might to broaden the acceptable breadth for visual aesthetic experience. Neither does the use of embroidered garments from Guatemala or masks from West Africa, which might be seen as "exotica" unrelated to the folk and popular arts of the pupil's own cultural context. Therefore, the second objection to the SWRL program is the somewhat parochial nature of much of its content. Ronald Silverman, in the California Art Education Association newsletter, notes that the program "reflects both the qualitative nature of great art and significant aesthetic components within natural and manmade objects." He continues by saying that children using this program "will be guided to analyze 1500 art works from major collections. In all they will see almost 6000 images which will alert them to aesthetic qualities in the environment as well as in established works of art."[14] Figure 115 provides examples of activities involving analysis of art objects. As impressive as the statistics quoted by Silverman undoubtedly are—and it should be understood that the magnitude of visual experiences in this program is impressive and valuable—one can only regret that the breadth of objects pictured and

114. Summary of program filmstrips from SWRL

	VISUAL ANALYSIS FILMSTRIPS	PRODUCTION FILMSTRIPS	CRITICAL ANALYSIS FILMSTRIPS
Purpose	To show objects in the environment that can serve as subject matter for student art works. Characteristic features and relationships in the objects are pointed out in detail.	To show the teacher how to demonstrate the art production activities, augmenting the procedures described in the A&M Guides,* and to show examples of completed products.	To show examples of works by adult artists that exhibit characteristics related to the works the students themselves have created. These examples serve as a basis for discussing (describing, interpreting, analyzing, and comparing) the qualities in both the student and adult artist productions.
When Used	Previewed by the teacher, then presented to students during the instructional acitvity.	Viewed by the teacher before the beginning of the instructional activity while reviewing activity procedures in the A&M Guide.	Previewed by the teacher, then presented to students as needed during the instructional activity to stimulate discussion of artistic concepts and techniques.
Related Print Materials	The Visual Analysis section of the A&M Guide.*	The Demonstration section of the A&M Guide.	The Critical Analysis Guides.

Note: From Greer, *SWRL Elementary Art Program,* p. 18. Reprinted by permission of the Southwest Regional Educational Laboratory.
      *The A&M (Activities and Materials) Guides are documents that provide additional information on art processes recommended in various SWRL units.

studied does not include those materials which surround our youngsters today and which can readily serve as a starting point for their understanding of their own present responses and future aesthetic experiences.

A third disadvantage of this program is its neglect of the kinds of information this volume views as critical to the study of art as a school subject. The program omits consideration of ideas about the nature of aesthetic response to all objects in the environment, the heart of what is seen here as basic art content in the school. To simplify (and, perhaps, oversimplify) these two ideological orientations, the SWRL program and all the others currently available study

UNIT 2   Image Analysis: Suggested Activities

ACTIVITY 1 (*Visual Essay*)

Twelve art objects (paintings and fabrics) that are "warm" colored are shown. Red, orange, yellow, and colors that contain them are considered "warm." These colors suggest warmth. Artists use this effect when creating images.

> Show all 12 frames, pausing briefly at each image. Then turn off the projector. Ask how these images are all alike. When someone suggests similar colors, turn on the projector and reshow the images in reverse order (back to frame 1). Ask students to name the major colors in each image.

> Show frame 1. Ask students to list adjectives for this image; list the words on the chalkboard. Be sure students give words derived from viewing the image. If unsure, ask students to come to the screen and point out the particular source *in the image*. Repeat this activity for four or five more frames. Turn off the projector and discuss word similarities from the list. "Warm" adjectives will probably predominate. Discuss the reason: warm colors are suggestive of warm things in general.

> Discuss warm colors and their meanings with the class. The sun, fire, and other sources of warmth are suggested by predominately red, orange, and yellow colors. These colors are more bright, exciting, or vibrant, and are used to depict things with those characteristics.

ACTIVITY 2 (*Visual Essay*)

Thirteen art objects (paintings and fabrics) that are "cool" colored are shown. Blue, green, gray, and colors that contain them are considered "cool." These colors suggest a lack of warmth. Artists use this color effect when creating images.

> Show all 13 frames without comment, pausing briefly at each image. Then turn off the projector. Ask how the images are all alike. When someone suggests similar colors, turn on the projector and reshow the images in reverse order (back to frame 1). Ask students to name the major colors in each frame.

> Show frame 1. Ask students to list descriptive adjectives for this image; list the words on the chalkboard. Be sure students give words derived from the image. If unsure, ask students to come to the screen and point out the particular source *in the image*. Repeat this activity for four or five additional frames. Turn off the projector and discuss word similarities from the list. "Cool" adjectives will probably predominate. Discuss the reason; cool colors are suggestive of cool things in general.

> Discuss cool colors and their meanings with the class. The sky, water, grass, and other sources of coolness are suggested by predominately blue, green, and gray colors. These colors are more placid, sad, or stable, and are used to depict things with those characteristics.

UNIT 2   Cultural-Historical Context

ACTIVITIES 1 AND 2

That color affects our state of being in different ways is commonly accepted in our society. Interior decorators create colorful environments designed to soothe or excite us, and advertisers skillfully employ color to sell products.

Some cultures of the past have believed that color not only affects us psychologically, but has a direct effect on our physical body.

Visual artists are keenly aware that color affects the viewer. They deliberately use color to elicit specific responses, and the communication involved depends to a large extent upon the viewer's symbolic and psychological understanding of color.

Many of the meanings commonly attached to colors in our culture are deeply rooted in the past. For example, policemen probably wear blue uniforms because the Romans dressed their servants in that color. Similarly, black as mourning, red as danger, and yellow for quarantine are all firmly rooted in the past.

The color red is a warm color and suggests blood, health, friendship, danger, and rage. Christmas, St. Valentine's Day, and the American flag are associated with red in our culture. Orange, another warm color, indicates autumn, exuberance, Thanksgiving, Halloween, and joviality. In Hindu and Buddhist culture and art, orange symbolizes a surrender of tensions. Yellow, a third warm color, symbolizes sunset, vitality, cheerfulness and high spirit, but also caution. Green, a cool color, is associated with nature, water, refreshment, and rest. However, it also suggests disease, ghastliness, and terror. Blue, another cool color, symbolizes royalty, water, ice, sky, contemplation, melancholy, gloom, and fearfulness. Purple, a third cool color, suggests mystery, royalty, dignity, loneliness, desperation, shadows, and misty atmosphere. White is associated with light, winter, purity, and brightness of spirit. Black indicates darkness, emptiness, mourning, depression, negation of spirit, and death.

In thinking about these cultural meanings, it is clear that colors have different symbolic meanings depending upon their context. Visual artists deliberately create contexts in which symbolic meaning of color is appropriate and supportive of subject matter or form.

Pablo Picasso's "Portrait of Sebastian Innes Vidal" and David Tenier's "The Smoker" illustrate how artists use color to communicate moods and ideas.

In Picasso's painting a cool blue tonality dominates. The blueness of the painting is intensified by a contrasting small, bright red spot. The overall mood is one of melancholia and gloom. Using blue to suggest this mood heightens the expressive power of the painting.

In David Tenier's painting a golden brown tonality dominates. A cool white cloth provides contrast to emphasize the figures' warmth and earthy vigor. The two people in the painting express enjoyment of physical pleasure. Yellow and red colors are used in their faces to heighten the feeling of vitality and cheerfulness. No melancholia or contemplation is evident in Tenier's painting.

Note: From Greer, *SWRL Elementary Art Program,* pp. 12–13. Reprinted by permission of the Southwest Regional Educational Laboratory.

art; the recommendation here is to study visual aesthetic experience in order to more effectively study art. It is an oddity of history (as we saw in our reference to Barkan's writing in chapter 6) that the first concept of art teaching is called aesthetic education, when it patently avoids attention to matters of aesthetic import.

These objections notwithstanding, the SWRL art program, even more than the Ohio art guide and the Plummer volume, provides the elementary teacher with thoughtful and contemporary curriculum ideas. The limitations in all three of these programs seem to be the result of misdirected theory and the need to compromise with current practice. Let us take the second problem first. Publicly sponsored projects such as the Ohio art guide and the SWRL program must be responsive in some measure to public expectations. Even if the collective authors of these projects were to agree unreservedly with the position of this book—that studio production should be greatly curtailed as a *required* class activity—the expectations of teachers, administrators, parents, and the pupils themselves would demand that it be kept on and emphasized in the mandatory curriculum. After all, if our children do not bring home clay pots and crayon drawings, it is obvious that they are not "studying" art. Further, there is no evidence in previous writings that any members of the groups that prepared these documents do think precisely the way this volume does about productive activities.

The problem of misdirected theory is less easily explained. Although there is considerable agreement among art educators that the valuational definition of aesthetic experience, particularly as it has been developed by Dewey, (the preference of this volume), is the most plausible, it is rare that its implications are carefully applied. If we accept that aesthetic response is the general human behavior of which response to art is one (albeit special) instance, then it is reasonable that the proper initial focus of art study must be on the general response. To restrict the content of what is examined in the art class to the fine arts, or to unduly emphasize their importance, is to distort or negate the educational consequences of this view of the nature of aesthetic experience.

What all three of the programs reviewed here do succeed in doing is to present a view of art as a serious academic study, a position long overdue in the field. This increasingly recognized view is also reflected in the ideological stance of the J. Paul Getty Trust, which sponsored the 1983 Summer Institute in Los Angeles for elementary teachers and administrators. The institute represents a first step in what is hoped to be a substantial and influential reordering of curricular priorities in the field toward a view of school art as a serious subject that must be systematically taught and studied.

The reader is urged to examine and assess the programs described in this chapter, as well as other elementary art curriculum suggestions found in the Bibliography and elsewhere, before making a choice of teaching practice. However, it is hoped that the theories and recommended practices of this volume will be that choice.

CHAPTER 9

newer media
and
elementary art

In order to provide only those materials judged to be critical to the task of teaching elementary art, this volume has kept its contents brief and relevant. Therefore, devoting an entire chapter to one particular domain of art media should impress the reader with the importance attached here to its potential. No other area of art media is as inherently exciting for pupils, as rampant with educational possibilities, and, regrettably, as unrecognized and unattended to by art education as the newer media.

Since the 1965 Newer Media in Art Education Project,[1] the term "newer media" has meant those concepts and mechanisms developed and used for the most part during the present century that collectively constitute a new and significant area of art forms or dramatically enhance the teaching of the arts. These newer concepts and mechanisms include, for example, television, videotape recording, motion pictures, slide and slide-tape sequences, and photography, although media such as slides and photography are hardly new to art and art education, except as they are defined here. This is not to suggest that the "older" media such as paint, clay, and crayons are any less worthy for their age. All media have merit insofar as they can help to expand the horizons of the aesthetically literate consumer of art. It is simply that these newer media appear to deserve special attention because of their unique qualities and their infrequency of use in the teaching of art.

A SURVEY OF THE NEWER MEDIA

A quick survey of these media should provide a firm basis for further discussion of their possible uses in the elementary curriculum. The following classifications are to some extent arbitrary and made for the purposes of clarity and convenience. In the main, however, they are substantive.

projected media

Perhaps the most prolific and versatile of the newer media are those which are literally projected on a screen. The simplest and most widespread is the *slide*. Ever present in our visual society and long the backbone of art history classes, the slide simply stores and reproduces a single pictorial unit. What is new is the arrangement of a series of slides in a dramatic or visual rather than informational sequence, with implications as an art form. Adding to such a sequence the element of sound in the form of a disc or audiotape, the *slide-sound sequence* becomes an art form something like the motion picture and television, but different enough to have its own unique character and potential.

Most relevant to the classroom is the fact that a slide-sound sequence is one of the least expensive newer media forms. Cameras for making slides can be moderately priced, "instamatic," fixed-focus mechanisms, and many pupils might have the use of family cameras of this type. Also, audiotape machines are by now part of every school's audio-visual inventory. Professional or existing homemade slides can be used for the sequence, or elementary pupils can easily make slides from any flat pictorial material such as books, magazines, and reproductions by using a unit such as the Kodak Ektographic Visual Maker Kit. This process uses a Kodak Instamatic camera with a special lens, flash bulbs, and a tripod-like platform and does not require the user to compute or adjust the lens opening or time of the shot. At first under supervision and later on their own, even primary children can make successful slides for a sequence.

Sound can be added to the sequence from commercial phonograph records with a record player or from a tape recorder, which would handle spoken narrative, music, or any form of sound. The addition of the factor of sound to visual stimuli completely changes the quality of the aesthetic experience, providing cues to the understanding and interpretation of what is seen different enough to make the slide-sound sequence a unique art form.

The *filmstrip* is essentially a series of slides on a single strip of film, projected on a screen by a special filmstrip projector or filmstrip adapter on a slide projector. The obvious advantage of a filmstrip is the ease of storage and handling of a sequence of visual and verbal units on a single strip of film. Its disadvantage is that the sequence is fixed and cannot be changed. Thus the filmstrip is more notable as an instructional device than as an art form.

The *motion picture* (or film, cinema, or movie) is another so-called newer media form and one that has been treated in the school almost exclusively as an instructional device. Nevertheless, it has a considerable potential as an art medium in itself. These possibilities will be discussed later in this chapter. Happily, there are ample resources of good quality films on art and films as art to use in the classroom. Furthermore, technology and commerce have furnished cameras and projectors that are reasonably low-priced, easy to operate, and of adequate quality for most artistic requirements in the school situation. The elementary teacher can contact school district or county audio-visual personnel for information on available or appropriate equipment.

A further notable special feature in film hardware is the film cartridge projector. With a built-in rear screen capacity or as a wall screen projector, these machines function in the same way as an audio cassette player, using a loop film cartridge or cassette. They provide simplicity of handling so great that they can be used as self-instructional devices even by the youngest school child. Unfortunately, all such mechanisms or "hardware" are dependent upon supporting "software"—the films, tapes, and cassettes—available commercially for the size of projector or recorder, and the range of film cartridges on art for this equipment is quite limited. The teacher cannot easily make these materials, as in the case of audiotape or videotape, as we shall see later in this chapter.

Film as an art form combines the input of moving sequential visual images, words, and music all in one art form which the individual appears to perceive as a kind of substitute life experience—a type of reality other art forms do not as successfully provide. Film is obviously a very special twentieth-century art form, very much a part of the aesthetic lives of the young (especially through the offices of television) and well worth our concern in art education.

Overhead and *opaque projections* are also available newer media, though their applications in teaching art are relatively limited. The overhead projector is an arrangement of light source and lenses in a unit the size of a desk top. The image is projected from a 9 × 12″ specially prepared acetate transparency. The advantage of this machine is that one can superimpose one transparency over another and even write or diagram on them with wax pencil. Diagramming the composition of a painting or building, for example, is quite easy in this medium. On the other hand, transparencies of art works must be prepared commercially and the range of such software in the art area is severely limited. In the late 1960s there was a short flurry of activity in developing art transparencies, but their fragility and difficulty of storage as compared with slides seemed to curtail this growth.

The opaque projector is a larger machine, though still portable, which can project any flat pictorial material on to a screen. It does not require transparencies; any book, magazine, or drawn or painted image can be utilized. As with the overhead projector, the person projecting can add writing or drawing to the image before or during the projection. However, the rather cumbersome size of the machine and its relatively imperfectly reproduced image have kept the opaque projector an infrequently used audio-visual item in an art context.

A final projected media process of note for us here is *holography.* By the use of laser beam projection of a specially prepared slide, the holographic projection shoots a three-dimensional image into space, an image one can walk around and look at on all sides. The relevance of this process to art, so much of which is in three-dimensional form (for example, sculpture, architecture, and many crafts), is apparent; yet little has been done commercially in this direction. The process known as "solid photography," developed in 1976, is an interesting step. In it multiple cameras electronically transfer any three-dimensional image to a computer controlling the sculpting of that image in a fully round, precise reproduction. An exact replica of Michelangelo's *Pieta* or an authentic model of the Parthenon could be provided as art study objects for the schools by this technique. However, the unavoidable loss of scale or size and its attendant distortion of aesthetic impact would—at least in theory— dilute the educational uses of such models.

television and videorecording

The possibilities of television and, particularly, of videotape recording (VTR) have also largely been overlooked by art education. The video process in general, which is now a major information, entertainment, and advertising industry, intrudes into almost every home and exists in one form or another in almost every school. Although television operates in broadcast and closed circuit or cable systems, perhaps its most important contribution to art teaching is to be found in its videorecording and playback capability. Any broadcast or cable program can be recorded and replayed at a later time, although questions of copyright infringement inherent in this process have not yet been settled in the courts. A videocamera unit on a videorecorder can film in color and sound any scene to which the camera can be taken. In the sense, therefore, of most definitions of motion pictures, the portable video system enables pupils to make movies with several considerable advantages over the movie camera. The videotape is, in effect, processed as it is shot; there is no waiting period for film processing. Furthermore, the monitor or camera viewer allows the final picture rather than the scene being filmed to be viewed as it is being shot. There is no problem of sound since visual and audio are recorded together and thus automatically synchronized. Videotape can be erased like audiotape and used repeatedly and can easily be reproduced. Broadcast or cable material of either a commercial or an educational nature can be recorded and used or mixed with pupil-made tape.

Videotape has some disadvantages, such as the relatively high price of videosystems and videotape as compared with cameras and film. It is hoped that wider use and greater sales will ultimately lower this cost. More serious from a technical sense is the difficulty of editing videotape. Unlike movie film, which can be cut and manually reconnected, videotape must be edited by re-recording, most easily with a separate video-editing machine. This factor, in turn, raises the price of a videosystem. However, weighing together all of these considerations, videorecording is still the single most valuable newer media contribution to art teaching. Its unquestioned facility for providing access to a wide range of visual and verbal materials (theoretically, anything that is broadcast, projected, or observed can be recorded) makes it the potentially ideal single media system for the school and for art activities. The number of excellent educational broadcasts related to art grows each year and these might be recorded and used in the school. Pupils can see a well-made tour of the Louvre or films made by children at or near their grade level in another state or their own video productions, all on one equipment system. In theory at least, videorecording replaces slide-sound, motion pictures, filmstrips, and overhead and opaque projection, though each of these processes has its own unique virtues.

reproduced media

This category represents some of the oldest of the newer media. It includes *paperback books,* which became popular and numerous in the 1940s. What is new about paperbacks is that they now represent a large part of what is printed, are available with good quality visuals, and are reasonable in price as com-pared with hardbound volumes. Thus they provide a resource of considerable breadth for those teaching art. A second such medium is the *flat reproduction.* Again, this is not a new form except in terms of quality and scope. As with slides, though not in such profusion, much of the art of the past and present is available in good quality and reasonably priced reproductions for school use. Interestingly enough, there is a firm in West Germany which apparently can reproduce paintings with such authentic duplication of canvas, pigments, brushstrokes, and so forth, as to confuse even the experts on art forgery. Also, a museum team has reproduced, with careful photography, Michelangelo's Sistine ceiling at one-third of its original scale, so that one might see this work by visiting New York City rather than Rome. A third reproduced medium in limited but useful numbers is the *three-dimensional reproduction.* Since so many visual art works are in the round or part-round, this type of material is highly important to art teaching. However, with those three-dimensional works of art too large to be duplicated in actual size, the critical aesthetic factor of scale is lost. It might be said with justification that there is no way to properly experience Auguste Rodin's *Burghers of Calais* or the massive scale of the walls of a Gothic cathedral except with the same size of reproduction. There are, after all, some things media cannot do.

Nevertheless, three-dimensional materials such as the Boston Children's Museum suitcase exhibits (in which careful three-dimensional reproductions, in scale for the most part, and explanatory verbal materials on the arts of a particular culture are packaged in a suitcase for loan to schools and other learning situations) are available in some communities. Once again, greater use of reproductions of this sort would insure their expansion of coverage of art in the round and the lessening of their cost as well.

Photography is also in one sense a reproduced medium, one that is familiar to all of us and far from new. What is fairly recent is its school use, not only as a means of teaching art but as an art form itself. Even twenty years ago, photography classes in the high school were fairly rare. This is no longer the case. As with the motion picture, the technology of photography has given us easy-to-use cameras at reasonable prices and many children have access to such cameras at home.

Although photography is not a widespread part of the elementary art curriculum today, it is present in many experimental situations in the schools and most certainly a well-established part of the art world. Museums often have photography exhibits and some even have permanent photography galleries. Photography exhibits are reviewed in the news media and the photographer is looked at by most of us as a legitimate artist. The demise of the big picture magazines has curtailed somewhat our easy access to large numbers of first-rate photographs, but newspapers and other magazines today are heavily visual as a compensation. Photography is unquestionably an appropriate medium for art activities in the classroom and one that younger children will find contemporary, provocative, and well within their capability to handle.

Unless there is a resident art specialist in the school or a teacher among the faculty who is adequately knowledgeable about photography, it is recommended that the classroom teacher use a simple, fixed-focus, "instamatic" camera of any make and follow the process of developing the film and making prints with the pupils on the most basic level. Each elementary school should have a darkroom as part of its media facilities. This is by no means as expensive as it sounds; a usable darkroom containing an enlarger and equipment for developing film can be set up even in a large closet—preferably with a sink—and can cost as little as a few hundred dollars.

programmed instruction

The decade of the 1960s saw an explosion of interest in programmed instruction, the orderly, progressive, consistently reinforced sequencing of bits of information. The programmed instruction approach grew out of the testing materials and machines of psychologist Sidney Pressey in the 1920s and was supported by the learning theories of B. F. Skinner and others in the 1950s. As interest expanded in this process, increasingly sophisticated machines were developed to administer the program to the pupil.

The theory and practice of programmed instruction is based on the following principles: (1) reducing the knowledge to be learned to its smallest discrete bits of information; (2) sequencing these bits so that learning bit B depends upon learning bit A; (3) organizing the knowledge so that the learner can control the rate of study; (4) continually reinforcing the learning by the intrinsic reward of success; and (5) intermittently testing both to monitor learning and to reinforce it. It is not difficult to see that this process is a strong idea for educational efficiency, provided what is to be learned is didactic or informational in nature. Although there are large areas of this sort even in elementary art, including historical, critical, and technical information, art educators have emphasized attitudinal learning and looked upon programmed instruction as only minimally relevant to their field. Thus very little was done in art programmed material during or since that time. It is quite reasonable to suggest, of course, that programmed instruction was in many ways part of the development of performance-based and competency-based education and is in this way very much still with us even in art education.

As interest in programmed instruction dwindled, the teaching machines were set aside, but a few *written programs,* the software of the approach, can be examined as illustrative of the procedure. Figure 116 is one small portion of a written program for elementary art on the subject of color in art as part of the pupils' technical information. As one can readily see, the information is carefully sequenced and undeniably useful. However, art educators most commonly believe that this type of knowledge can be taught or learned more easily and effectively during the process of making works of art, rather than in the comparative artistic vacuum of a program.

A second type of programmed instruction involved *computer-assisted learning.* Fundamentally any use of a computer qualified in this category. Most frequently the computer was used in conjunction with a program, for both motivation and testing. The discomfort of art educators with programmed instruction in general was even more acute in the case of computer-assisted instruction, and no situation in which elementary art is being taught in this fashion has been publicized. Nevertheless, there is considerable experimentation with art programs using the video screen and computer for self-instructional learning. In such systems, the computer can be programmed to review and correct the patterns created by the learner.

One such program was developed by Philip E. Callahan. His computerized tutoring design program evaluates certain electronically drawn images representing *balance* and *positive and negative space* (see Figure 117). First the student is drilled with selectable routines emphasizing these design factors. Then he or she attempts an electronic drawing visualizing the first element studied. As each routine is completed, the student attempts an electronic drawing visualizing the element identified in the next routine. The electronic drawing is done by depressing a particular computer terminal key which, in turn, moves a drawing cursor on the video display screen, allowing the student to create or erase points or lines on the screen. Once the student completes a drawing, the image is evaluated and the results displayed on the screen in numerical equivalents, such as "Negative space exceeds Positive by 89 percent" (see Figure 117). This numerical analysis provides a quantitative base for comparing further explorations.

116. A page from a programmed instructional package

9. Color helps you to describe different kinds of objects, so that other people know exactly what you are talking about. When you say "My bike is blue", "The tree is green", "The evening sky is red", you are _____ three different kinds of things, the bike, the tree and the sky.

9. describing

10. There are many, many colors of paint. To teach you how to mix your own colors of paint we have chosen 3 main colors. We will call these first three colors **primary colors.** We will use these _____ _____ to begin to study color.

10. primary colors

11.

The first letters of 3 **primary colors** are shown on this chart. You already know and can recognize these

_____ _____

as red, yellow and blue.

11. primary colors

12. When you want to paint a picture of the leaves on a tree and have just the primary colors (red, yellow and blue) you can mix a new color, green. You can make green by_____ the primary yellow with the primary blue.

12. mixing

13. When you mix two primary colors such as blue and yellow together, the result is a new color green. We call this new color green a secondary color. Green is a _____ _____.

13. secondary color

14. Green is made by_____ blue and yellow paints.

14. mixing

15. Another secondary color is made by ___(a)___ red and **yellow** together. Red and yellow are two of the ___(b)___ colors.

15. a) mixing
    b) primary

16. The name of this new secondary color is orange. We make it from red and yellow. Orange is not one of the primary colors. It is a _____ color.

16. secondary

17. Purple is another **secondary color** that is made by mixing two primary colors. It is made by mixing blue with _____ .

17. red

Note: From Florence Hayner, *Elementary Color* (Rochester, N.Y.: Graflex, Inc., 1963), p. 2. Reprinted by permission of Telex Communications, Inc. (formerly Graflex, Inc.)

117. The patterns on these video display screens show the kinds of designs students learn to develop in Callahan's computerized tutoring design program. Courtesy of Philip E. Callahan

Assisted by an increasing volume of advertising in all the news media, some art educators are hailing the computer as the new panacea that will cure all the "ailments" of art teaching, in the same way that its ancestor, the teaching machine, was greeted as the savior of education two decades ago. Just as the earlier mechanism did not succeed in accomplishing everything its proponents predicted, so the computer is unlikely to achieve all that its supporters claim it will. Nevertheless, one can create images of a sort on the computer; it can respond to our actions insofar as we can program such responses; and, further, no one can foresee just how sophisticated these possibilities might become with future advances in technology.

One exotic and visionary use of the computer as a visual and verbal data storage device was described in 1966.

CLASS: "The Visual Arts in World Cultures."
PLACE: Any American high school.

At 10:23, Mr. Dobbs, the art teacher, begins his second lecture to the visual arts lecture group of 30 pupils. [Although the Federal Education Act of 1972 restricted class size to a maximum of 18 pupils, lecture groups of up to 40 students are permissible under the law.] Having dealt with primitive habitations and post and lintel construction in architectural design during the first lecture, he is ready to describe the discovery and uses of the arch as a building principle. As he presents his ideas, he presses the button marked *visual* on his wrist-band instrument panel. The room lights dim and the classroom screen glows with 3-D color images of the Coliseum, the Arch of Titus, the aqueduct at Segovia, etc. The silken tones and fine diction of Richard Burton take over the lecture from Mr. Dobbs with a synopsis of factual data about the structures. At the appropriate moment diagram overlays analyzing the directions of stress appear on the screen. At this point several students tap the photo duplication button on their desk instrument panels: the diagrammatic analysis on the screen in color photocopy form will be a useful illustration in their note book projects. By the end of the lecture session each of the students has selected an individual or small group project for the following study period. Several have chosen programmed sequences presenting architectual history in greater detail, to be viewed on their individual desk units; some will work together on a series of models of arch-structured buildings, others on group murals; two younger students have elected to prepare a sound 8 mm film on the "Uses of the Arch as a Decorative Motif in our Community." Meanwhile, Mr. Dobbs jots down a reminder to request that film clips from the movie set restoration of the Hadrianic Baths at Lepcis Magna (from the Hollywood epic "Goddesses of the Western World") be stored in the school district computer memory banks. Next school quarter, this lecture will be improved by the extra visuals—though without the goddesses, of course, he tells himself.[2]

Obviously it will be many years before the visual arts are of sufficient importance in public education to warrant the expense necessary to develop a system of this sort. We should note, however, that a Japanese firm did market a mechanism to obtain still photographs in black and white from the televised screen image. What seemed to be fantasy or science fiction in 1966 became a mundane fact a few years later.

A third type of programming quite different from the first two is the *multi-media package*. Any systematic scheme for presenting information is essentially a "program" (for example, a textbook), and a multi-media kit presents such an outline of information through more than one medium. Since the information to be learned has to be very carefully and systematically arranged or programmed in order to be presented by several media, the product is classified as programmed material, even though all the criteria of sequencing, reinforcing, and testing are not always met in these packages. The simplest illustration of this medium is the slide-sound combination, as in the case of a slide sequence on a slide projector with accompanying audiotape on a tape recorder. Compact units are also available on the market, with a built-in slide-sound capacity. Even filmstrips with frames having verbal content are in a very rudimentary fashion multi-media packages, as are films with a spoken text. Usually, however, the process refers to a package or kit with two separate media sources concurrently presenting the desired material.

While there are relatively few multi-media packages in art as compared with other subject areas, some have been developed. Much more prevalent several years ago was the use of this instructional medium as an art technique. Artists designed and exhibited multi-media presentations with several simultaneous images on one or more screens, often with sound. Today, the technique as an art form has lost its popularity, but it might still be a provocative idea for use with elementary pupils.

A last technique in this category is, like multi-media kits, programmed only in the sense of its careful preparation. This is the *single concept loop film*. Using the rear screen or wall loop projector (usually 8 or Super 8 mm. in size), which was previously described under "Projected Media," the single concept film tries to do just what its name implies. It presents a single process or a very limited segment of information in visual as well as verbal terms. Its function like most items in this category is self-instructional and since the film cartridge holds under five minutes of film in a loop, it can be left running to be seen several times to ensure that the concept is learned.

Most single concept art films deal with technical art processes, though any content reducible to single concepts is, of course, appropriate. Like other newer media described in this chapter, the problem here is again the one of range of software available. Unless, as in the case of the VTR, the teacher can make his or her own materials, art teaching is dependent upon commercial sources for software, and since art is only a very limited part of the curriculum, the range of such sources is not as great as one might wish. For this reason and for other reasons noted in this section, it is recommended that art and classroom teachers concentrate on television and VTR if these systems are available.

NEWER MEDIA AS CONTENT AND METHOD

None of these media are essentially visual art forms; media such as film and television are basically dramatic forms, especially in their sequential or linear character. On the other hand, there is no theoretical or practical reason why art teachers or classroom teachers teaching art cannot use these media to promote the ends of art education. That they have not done so to more than a very limited extent is more than a little puzzling, particularly in the light of the easy acceptance of newer media such as photography and motion pictures as bona fide art forms by both the erudite and the popular press. In any case, these media unquestionably pervade today's society and represent excellent examples of art forms with which all the pupils of any level, class, or region are thoroughly familiar. The child who has never knowingly seen a lithograph or a bronze sculpture or a mural painting has seen enormous numbers of photographed media and electronic media even before starting kindergarten. Thus, newer media can be a fine source for developing canalized curricula, literally starting instruction on the present level of the learner. Further, for many in the arts, these media constitute an intrinsically significant art form—one which is not only extensively available, close to the everyday experience of the young, but, indeed, capable of powerful aesthetic impact as a work of art. If for no other reason, the last one alone should ensure our attentiveness to these media in the classroom.

What can be done with these media in the teaching of art? Let us start with the most valuable medium of them all, videotape recording. The following video projects are recommended not as "sure fire" panaceas, but as models on which the careful teacher can build elementary art curriculum.

using the VTR in the classroom

The format for curriculum planning that was employed in the previous chapter is used again here; the following projects are examples—in this case without grade-level designation—of looking, talking, making, and reading activities.

1. *Stained Glass.* A television program concerning stained glass as a craft form appears on the local or state educational broadcasting channel. It is videotaped by the teacher or the district audio-visual people (with appropriate permission) and shown to the class. Discussion centers on how stained glass is made, the various uses to which it might be put, and its particular and unique aesthetic qualities. Pupils are encouraged to note and report details and locations of examples of stained glass they find in their community. When possible or desirable, pupils can photograph those examples which are not easily accessible so that others in the class might see them.

2. *Classic Film.* In the same way, a videotape of Robert Flaherty's film *Man of Aran* can be made from a broadcast of the film and screened for the class. Discussion might focus on the hardships the Aran islanders face daily, the cinematic ways in which Flaherty dramatized their lives, and—if pupils appear to be interested in pursuing this direction—the function of film in exploring how people confront and negotiate their physical and social environments. An art specialist or knowledgeable classroom teacher could develop the second point, Flaherty's technical treatment of the content, into an examination of basic design concepts when this material appears appropriate to the particular class.

3. *Building Construction.* Prepared by careful in-class planning, a group or entire class can make use of the videorecorder's mobility by visiting a local building site (preferably, but not necessarily, a private house) several times, filming some of the steps of building construction, interviewing the

workmen, and recording, with picture and sound, explanations of the functions of plans, blueprints, construction machines, skilled trades, and so forth. The completed videotape, along with ancillary materials prepared by the pupils, such as drawings, models, and photographs of the building project, can be presented to other classes in the school.

Of course, the same project can be done with a movie camera as well as with a videorecorder. However, the disadvantages of film are revealed by the procedures of a project such as this one. Not only is there a cumbersome time lag while movie film is developed, but there is the problem—except with specialized and expensive equipment—of synchronizing sound with picture. Film cannot be erased and used again, while the videotape can simply be reused for other projects repeatedly. The drawback of videotape editing, on the other hand, is probably best solved by obtaining again the assistance of district audiovisual personnel. In fact, editing the videotape could well be a class or small group art project involving a visit to the audio-visual facility and participation in the editing process. Also, the class or pupil group involved in such a project can be organized into a production team, with some pupils handling the camera, others monitoring sound, preparing scripts—in the sense of planning sequences to be taped—locating necessary materials, or narrating. The potential for a multitude of learnings, many unrelated to art, of course, will be obvious to the reader.

4. *The Television Story.* Opportunities for imaginative humor, dramatic invention, or psychological or social problem examination are endless within the format of a short—up to fifteen minutes—television story, written, produced, acted, and filmed by pupils. Unlike most studio art media, this activity is usually a collective, cooperative enterprise and promotes the values inherent in such school processes. Also, making a videotape requires only very minimal manipulative skill rather than art skills per se. Examples of a television story might be what happens to and how it feels to be a new pupil in a school or a situation comedy about a family of Martians living in the pupils' community and what they might find amusing in that environment.

For those who worry about the issue that this project does not seem to be about art and is, in fact, more drama than art in process, we can be quickly reassuring. Just as filmmakers and television directors attend to the visual arrangements of the screened images, to the extent that such care is relevant or within the limits of their competence, children can be led to see that all the artistic factors of their screened pictures can help to make their programs more effective in promoting the ideas, emotions, or information they wish to convey. For example, sharp contrasts of value (dark and light) usually elicit a greater intensity of response to a particular scene than an even lighting overall. In the sense that we mean it here, this dramatic quality is the same in a Rembrandt portrait as in a television scene that is meant to be intense. Thus factors of aesthetic character can be learned as well from the television screen as from the usual art materials common to present elementary art activities. The deciding element is the teacher's effort to direct the attention of pupils to these factors.

5. *Commercial Advertising.*   Videotapes made by the teacher, or at the teacher's request by someone else, of several current television commercials can be used as content for an examination of the function of advertising and the use it makes of the visual arts to persuade the viewer. In these projects the visual material of the tape can be expanded by collecting magazine and newspaper advertisements, photographing billboards, or bringing in mail ads. Since advertising is so large a part of our society and since some of it appears to be directed at a younger and younger audience, it would seem quite appropriate for the school to help children to understand it. In doing so, we can once again promote considerable art learnings.

These few video projects are, of course, only the tip of the iceberg. The imaginative classroom teacher or art specialist can develop a wide variety of such projects relating to the specific grade level, locale, or background of the pupils. Perhaps the best guide for promoting project ideas is for the teacher to follow, whenever possible, his or her dominant interests in art or media, so that genuine enthusiasm can help to spark the response of the pupils.

using the motion picture in the classroom

Although the VTR is the most effective general purpose media system one might use in teaching art, there is little question that movies (some of which are, in fact, television programs or films made specifically for television) contain the most significant body of content materials for our use. Perhaps 50,000 full-length feature films have been produced since the earliest days of cinema. If one includes short films and commercials, industrial and educational films, the number would be much higher. Of these, only a small number deal with the fine, folk, or popular arts as subject matter. A greater number are themselves works of art in either the cinematic or visual sense. Most films concentrate on providing entertainment, and though they may be superb in that context, they do not easily serve as consistent examples of attentiveness to aesthetic values for teaching. Almost every film has scenes or sequences or some characteristic of artistic merit, but it is easier in teaching art to use those in which such material seems to have been the primary concern in making them.

Occasionally, films involve content which might be considered inappropriate to the elementary level. The reader will be able to identify numerous examples from his or her own experience of films which contain violence or sexuality or propaganda which neither school nor community—nor the teacher, for that matter—would find acceptable for the elementary age levels. These films are, of course, unavoidably lost to our use, even though they may include other excellent material. Nevertheless, even with these restrictions, the number of films we can use in teaching art is considerable. This body of material can be divided into three basic categories: (1) nonfiction films about art, (2) dramatic films containing useful information about art or artists, and (3) films which themselves aspire to function as works of art—particularly in visual terms.

As with the VTR project involving *Man of Aran,* suggested earlier, these films can be videotaped (with appropriate permission) and shown on a television monitor, or they can be rented in 16 mm. and screened with a school projector. In some instances, the school district or the central audio-visual agency might own one or more of these films and it will be unnecessary to expend a rental fee for their use. To the extent that an art specialist is available, discussion prompted by viewing these films can be directed toward their visual properties or their art content. In the absence of an art specialist, however, the classroom teacher should not hesitate to promote dialogue regarding any aspect of the film about which he or she feels confident. The reader will recall that the position of this volume is that persons untrained in art in our culture have a great deal more insight into and information about the visual arts than they themselves realize.

Filmmaking, the other aspect of using motion pictures in the classroom, requires the purchase of some basic equipment and supplies. Although VTR is a more desirable system for the school because of its recording and projecting capabilities, the movie camera is also highly recommended. While it has some disadvantages as compared with the video camera and videorecorder, the relative simplicity of its editing process is a highly attractive feature.

The basic equipment for filmmaking in the classroom, the camera, is simple to operate. Depending on how the class is organized into a "production team," one or more fixed-focus Super 8 cartridge cameras are adequate. An affluent school or school district might invest in cameras with a gross but useful zoom lens capacity (a two-to-one zoom ratio, for example) and some sort of built-in light metering device so that the problem of shooting without adequate light is lessened. Also, at least one and preferably several film editors and splicers and a Super 8 film projector are necessary. The interested teacher can price these items through a local camera shop or through the district purchasing agency. In addition to this basic equipment, the budget for filmmaking must include the continuing expense of buying cartridge film and having it developed, if that is a separate cost.

Animation as a film project is not recommended since it requires a more expensive single frame capacity camera and is cumbersome and tiring for most elementary pupils. Nor do we particularly endorse drawing or painting on film stock, which is undoubtedly entertaining but negates the photographic function of film. Since the kind of project both in making and looking at motion pictures is fundamentally the same as with VTR, suggested projects will not be repeated here. Film materials which cannot be obtained through use of the video system are available in 16 mm., and until most of the relevant art materials are transferred to one system, the conscientious elementary teacher will have to deal with several.

using slide sequences in the classroom

Another excellent media area for art activities and one which is considerably less expensive than either the videotape recorder or the motion picture is the slide or slide-sound sequence, which was described earlier in this chapter. The following projects are examples of what might be done with this medium.

1. *Historical Buildings.* Every American community has structures from the past which illustrate periods of our history and often exhibit a high level of art quality as well. In fact, many communities now have citizen groups involved in efforts to preserve these structures. Armed with simple cameras and slide film, children can photograph these buildings, either as a class field trip or after school with parents or other adults. When earlier photographs of those same buildings or other relevant visual materials (drawings, paintings, or prints that provide related information) are available, slides can be made with the Ektagraphic Kit and added to the sequence. Sound to match the image sequence can include narration by the children, music of the period of the building, or other related sound on records or tape.

2. *The Visual Biography.* Most of us have among our personal possessions a visual record of our own lives in the form of snapshots of ourselves growing up, school yearbook photos, pictures of family and friends, homes we have lived in, and places we have traveled to. The teacher can select significant photos of his or her own life and make slides of them, adding appropriate sound to the sequence if desired. This visual biography, shown to the class early in the year, can help the pupils know the teacher as a full-fledged person, with antecedents and aspirations. It can also prompt a wide variety of discussions ranging from what life was like during the teacher's school days, to the description of places in the country or in the world where the teacher has traveled. The art content of such a project is located in the awareness that it provides of how important visual images have become in our present society and how they can help to reveal (and conceal) the events of our lives. Each pupil can prepare similar visual biographies.

3. *Signs That Help Us.* Since so much of how we move around our complex society, both physically and psychologically, is guided by signs, children can develop slide sequences—with or without sound—exploring signs and their varied messages. Using photography or the Ektagraphic process, slides can be arranged in series representing clusters of messages or directions: vehicle and foot traffic signs, boundary signs such as "No Trespassing," historical signs such as commemorative plaques, and unofficial signs such as graffiti. Again, if the teacher wishes to do so, dialogue might emphasize how these signs are arranged or designed and how they might be improved. This discussion, in turn, could lead to a production project in the making of signs for the classroom or school.

4. *The Art Around Us.* Just as in the case of historic buildings, most communities have works of art, both public and private, in a wide variety of media, which are either unrecognized as such or known only to those who own them. If our concept of art includes, as has been suggested here, works of

folk and popular art, the visual aesthetic resources of even the poorest neighborhood or family can be quite impressive, and elementary pupils can locate
and make slides of these items. For example, although Chicago has a massive
Picasso scuplture, many small towns have war memorials and sculptures in
parks and in public and private buildings. Some towns still have undestroyed
WPA murals in post offices, and a good number of cities now have murals
painted by trained or untutored minority group artists (see Figure 23, page 20).
Many families—if not almost all—have treasured objects of family history,
sewing, knitting, rugs, china, metalwork, furniture, or jewelry that serve or
can assume the status of art objects. Children can collect or locate these items
and make slides of them, either in individual sequences or in group projects.
The presentation of and discussion about these slides would follow a format
by now familiar to the reader.

One point is important enough to note again. When the material being
considered—in slides, discussion, or any medium whatever—is not clearly of
a "fine arts," museum status, the teacher must be careful to avoid a discrimina-
tory attitude. There is no question that there are qualitative distinctions
among works of art, whatever their origin or function. However, these distinctions should, at best, be the product of careful, unbiased analysis rather
than based on a priori assumptions of superiority and inferiority. A well-done
quilt can be more worthwhile in aesthetic terms than a mediocre painting. If
they do nothing else, elementary art programs should strive to eliminate the
various elitisms that permeate the visual arts.

using photography in the classroom

Up to now we have been talking about the screened or projected image. There
are also excellent possibilities for the elementary art program in the printed
photographic image. At best, when both facilities and the knowledgeable
teacher are available, children should shoot, develop, and print their own
photographs (see Figure 118). Earlier in this chapter we provided a description
of the basic equipment required for this process and some very simple guidelines for its use. Obviously, since they deal with still-film images, each of the
suggested slide projects described previously could also be done with exhibits
of printed photographs. Some additional recommended projects specific to
this medium are offered here.

1.   *The Photo Mural.*   A group or entire class project combines pupil-
shot and printed photographs in a montage or collage mounted on a wall. The
photographs can all relate to one theme, or they can simply be individual statements brought together as the work of a group. Just as with a painted mural,
the photo mural can promote a sense of collective identity and, simultaneously, can reveal the value of unique individual contributions. It can also be a useful exercise in arrangement no less than the often uninspiring design exercises
found in some art textbooks.

118. In a photo-saturated society such as ours, children's interest in taking and talking about photographs is usually instantaneous and abiding.

2. *The Design Portfolio.* Pupils might search for and photograph examples which illustrate the design principles they have learned or are learning in art activities (see chapter 4 for a review of design materials). For example, pupils can look for the *repetition of shapes* in buildings, natural scenery, or the display of goods in a supermarket and photograph these examples. Each pupil, several groups, or the entire class can develop a portfolio of photos picturing all the design principles they have learned and illustrated.

3. *The Sports Event.* Any public event involving numbers of people is, of course, a rich source of photographic images. Since our culture has so many public sports activities and since they are apt to be of interest in themselves to elementary pupils, they can serve admirably as photographic material. From auto races to sandlot baseball, the "game" can be photographed endlessly since its visual aspects change constantly.

These are a few of the ways this volume proposes for using the newer media. Television, motion pictures, slides, and photography are, cumulatively, highly valuable additions or alternatives to school art programs. What is particularly important to remember is that these media—indeed, all media and activities—must be used in the service of the one proper goal for elementary art education; that goal is aesthetic literacy, the development of young people who possess affection for and understanding of all the visual arts.

This volume has presented the basic information the elementary teacher needs to organize and supervise an art curriculum for the 1980s. The suggestions made here are radical in the sense that they move away from the time-honored elementary art dependence on studio performance. On the other hand, there is every reason to predict that ideas about the teaching of art are developing in the direction proposed here and that within a few years these ideas will seem quite traditional. When this happens it will be time for another book with an even more advanced outlook. If we believe that art is an important part of our lives, ideas about teaching it should be fertile, forward-looking, and constantly changing.

notes

CHAPTER 1. THE PURPOSES AND NATURE OF ART

1. Melvin M. Rader and Bertram E. Jessup, *Art and Human Values* (Englewood Cliffs, N.J.: Prentice-Hall, 1976), pp. 10–11.

2. Arnold Berleant, *The Aesthetic Field* (Springfield, Ill.: Charles C. Thomas, 1970), p. 49.

3. Arthur D. Efland, "Conceptions of Teaching in Art Education," *Art Education* 32, no. 4 (April 1979): 21.

4. Berleant, *Aesthetic Field*, pp. 122–23.

5. Ibid., pp. 114–24.

6. Ibid., p. 143.

7. Jerome Stolnitz, *Aesthetics and the Philosophy of Art Criticism* (Boston: Houghton Mifflin, 1960), p. 63.

8. Rudolf Arnheim, *Towards a Psychology of Art* (Berkeley: Univ. of California Press, 1966), p. 182.

9. For examples of writings which criticize the statement function of art (i.e., the function of information transmittal between artist and viewer), see E. H. Gombrich, "The Visual Image," *Scientific American* 227, no. 9 (September 1972): 82–96, and Vincent Lanier, "One Word Is Worth a Thousand Pictures," in *Essays in Art Education: The Development of One Point of View*, 2nd ed. (New York: MSS Information Corp., 1976), pp. 81–90.

10. Berleant, *Aesthetic Field*, pp. 24–38.

11. Stolnitz, *Aesthetics*, pp. 109–212.

12. Rader and Jessup, *Art and Human Values*, pp. 78, 81, 125, 147.

13. Morris Weitz, "The Role of Theory in Esthetics," in *A Modern Book of Esthetics*, ed. Melvin M. Rader (New York: Holt, Rinehart and Winston, 1966), pp. 199–208.

14. Efland, "Conceptions of Teaching," p. 23.

15. Weitz, "Role of Theory," p. 207.

16.   John Dewey, *Art as Experience* (New York: Minton, Balch & Co., 1934), p. 326.

17.   Donald Arnstine, "The Aesthetic as a Context for General Education," *Studies in Art Education* 8, no. 1 (Autumn 1966): 16.

18.   Weitz, "Role of Theory," p. 208.

19.   David W. Ecker, "Justifying Aesthetic Judgments," *Art Education* 20, no. 5 (May 1967): 5–6.

OVERVIEW: PART II. THE TEACHING OF ART

1.   The literature of the early sixties provides some debates on the question of whether art education is a discipline or a field of study. For example, see Elliot W. Eisner, "On the Impossibility of Theory in Art Education," *Studies in Art Education* 4, no. 2 (Fall 1963): 1–8, and David W. Ecker, "On the Possibility of Theory in Art Education," *Studies in Art Education* 6, no. 2 (Spring 1965): 1–6. The issue was perhaps devoid of substance, but it *was* evidence of two tendencies. One was an increasing recognition that the teaching of art can be studied in a scholarly manner rather than being, as before that time, largely a matter of pure intuitve speculation. The second tendency was an awareness of the even now unresolved question of the degree to which other disciplines should influence or structure the field.

2.   See Bibliography (Resources on Art Education, Periodicals).

3.   Laura H. Chapman, *Instant Art, Instant Culture: The Unspoken Policy for American Schools* (New York: Teachers College Press, 1982), p. 68.

CHAPTER 6. THEORY AND PRACTICE IN TEACHING ART

1.   Happily for art education, some theorists remain unafraid of the charge of iconoclasm. Brent Wilson describes what he considers the "conventional, ritualistic, rule-governed and compulsory" character of school art as opposed to the spontaneity and freedom of children's play art ("The Super-heroes of J. C. Holz," *Art Education* 27, no. 8 [November 1974]: 2–9). Arthur Efland questions the alleged creativity and free expression of much child art in the schools by proposing that there is, in fact, a "school art style" which imposes limitations on the visual statements of our pupils sometimes as formal as the adult conventions from which we claim they have been freed ("The School Art Style: A Function Analysis," *Studies in Art Education* 17, no. 2 [1976]: pp. 37–43).

2.   William G. Whitford, *An Introduction to Art Education* (New York: D. Appleton-Century Co., 1937), pp. 3–12.

3.   Royal B. Farnum, "The Early History of American Art Education," in *Art in American Life and Education*, ed. Guy M. Whipple (Bloomington, Ill.: Public School Pub. Co., 1941), p. 446.

4.   Walter H. Klar, Leon L. Winslow, and C. Valentine Kirby, *Art Education in Principle and Practice* (Springfield, Mass.: Milton Bradley Co., 1933), p. 27.

5.   Arthur W. Dow, *Theory and Practice of Teaching Art* (New York: Teachers College, Columbia University, 1908), p. 55.

6.   There appears to be some historical evidence that, in fact, the art works of children in Cizek's classes were anything but the products of uninfluenced, creative self-expression, but, rather, often highly "mannered," or influenced results of forceful teaching. See Paul Duncum, "The Origins of Self-Expression: A Case of Self-Deception," *Art Education* 35, no. 5 (September 1982): 32–35.

7.   Wilhelm Viola, *Child Art and Franz Cizek* (New York: John Day, 1936), p. 6.

8.   Donald Laging, "Art in Everyday Living," *Art Education Today: An Annual Devoted to the Problems of Art Education* (Bureau of Publications, Teachers College, Columbia University, 1942): p. 57.

9.   Italo L. de Francesco, *Art Education: Its Means and Ends* (New York: Harper & Bros., 1958), pp. 30–59.

10. Viktor Lowenfeld, *Creative and Mental Growth* (New York: Macmillan, 1947); Victor D'Amico, *Creative Teaching in Art* (Scranton, Pa.: International Textbook, 1942); Herbert Read, *Education Through Art* (London: Faber & Faber, 1943).

11. Arthur D. Efland, "The Transition Continued: The Emergence of an Affective Revolution," *Studies in Art Education* 13, no. 1 (Fall 1971): 13–24.

12. Elliot W. Eisner, Barbara Laswell, and Charles Weidner, "What Do Prospective Art Teachers Believe About the Teaching of Art?" (Unpublished research report, Stanford University, 1973), p. 16.

13. J. P. Guilford et al., "A Factor-Analytic Study of Creative Thinking, II., Administration of Tests and Analysis of Results," *University of Southern California Psychological Laboratory Reports* 8 (1952).

14. Manuel Barkan, *Through Art to Creativity* (Boston: Allyn & Bacon, 1960).

15. Harlan E. Hoffa, "Overview: Outcome and Effect," *Art Education Bulletin* 18, no. 4 (April 1961): 66.

16. Harlan E. Hoffa, *An Analysis of Recent Research Conferences in Art Education* (Bloomington: Indiana University Foundation, 1970).

17. Manuel Barkan, "Transition in Art Education: Changing Conceptions of Curriculum Content and Teaching," *Art Education* 15, no. 7 (October 1962): 12–18; Kenneth M. Lansing, "Editorial," *Studies in Art Education* 4, no. 1 (Fall 1962): 1–3; Vincent Lanier, "Schismogenesis in Contemporary Art Education," *Studies in Art Education* 5, no. 1 (Fall 1963): 10–19.

18. Manuel Barkan, Laura H. Chapman, and Evan J. Kern, *Guidelines: Curriculum Development for Aesthetic Education* (St. Louis, Mo.: Central Midwestern Regional Educational Laboratory, 1970).

19. Manuel Barkan, "Curriculum Problems in Art Education," in *A Seminar in Art Education for Research and Curriculum Development*, ed. Edward L. Mattil (University Park: The Pennsylvania State University, 1966), p. 243.

20. Barkan had already declared his position in an earlier article. See Barkan, "Transition in Art Education," pp. 12–18.

21. Vincent Lanier, "A Plague on All Your Houses: The Tragedy of Art Education," *Art Education* 27, no. 3 (March 1974): 12–15.

22. Efland, "The Transition Continued," p. 24.

23. June K. McFee, "Urbanism and Art Education in the U.S.A.," *Art Education* 22, no. 6 (June 1969): 16–18.

24. Paolo Freire, *Pedagogy of the Oppressed* (New York: Herder and Herder, 1970). Critical consciousness, or what Freire calls *conscientizacao* in Portuguese, refers to learning to perceive social, political, and economic contradictions and to take action against the oppressive elements of reality. This definition can be found in the translator's note on p. 19.

25. Vincent Lanier, "The Teaching of Art as Social Revolution," *Phi Delta Kappan* 50, no. 6 (February 1969): 314–19, and Vincent Lanier, "The Unseeing Eye: Critical Consciousness and the Teaching of Art," in *The Arts, Human Development and Education*, ed. Elliot W. Eisner (Berkeley, Calif.: McCutchan, 1976), pp. 19–29.

26. Hans Giffhorn, "Ideologies of Art Education," *Studies in Art Education* 19 (Spring 1978): 52.

27. Jean Ellen Jones, *Teaching Art to Older Adults: Guidelines and Lessons* (Atlanta: Georgia State University, 1980).

28. Edmund B. Feldman, "Art Is for Reading: Pictures Make a Difference," *Teachers College Record* 82, no. 4 (Summer 1981): 649–60.

29. The IMPACT project was a one million dollar experimental program funded by the U.S. Office of Education in five dissimilar and geographically widespread communities. Its purpose was to determine the influence on general pupil learning of an expansion of involvement in the arts.

30. Betty Edwards, *Drawing on the Right Side of the Brain* (Los Angeles: J. P. Tarcher, 1979), and Hermine Feinstein, "A College Drawing Curriculum Integrating Langer's Theory of Symbolization and Aspects of Hemispheric Processes" (Unpublished Ph.D. diss., Stanford University, 1978), chapters 1, 2, and 5.

31.   *The American Journal of Art Therapy,* published quarterly by Elinor Ulman in Washington, D.C.

32.   Duke Madenfort, "Educating for the Immediately Sensuous as Unified Whole," *Art Education* 26, no. 7 (October 1973): 6–11; Merle Flannery, "Images and Aesthetic Consciousness," *Art Education* 27, no. 3 (March 1974): 4–7; and Robert Bersson, "Against Feelings: Aesthetic Experience in Technocratic Society," *Art Education* 35, no. 4 (July 1982): 34–39.

33.   Ann S. Richardson, "Art Means Language," *Art Education* 35, no. 5 (September 1982): 11.

34.   Laura H. Chapman, *Approaches to Art in Education* (New York: Harcourt Brace Jovanovich, 1978), pp. 19–20.

35.   *School Arts,* published monthly September through June (Worcester, Mass.: Davis Publications); *Arts and Activities,* published monthly except for July and August (San Diego, Calif.: Publishers' Development Corp.).

36.   Hugo B. Froehlich and Bonnie E. Snow, *Textbooks of Art Education* (New York: The Prang Educational Co., 1904).

37.   Guy Hubbard, *Art for Elementary Classrooms* (Englewood Cliffs, N.J.: Prentice-Hall, 1982).

38.   These surveys include: U.S. Department of Health, Education and Welfare, *The Condition of Education* (Washington, D.C., 1975); *Music and Art in the Public Schools,* National Education Association, Research Monograph 1963 M3 (Washington, D.C., 1963); and Reid Hastie and David Templeton, *Art Education in the Secondary Schools,* Research Report 1–63 (Minneapolis: University of Minnesota, Department of Art Education, 1963). I am not including the National Assessment of Educational Progress findings in art in this reference. This program of evaluation conducted in 1974–75 and in 1978–79 by the Education Commission of the States did not attempt to discover or describe what occurred in art in American classrooms; it did attempt to measure what learnings were accumulated in the contexts of the questions asked (National Assessment of Educational Progress, *Art and Young Americans, 1974–79: Results from the Second National Art Assessment,* Report No. 10-A-01 [Denver: Education Commission of the States, 1981]). I have also neglected Chapman's survey of teacher attitudes and actions regarding art, because her respondents were elementary and secondary art teachers rather than classroom teachers (Laura H. Chapman, "Teacher Viewpoint Survey: The Results," *School Arts* 78, no. 9 [May 1979]: 2–5).

39.   An example of this kind of art dialogue is:

> It is just possible that, with their extra-sensitized intuition, artists may have unconsciously predicted the discovery of atomic energy long before "the bomb" became a familiar houshold word, for the history of break-up in art antedates the history of nuclear break-up. (Katherine Kuh, *Break-up: The Core of Modern Art* [New York: New York Graphic Society, 1965], p. 13)

With this kind of "heavy" statement by a respected and popular art critic, a statement which is disturbingly questionable, how can those untrained in art help but feel inadequate about art? Another example, in this case about the teaching of art, is:

> Art teaching that is infused with an aesthetic quality requires an adherence to the relevant factors that operate in any single person-process-product combination. This is a complex and easily disturbed series of relationships that requires alert sensibilities leading to intuitive juggling of elements on the part of the instructor. It is the peculiar and open-ended inter-dependence of these three parts, frequently in unconscious or accidental relationship that determines the depth of validity of the student's aesthetic experience. (Irving Kaufman, *Art and Education in Contemporary Culture* [New York: Macmillan, 1966], p. 477)

Any serious-minded student aspiring to be a teacher cannot help but be terrified away from art by this injunction.

40.   Forbes Rogers, "In Pursuit of Significance," *Art Education* 28, no. 5 (September 1975): 5.

41.   Arts, Education and Americans Panel. *Coming to Our Senses: The Significance of the Arts for American Education* (New York: McGraw-Hill, 1977), p. 248.

42.   "What We Believe and Why," in *Report of the NAEA Commission on Art Education* (Reston, Va.: NAEA, 1977), p. 42.

43.   Fred R. Schwartz, "President's Message," *Vocational Alternatives in Art Education,* The Institute for the Study of Art in Education, ISAE/Abstracts 1, no. 1 (April 1975): 5.

44.   Stephen Dobbs (Ed.), *Arts Education and Back to Basics* (Reston, Va.: NAEA, 1979).

45.   Jacques Barzun, "Art and Educational Inflation," *Art Education* 31, no. 2 (October 1978): 5. The same point was made earlier within the field itself. See Vincent Lanier, "Hyphenization Takes Command," *Art Education* 14, no. 6 (June 1961): 6.

46.   Harry S. Broudy, *Enlightened Cherishing* (Urbana: Univ. of Illinois Press, 1972), p. 58.

47.   Kenneth M. Lansing, *Art, Artists, and Art Education* (New York: McGraw-Hill, n.d.), p. 130.

48.   John Dewey, *Art as Experience* (New York: Minton, Balch & Co., 1934), pp. 4–5.

49.   Herbert J. Gans, *Popular Culture and High Culture* (New York: Basic Books, 1974), p. 127.

50.   See Vincent Lanier, *Teaching Secondary Art* (Scranton, Pa.: International Textbook, 1964), pp. 74–78, and Elliot W. Eisner, *Educating Artistic Vision* (New York: Macmillan, 1972), p. 2.

51.   Arthur D. Efland, book review of *Curricular Considerations for Visual Arts Education: Rationale, Development and Evaluation,* edited by George W. Hardiman and Theodore Zernich, *Studies in Art Education* 17, no. 3 (1976): 71.

52.   "What We Believe and Why," p. 41.

53.   Edmund B. Feldman, *Becoming Human Through Art* (Englewood Cliffs, N.J.: Prentice-Hall, 1970), p. vi.

54.   Laura H. Chapman, *Instant Art, Instant Culture: The Unspoken Policy for American Schools* (New York: Teachers College Press, 1982), p. 32.

55.   For example, see Elliot W. Eisner, "Examining Some Myths in Art Education," *Studies in Art Education* 15, no. 3 (1973–1974).

56.   Clyde R. Appleton, "Black and White in the Music of American Youth," *New York University Educational Quarterly* 5, no. 2 (Winter 1973): 24.

57.   Record album cover text, *The Best from the Russia We Love,* Westminster Gold Series, no. W6S–8103.

58.   Anne Heath, "From Theory to Practice: The Initiation of an Art Specialist Credential" (Unpublished Ph.D. diss., University of Oregon, 1977).

CHAPTER 7. ART AND CHILD DEVELOPMENT

1.   Howard Gardner, *The Arts and Human Development* (New York: Wiley, 1973), pp. 23–24.

2.   For an early source, see Helga Eng, *The Psychology of Children's Drawings* (London: Routledge and Kegan Paul, 1931).

3.   Howard Gardner, *Artful Scribbles* (New York: Basic Books, 1980), pp. 72–73.

4.   Brent Wilson and Marjorie Wilson, "The Use and Uselessness of Developmental Stages," *Art Education* 34, no. 5 (September 1981): 5.

5.   Rudolf Arnheim, *Art and Visual Perception* (Berkeley: Univ. of California Press, 1954).

6.   Jean Piaget and Barbel Inhelder, *The Child's Conception of Space* (New York: Humanities Press, 1956).

7.   Suzi Gablik, *Progress in Art* (New York: Rizzoli, 1976).

8.   Dale Harris, *Children's Drawings as Measures of Intellectual Maturity* (New York: Harcourt, Brace and World, 1963).

9.   Burrhus F. Skinner, *About Behaviorism* (New York: Random House, 1976).

10.   Viktor Lowenfeld, *Creative and Mental Growth* (New York: Macmillan, 1947).

11.   Elliot W.Eisner, *Educating Artistic Vision* (New York: Macmillan, 1972), p. 90.

12.   Herbert Read, *Education Through Art* (London: Faber and Faber, 1943).

13.   Henry Schaefer-Simmern, *The Unfolding of Artistic Activity* (Berkeley: Univ. of California Press, 1950).

14.   June K. McFee, *Preparation for Art* (Belmont, Calif.: Wadsworth, 1970).

15.   Everett S. Allen, "The Utter Mess of Human Failing," *The Arizona Daily Star,* 17 Jan. 1982, sec. C2, p. 4.

16.   See chapter 6, note 47.

17.   Irvin L. Child, *Development of Sensitivity to Aesthetic Values* (New Haven, Conn.: Yale University, 1964).

18.   Harold J. McWhinnie, "A Review of Some Research on Aesthetic Measure and Perceptual Choice," *Studies in Art Education* 16, no. 2 (1975): 42–53.

19.   Diana Korzenik, "Role Taking and Children's Drawings," *Studies in Art Education* 15, no. 3 (1973–1974): 17–24.

20.   Barry E. Moore, "A Description of Children's Verbal Responses to Works of Art in Selected Grades One Through Twelve," *Studies in Art Education* 14, no. 3 (Spring 1973): 27–34.

21.   For a description and critical review of this series, see Jessie Lovano-Kerr and Jean C. Rush, "Project Zero: The Evolution of Visual Arts Research During the Seventies," *Review of Research in Visual Arts Education* 15 (Winter 1982): 61–81. The same article provides a bibliography of publications reporting the Project Zero studies in this area.

22.   Gardner, *Artful Scribbles,* pp. 268–69.

23.   Edmund B. Feldman, *Becoming Human Through Art* (Englewood Cliffs, N.J.: Prentice-Hall, 1970), p. 158.

CHAPTER 8.   THE ELEMENTARY ART CURRICULUM

1.   For an earlier application of this organization see Vincent Lanier, *Teaching Secondary Art* (Scranton, Pa.: International Textbook 1964).

2.   Alexander S. Neill, *Summerhill* (New York: Hart Pub., 1960).

3.   Vincent Lanier, "Talking About Art: An Experimental Course in High School Art Appreciation," *Studies in Art Education* 9, no. 3 (Spring, 1968): 32–44.

4.   California State Board of Education, *Art Education Framework* (Sacramento, Calif.: State Department of Education, 1971).

5.   State of Ohio Department of Education, *Guidelines for Planning Art Instruction in the Elementary Schools of Ohio* (1970), p. 133.

6.   An interesting illustration of a technique measuring one aspect of response is found in Tom Turicchi's psychographic research firm in Richardson, Texas. Turicchi attaches electrodes to two fingers of six carefully selected subjects and records on a machine much like a lie detector their galvanic skin response (GSR), blood pressure, and pulse as they listen and react to popular songs. The subjects also consciously rate what they hear. What they "really" feel, as demonstrated by the physiological responses, provides the basis for predictions on the popularity of the songs with a profitable 92 percent accuracy.

7.   State of Ohio Department of Education, *Guidelines,* p. 4.

8.   Gordon S. Plummer, *Children's Art Judgment: A Curriculum for Elementary Art Appreciation* (Dubuque, Iowa: W. C. Brown Co., 1974), p. xi.

9.   Ibid., p. 107.

10.   Ibid., p. 22.

11.   W. Dwaine Greer, *SWRL Elementary Art Program* (Bloomington, Ind.: Phi Delta Kappa, 1981), p. 2.

12. Ibid., p. 5.

13. Ibid., p. 1.

14. Ronald H. Silverman, "Curriculum Corral," *The Painted Monkey,* California Art Education Association Newsletter 7, no. 9 (May–June 1982): 2.

CHAPTER 9. NEWER MEDIA AND ELEMENTARY ART

1. Vincent Lanier, *Final Report of the Uses of Newer Media in Art Education Project,* NAEA, National Defense Education Act Project No. 5–16–027 (Washington, D.C.: NAEA, 1966).

2. Vincent Lanier, "Newer Media and the Teaching of Art," *Art Education* 19, no. 4 (April 1966): 5.

bibliography

RESOURCES ON ART

advertising design

Antebi, Michael. *Art of Creative Advertising.* New York: Reinhold Book Corp., 1968.
Maurello, Samuel Ralph. *Commercial Art Techniques.* New York: Tudor Pub. Co., 1963.
Rodewald, Fred C. *Commercial Art as a Business.* 2d rev. ed. New York: Viking Press, 1971.

architecture

Allen, Edward. *How Buildings Work: The Natural Order of Architecture.* New York: Oxford Univ. Press, 1980.
Catanese, Anthony J., and Snyder, James C. *Introduction to Architecture.* New York: McGraw-Hill, 1979.
Ching, Frank. *Architectural Graphics.* New York: Van Nostrand, Reinhold, 1975.
_____. *Building Construction Illustrated.* New York: Van Nostrand, Reinhold, 1975.
Kahn, Ely J. *A Building Goes Up.* New York: Simon and Schuster, 1969.
Moore, Charles. *The Place of Houses.* New York: Holt, Rinehart and Winston, 1974.
Trogler, George E. *Beginning Experiences in Architecture.* New York: Van Nostrand, Reinhold, 1972.

ceramics

Nelson, Glenn C. *Ceramics: A Potter's Handbook.* 3d ed. New York: Holt, Rinehart and Winston, 1971.
Roettger, Ernst. *Creative Clay Design.* New York: Van Nostrand, Reinhold, 1972.

Speight, Charlotte F. *Hands in Clay: An Introduction to Ceramics.* Sherman Oaks, Calif.:
     Alfred Pub. Co., 1979.

drawing and painting

Hawthorne, Charles W. *Hawthorne on Painting.* New York: Dover Pub. Co., 1960.
Henri, Robert. *The Art Spirit.* Philadelphia: J. B. Lippincott Co., 1951.
Kaupelis, Robert. *Learning to Draw.* New York: Watson-Guptill, 1966.
Nicolaides, Kimon. *The Natural Way to Draw; A Working Plan for Art Study.* Boston: Hough-
     ton Mifflin, 1969.
O'Hara, Eliot. *Making Watercolor Behave.* New York: Minton, Balch & Co., 1932.
Purser, Stuart. *Drawing Handbook.* Worcester, Mass.: Davis Publications, 1977.

filmmaking

Laybourne, Kit. *The Animation Book: A Complete Guide to Animated Filmmaking from Flip-
     Flop Books to Sound Cartoons.* New York: Crown, 1979.
Pincus, Edward. *Guide to Filmmaking.* Chicago: Regnery, 1972.

history of art

Gardner, Helen. *Gardner's Art Through the Ages,* rev. by Horst de la Croix and Richard G.
     Tansey. 5th ed. New York: Harcourt, Brace & World, 1970.

Gombrich, E. H. *The Story of Art.* Oxford: Phaidon Press, 1972.
Hartt, Frederick. *Art: A History of Painting, Sculpture and Architecture.* 2 vols. Englewood
     Cliffs, N.J.: Prentice-Hall, 1976.
Janson, H. W. *History of Art for Young People.* New York: Harry N. Abrams, 1971.
Lowry, Bates. *The Visual Experience: An Introduction to Art.* Englewood Cliffs, N.J.: Prentice-
     Hall, 1961.
_____. *Phaidon Encyclopedia of Art and Artists.* New York: E. P. Dutton, 1978.

industrial and product design

Dreyfuss, Henry. *Designing for People.* New York: Simon and Schuster, 1955.
Levens, Alexander S. *Graphics, Analysis and Conceptual Design.* 2d ed. New York: Wiley, 1968.
Niece, Robert Clemens. *Art in Commerce and Industry.* Dubuque, Iowa: W. C. Brown Co.,
     1968.
Reed, Herbert. *Art and Industry: The Principles of Industrial Design.* Bloomington: Indiana
     Univ. Press, 1961.

interior design

Bennet, Corwin. *Spaces for People: Human Factors in Design.* Englewood Cliffs, N.J.: Prentice-
     Hall, 1977.
Deasy, C. M. *Design for Human Affairs.* Cambridge, Mass.: Schenkman Pub. Co., 1974.
Faulkner, Sarah. *Planning a Home: A Practical Guide to Interior Design.* New York: Holt,
     Rinehart and Winston, 1979.

Whiton, Augustus S. *Interior Design and Decoration.* 4th ed. Philadelphia: J. B. Lippincott, Co., 1974.

jewelry

Bovin, Murray. *Jewelry Making for Schools, Tradesmen and Craftsmen.* Forest Hills, N.Y.: Bovin Publishing, 1967.
Morton, Philip. *Contemporary Jewelry: A Studio Handbook.* 2d ed. New York: Holt, Rinehart and Winston, 1976.
Von Neumann, Robert. *The Design and Creation of Jewelry.* Philadelphia: Chilton Books, 1972.

landscape design

Laurie, Michael. *Introduction to Landscape Architecture.* New York: American Elsevier Pub. Co., 1975.
McHarg, Ian L. *Design with Nature.* Garden City, N.Y.: Natural History Press, 1969.
Rutledge, Albert J. *Anatomy of a Park: The Essentials of Recreation Area Planning and Design.* New York: McGraw-Hill, 1971.
Simonds, John Ormsbee. *Landscape Architecture: The Shaping of Man's Natural Environment.* New York: McGraw-Hill, 1961.

photography

Berryman, Gregg. *Notes on Graphic Design and Visual Communication.* Los Altos, Calif.: W. Kaufmann, 1980.
Cyr, Don. *Teaching Your Children Photography: A Step by Step Guide.* Garden City, N.Y.: Amphoto, 1977.
Davis, Phil. *Photography.* 3d ed. Dubuque, Iowa: W. C. Brown Co., 1979.
Holter, Patra. *Photography Without a Camera.* New York: Van Nostrand, Reinhold, 1972.
Langford, Michael J. *Step by Step Guide to Photography.* New York: Alfred A. Knopf, 1978.
Swedlund, Charles. *Photography: A Handbook of History, Materials and Processes.* New York: Holt, Rinehart and Winston, 1974.

printmaking

Heller, Jules. *Printmaking Today: An Artist's Handbook.* 2d ed. New York: Holt, Rinehart and Winston, 1972.
Rosen, Randy. *Prints.* New York: E. P. Dutton, 1978.
Ross, John, and Romano, Clare. *The Complete Printmaker.* New York: Free Press, 1972.
Saff, Donald. *Printmaking: History and Process.* New York: Holt, Rinehart and Winston, 1978.
Sternberg, Harry. *Woodcut.* New York: Pitman, 1962.

sculpture

Coleman, Ronald L. *Sculpture: A Basic Handbook for Students.* Dubuque, Iowa: W. C. Brown Co., 1968.
Kelly, James J. *The Sculptural Idea.* 2d ed. Minneapolis, Minn.: Burgess Pub. Co., 1974.
Rogers, Leonard R. *Sculpture.* London: Oxford Univ. Press, 1969.

television and film criticism

Corbett, D. J. *Motion Picture and Television Films*. New York: Focal Press, 1968.
Price, Jonathan. *Video Visions: A Medium Discovers Itself*. New York: New American Library, 1977.

understanding art

Anderson, Donald M. *Elements of Design*. New York: Holt, Rinehart and Winston, 1961.
Feldman, Edmund B. *Varieties of Visual Experience*. Englewood Cliffs, N.J.: Prentice-Hall, 1973.
Kainz, Luise C., and Riley, Olive L. *Understanding Art*. New York: Harry N. Abrams, n.d.
Krause, Joseph H. *The Nature of Art*. Englewood Cliffs, N.J.: Prentice-Hall, 1969.
Morman, Jean Mary. *Art: Of Wonder and a World*. Blauvelt, N.Y.: Art Education, 1967.
Richardson, John A. *Art: The Way It Is*. Englewood Cliffs, N.J.: Prentice-Hall, 1973.

urban planning

Fish, Gertrude Sipperly. *The Story of Housing*. New York: Macmillan, 1979.
Gallion, Arthur B. *The Urban Pattern: City Planning and Design*. 3d ed. New York: Van Nostrand, Reinhold, 1975.
Halprin, Lawrence. *Cities*. Cambridge, Mass.: MIT Press, 1972.
Munzer, Martha. *Planning Our Town*. New York: Alfred A. Knopf, 1964.

weaving and fiber arts

Birrell, Verla. *The Textile Arts: A Handbook of Weaving, Braiding, Printing, and Other Textile Techniques*. New York: Schocken Books, 1973.
Held, Shirley E. *Weaving: A Handbook of the Fiber Arts*. 2d ed. New York: Holt, Rinehart and Winston, 1978.
Morrison, Phylis. *Spider's Games: A Book for Beginning Weavers*. Seattle: Univ. of Washington Press, 1981.

special areas

Andrews, Ruth (Ed.). *How to Know American Folk Art*. New York: E. P. Dutton, 1977.
Baird, Bil. *The Art of the Puppet*. New York: Macmillan, 1966.
Bishop, Robert. *New Discoveries in American Quilts*. New York: E. P. Dutton, 1975.
Cockcroft, Eva; Weber, John; and Cockcroft, James. *Towards a People's Art*. New York: E. P. Dutton, 1977.
Corbin, Particia. *All About Wicker*. New York: E. P. Dutton, 1978.
Daniels, Les. *Comix: A History of Comic Books In America*. New York: E. P. Dutton, 1971.
Fendelman, Helaine. *Tramp Art*. New York: E. P. Dutton, 1975.
Fine, Elsa H. *The Afro-American Artist*. New York: Holt, Rinehart and Winston, 1973.
Grigsby, Eugene, J., Jr. *Art and Ethnics*. Dubuque, Iowa: W. C. Brown Co., 1977.
Horton, Louise. *Art Careers*. New York: Franklin Watts, 1975.
Howlett, Carolyn C. *Art in Craftmaking*. New York: Van Nostrand, Reinhold, 1974.
Jacopetti, Alexandra. *Native Funk and Flash: An Emergency Folk Art*. San Francisco: Phelps-Schaefer, 1974.
Johnson, Pauline. *Creating with Paper*. Seattle: Univ. of Washington Press, 1958.
Keleman, Boris. *Naive Art*. New York: E. P. Dutton, 1977.

Kopp, Joel, and Kopp, Kate. *American Hooked and Sewn Rugs*. New York: E. P. Dutton, 1975.
Krevitsky, Nik. *Batik Art and Craft*. Rev. ed. New York: Van Nostrand, Reinhold, 1973.
Laury, Jean Ray. *Doll Making: A Creative Approach*. New York: Van Nostrand, Reinhold, 1970.
Laury, Jean Ray, and Aiken, Joyce. *Creating Body Coverings*. New York: Van Nostrand, Reinhold, 1973.
_____. *Levi's Denim Art Contest Catalogue of Winners*. Mill Valley, Calif.: Baron Wolman/ Equarebooks and Owens & Co., 1974, (unpaged).
Meilach, Dona Z. *Soft Sculpture and Other Soft Art Forms*. New York: Crown Publishers, 1974.
Rudofsky, Bernard. *Now I Lay Me Down to Eat*. Garden City, N.Y.: Anchor Press, Doubleday, 1980.
Stalberg, Roberta Helmer, and Nesi, Ruth. *China's Crafts*. New York: Eurasia Press, 1980.
Von Blum, Paul. *The Art of Social Conscience*. New York: Universe Books, 1976.
Webster, William E. *Contemporary Candlemaking*. Garden City, N.Y.: Doubleday & Co., 1972.

RESOURCES ON ART EDUCATION

books

Alschuler, Rose H., and Hatwick, La Berta W. *Painting and Personality*. Vol. 1 and 2. Chicago: Univ. of Chicago Press, 1947.
Anderson, Frances E. *Art for All the Children*. Springfield, Ill.: Charles C. Thomas, 1978.
Anderson, Warren. *Art Learning Situations for Elementary Education*. Belmont, Calif.: Wadsworth, 1965.
Art in American Life and Education. Fortieth Yearbook of the National Society for the Study of Education. Bloomington, Ill.: Public School Pub. Co., 1941.
Arts, Education and Americans Panel. *Coming to Our Senses: The Significance of the Arts for American Education*. New York: McGraw-Hill, 1977.
Barkan, Manuel. *A Foundation for Art Education*. New York: Ronald Press, 1955.
_____. *Through Art to Creativity*. Boston: Allyn & Bacon, 1960.
Barkan, Manuel, and Chapman, Laura H. *Guidelines for Art Instruction Through Television for the Elementary Schools*. Bloomington, Ind.: National Center for School and College Television, 1967.
Barkan, Manuel; Chapman, Laura H.; and Kern, Evan J. *Guidelines: Curriculum Development for Aesthetic Education*. St. Louis, Mo.: Central Midwestern Regional Educational Laboratory, 1970.
Battcock, Gregory. *New Ideas in Art Education*. New York: E. P. Dutton, 1973.
Baumgarner, Alice. *Conference on Curriculum and Instruction Development in Art Education*. Washington, D.C.: NAEA, 1967.
Beardsley, Monroe C. *Aesthetics from Classical Greece to the Present*. New York: Macmillan, 1966.
Beittel, Kenneth R. *Alternatives for Art Education Research*. Dubuque, Iowa: W. C. Brown Co., 1973.
Berleant, Arnold. *The Aesthetic Field*. Springfield, Ill.: Charles C. Thomas, 1970.
Brittain, W. Lambert. *Creativity, Art and the Young Child*. New York: Macmillan, 1979.
Broudy, Harry S. *Enlightened Cherishing*. Urbana: Univ. of Illinois Press, 1972.
Burkhart, Robert C. *Spontaneous and Deliberate Ways of Learning*. Scranton, Pa.: International Textbook, 1962.
Chapman, Laura H. *Approaches to Art in Education*. New York: Harcourt Brace Jovanovich, 1978.
_____. *Instant Art, Instant Culture: The Unspoken Policy for American Schools*. New York: Teachers College Press, 1982.

Churchill, Angiola, R. *Art for Pre-adolescents*. New York: McGraw-Hill, 1971.

Clark, Gilbert A., and Zimmerman, Enid. *Art/Design: Communicating Visually*. New York: Art Education, 1978.

Cole, Natalie E. *The Arts in the Classroom*. New York: John Day, 1940.

_____. *Children's Arts from Deep Down Inside*. New York: John Day, 1966.

Conant, Howard. *Art Education*. Washington, D.C.: Center for Applied Research in Education, 1964.

_____. *Seminar on Elementary and Secondary School Education in the Visual Arts*. New York: New York University, 1965.

Conant, Howard, and Randall, Arne. *Art in Education*. Peoria, Ill.: Charles A. Bennett, 1960.

Conrad, George. *The Process of Art Education in the Elementary School*. Englewood Cliffs, N.J.: Prentice-Hall, 1964.

D'Amico, Victor. *Creative Teaching in Art*. Scranton, Pa.: International Textbook, 1942.

D'Amico, Victor; Wilson, Frances; and Maser, Maureen. *Art for the Family*. New York: Museum of Modern Art, 1954.

de Francesco, Italo L. *Art Education: Its Means and Ends*. New York: Harper & Bros., 1958.

Dennis, Lawrence E., and Jacob, Renata M. (Eds.). *The Arts in Higher Education*. San Francisco: Jossey-Bass, 1968.

Dewey, John. *Art as Experience*. New York: Minton, Balch & Co., 1934.

_____. *Art and Education*. Marion, Pa.: Barnes Foundation Press, 1947.

Dimonstein, Geraldine. *Exploring the Arts with Children*. New York: Macmillan, 1974.

Dobbs, Stephen M. (Ed.). *Arts Education and Back to Basics*. Reston, Va.: NAEA, 1979.

Ecker, David W. *Improving the Teaching of Art Appreciation*. Columbus: The Ohio State University, 1966.

Eisner, Elliot W. *Educating Artistic Vision*. New York: Macmillan, 1972.

_____ (Ed.). *The Arts, Human Development and Education*. Berkeley, Calif.: McCutchan, 1976.

Eisner, Elliot W., and Ecker, David W. *Readings in Art Education*. Waltham, Mass.: Blaisdell, 1966.

Eisner, Elliot W., and Vallance, Elizabeth (Eds.). *Conflicting Conceptions of Curriculum*. Berkeley, Calif.: McCutchan, 1975.

Feldman, Edmund B. *Art as Image and Ideas*. Englewood Cliffs, N.J.: Prentice-Hall, 1967.

_____. *Becoming Human Through Art*. Englewood Cliffs, N.J.: Prentice-Hall, 1970.

_____ (Ed.). *Art in American Higher Institutions*. Washington, D.C.: NAEA, 1970.

Fisher, Elaine F. *Aesthetic Awareness and the Child*. Itasca, Ill.: F. E. Peacock, 1978.

Gaitskell, Charles. *Art Education for Slow Learners*. Peoria, Ill.: Charles A. Bennett, 1953.

Gray, Wellington B. *Student Teaching in Art*. Scranton, Pa.: International Textbook, 1968.

Greenberg, Pearl. *Children's Experiences in Art*. New York: Reinhold, 1966.

Grigsby, J. Eugene. *Art and Ethnics*. Dubuque, Iowa: W. C. Brown Co., 1977.

Hardiman, George W., and Zernich, Theodore. *Art Activities for Children*. Englewood Cliffs, N.J.: Prentice-Hall, 1981.

_____ (Eds.). *Foundations for Curriculum Development and Evaluation in Art Education*. Champaign, Ill.: Stipes, 1981.

Hastie, Reid (Ed.). *Art Education*. Sixty-fourth Yearbook, Part II, of the National Society for the Study of Education. Chicago: Univ. of Chicago Press, 1965.

Hastie, Reid, and Schmidt, Christian. *Encounter with Art*. New York: McGraw-Hill, 1969.

Hausman, Jerome J. (Ed.). *Report of the Commission on Art Education*. Washington, D.C.: NAEA, 1965.

_____ (Ed.). *Arts and the Schools*. New York: McGraw-Hill, 1980.

Hoffa, Harlan E. *An Analysis of Recent Research Conferences in Art Education*. Bloomington: Indiana University Foundation, 1970.

Hoffman, Donald; Greenberg, Pearl; and Fitzner, Dale (Eds.). *Lifelong Learning in the Visual Arts*. Washington, D.C.: NAEA, 1980.

Hubbard, Guy. *Art in the High School*. Belmont, Calif.: Wadsworth, 1967.

_____. *Art for Elementary Classrooms*. Englewood Cliffs, N.J.: Prentice-Hall, 1982.

Hubbard, Guy, and Rouse, Mary J. *Art: Meaning, Methods and Media*. Vols. 1–6. Westchester, Ill.: Benefic, 1973.

Hurwitz, Al, and Madeja, Stanley S. *The Joyous Vision*. Englewood Cliffs, N.J.: Prentice-Hall, 1977.

Jefferson, Blanche. *My World of Art*. 6 vols. (Grades 1–6). Boston: Allyn & Bacon, 1963.

Jones, Jean Ellen. *Teaching Art to Older Adults: Guidelines and Lessons*. Atlanta: Georgia State University, 1980.

Kainz, Luise C., and Riley, Olive L. *Understanding Art*. New York: Harry N. Abrams, 1967.

Kaufman, Irving. *Art and Education in Contemporary Culture*. New York: Macmillan, 1966.

Keiler, Manfred. *Art in the Schoolroom*. Lincoln: Univ. of Nebraska Press, 1951.

Kellogg, Rhoda. *Analyzing Children's Art*. Palo Alto, Calif.: National Press, 1969.

Knudsen, Estelle, and Christensen, Ethel. *Children's Art Education*. Peoria, Ill.: Charles A. Bennett, 1957.

Landis, Mildred M. *Meaningful Art Education*. Peoria, Ill.: Charles A. Bennett, 1951.

Lanier, Vincent. *Doctoral Research in Art Education*. Los Angeles: University of Southern California, 1962.

———. *Teaching Secondary Art*. Scranton, Pa.: International Textbook, 1964.

———. *Final Report of the Uses of Newer Media in Art Education Project*. NAEA Project No. 5–16–027. Washington, D.C.: NAEA, 1966.

———. *The Image of the Artist in Fictional Cinema*. Eugene: University of Oregon, 1968.

———. *Essays in Art Education: The Development of One Point of View*. 2nd ed. New York: MSS Information Corp., 1976.

———. *The Arts We See: A Simplified Introduction to the Visual Arts*. New York: Teachers College Press, 1982.

Lansing, Kenneth M. *Art, Artists and Art Education*. New York: McGraw-Hill, n.d.

Lark-Horovitz, S.; Lewis, H.; Luca, M. *Understanding Children's Art for Better Teaching*. Columbus, Ohio: Charles E. Merrill, 1967.

LeBaron, John. *Making Television: A Video Production Guide for Teachers*. New York: Teachers College Press, 1981.

Lewis, Hilda P. *Child Art: The Beginning of Self-Affirmation*. Berkeley, Calif.: Diablo, 1966.

Lidstone, John. *Self-Expression in Classroom Art*. Worcester, Mass.: Davis Publications, 1967.

Linderman, Earl W. *Invitation to Vision*. Dubuque, Iowa: W. C. Brown Co., 1967.

———. *Teaching Secondary School Art*. Dubuque, Iowa: W. C. Brown Co., 1971.

Linderman, Earl W., and Herberholz, Donald W. *Developing Artistic and Perceptual Awareness*. Dubuque, Iowa: W. C. Brown Co., 1964.

Linderman, Earl W., and Linderman, Marlene M. *Crafts in the Classroom*. New York: Macmillan, 1977.

Lindstrom, Miriam. *Children's Art*. Berkeley: Univ. of California Press, 1957.

Logan, Frederick. *Growth of Art in American Schools*. New York: Harper & Bros., 1955.

Loughran, Bernice B. *Art Experiences*. New York: Harcourt, Brace & World, 1963.

Lowenfeld, Viktor. *Creative and Mental Growth*. New York: Macmillan, 1947.

———. *Your Child and His Art*. New York: Macmillan, 1954.

Lowenfeld, Viktor, and Brittain, W. Lambert. *Creative and Mental Growth*. 6th ed. New York: Macmillan, 1970.

Luca, Mark, and Kent, Robert. *Art Education: Strategies of Teaching*. Englewood Cliffs, N.J.: Prentice-Hall, 1968.

McFee, June K. *Preparation for Art*. 2d ed. Belmont, Calif.: Wadsworth, 1970.

McFee, June K., and Degge, Rogena M. *Art, Culture and Environment*. Belmont, Calif.: Wadsworth, 1977.

Madeja, Stanley S. *Through the Arts to the Aesthetic*. St. Louis, Mo.: Central Midwestern Regional Educational Laboratory, 1977.

——— (Ed.). *Arts and Aesthetics: An Agenda for the Future*. St. Louis, Mo.: Central Midwestern Regional Educational Laboratory, 1978.

Manzella, David. *Educationists and the Evisceration of the Visual Arts*. Scranton, Pa.: International Textbook, 1963.

Mattil, Edward L. (Ed.). *A Seminar in Art Education for Research and Curriculum Development.* University Park: The Pennsylvania State University, 1966.

Mendelowitz, Daniel M. *Children Are Artists.* Stanford: Stanford Univ. Press, 1963.

Montgomery, Chandler. *Art for Teachers and Children.* Columbus, Ohio: Charles E. Merrill, 1968.

Morman, Jean Mary. *Art: Of Wonder and a World.* Blauvelt, N.Y.: Art Education, 1967.

Munro, Thomas. *Art Education: Its Philosophy and Psychology.* New York: Liberal Arts, 1947.

_____. *Evolution in the Arts.* Cleveland, Ohio: Cleveland Museum of Art, 1966.

Munro, Thomas, and Read, Herbert. *The Creative Arts in American Education.* Boston: Harvard Univ. Press, 1960.

Murphy, Judith, and Jones, Lonna. *Research in Arts Education.* Washington, D.C.: U.S. Office of Education, n.d.

NAEA. *Research in Art Education.* NAEA Yearbooks. Kutztown, Pa.: State Teachers College, 1951–1962.

_____. *Research Monographs 1 and 2.* Washington, D.C.: 1964, 1966.

_____. *Report of the NAEA Commission on Art Education.* Reston, Va.: 1977.

Oole, Eugenia M. *Art Is for Children.* Minneapolis, Minn.: Augsburg, 1980.

Packwood, Mary (Ed.). *Art Education in the Elementary School.* Washington, D.C.: NAEA, 1967.

Pappas, George. *Concepts in Art and Education.* New York: Macmillan, 1970.

Plummer, Gordon S. *Children's Art Judgment: A Curriculum for Elementary Art Appreciation.* Dubuque, Iowa: W. C. Brown Co., 1974.

Rader, Melvin M. *A Modern Book of Esthetics.* New York: Holt, Rinehart and Winston, 1966.

Rannells, Edward W. *Art Education in the Junior High School.* Louisville: University of Kentucky, College of Education, 1946.

Read, Herbert. *Education Through Art.* London: Faber and Faber, 1943.

Reed, Carl. *Early Adolescent Art Education.* Peoria, Ill.: Charles A. Bennett, 1957.

Rueschoff, Phil H., and Swartz, M. Evelyn. *Teaching Art in the Elementary School.* New York: Ronald Press, 1969.

Saunders, Robert J. *Relating Art and Humanities to the Classroom.* Dubuque, Iowa: W. C. Brown Co., 1977.

Sawyer, John R., and de Francesco, Italo L. *Elementary School Art for Classroom Teachers.* New York: Harper & Row, 1971.

Schaefer-Simmern, Henry. *The Unfolding of Artistic Activity.* Berkeley: Univ. of California Press, 1948.

Schultz, Harold, and Shores, J. Harlan. *Art in the Elementary School.* Champaign: University of Illinois, 1948.

Schwartz, Fred R. *Structure and Potential in Art Education.* Waltham, Mass.: Blaisdell, 1970.

Shinneller, James A. *Art: Search and Self-Discovery.* Scranton, Pa.: International Textbook, 1961.

Silver, Rawley. *Developing Cognitive and Creative Skills Through Art.* Baltimore, Md.: University Park Press, 1978.

Silverman, Ronald H. *A Syllabus for Art Education.* Los Angeles: California State University, 1972.

_____. *Art, Education and the World of Work.* Washington, D.C.: NAEA, 1980.

Smith, Ralph A. *Aesthetics and Criticism in Art Education.* Chicago: Rand McNally, 1966.

_____. *Aesthetics and Problems of Education.* Urbana: Univ. of Illinois Press, 1971.

_____. "Artists-in-Schools: Analysis and Criticism." Bureau of Educational Research, University of Illinois, Champaign, 1978. Mimeo.

Tamsma, Maarten. *Zienswijzer.* Amsterdam, Netherlands: Meulenhoff Educatief, 1974.

Uhlin, Donald. *Art for Exceptional Children.* Dubuque, Iowa: W. C. Brown Co., 1972.

Wachowiak, Frank, and Hodge, David. *Art in Depth.* Scranton, Pa.: International Textbook, 1970.

Wachowiak, Frank, and Ramsay, Theodore. *Emphasis: Art.* Scranton, Pa.: International Textbook, 1964.

Wickiser, Ralph L. *An Introduction to Art Education.* New York: World, 1959.

Winslow, Leon L. *Art in Secondary Education.* New York: McGraw-Hill, 1941.

Ziegfeld, Edwin, and Smith, Mary E. *Art for Daily Living: The Story of the Owatonna Art Education Project.* Minneapolis: Univ. of Minnesota Press, 1944.

periodicals

Art Education, published bi-monthly, January through November by the NAEA in Reston, Va.

Art Education Today: An Annual Devoted to the Problems of Art Education, published annually from 1935–1952 (excluding the years 1944–1947) by the Bureau of Publications, Teachers College, Columbia University, New York.

Arts and Activities, published monthly except for July and August by Publishers' Development Corp., San Diego, Calif.

Journal of Aesthetic Education, published quarterly by the University of Illinois in Urbana.

Review of Research in Visual Arts Education, published twice a year by the University of Illinois in Urbana.

School Arts, published monthly nine times a year by Davis Publications, Worcester, Mass.

Studies in Art Education, published three times a year by the NAEA in Reston, Va.

indices

Studies in Art Education, annotated for articles from 1959 to spring 1973. In Vol. 15, no. 2 (1973/74). Also, each year's no. 3 contains annotations for articles in previous volume issues.

Art Education, for articles from 1963 to October 1974: In April/May 1975.

index

Page numbers in italic type direct you to illustrations in this book.